W9-BYZ-753

Life Skills Math

by
Donald H. Jacobs
and
August V. Treff

AGS Publishing
Circle Pines, Minnesota 55014-1796
1-800-328-2560

About the Authors

Donald H. Jacobs, M.Ed., taught mathematics for many years in the Baltimore City Public Schools. He is currently with the Upton Home and Hospital School Program in the technology department. Other AGS textbooks that he has coauthored include *Basic Math Skills, Physical Science,* and *General Science.*

August V. Treff, M.Ed., was a mathematics teacher and department head, director of research and evaluation, and chief of accountability with the Baltimore City Public Schools. He is now an information analyst with Bank of America. His is also coauthor of AGS *Basic Math Skills.*

Photo credits for this textbook can be found on page 374.

The publisher wishes to thank the following educators for their helpful comments during the review process for *Life Skills Math.* Their assistance has been invaluable.

Bryan Backes, Special Education Instructor, Apollo High School, St. Cloud, MN; **Marcie Buchwald,** Special Needs Teacher, Southeast High School, Springfield, IL; **Ms. Bonnie Castelluccio,** Independent Study Teacher, City of Angels, Venice, CA; **Melanie Eick,** Disabilities Specialist, Oklahoma Department of Vocational and Technical Education, Stillwater, OK; **Ruth Greider,** Special Education Coordinator, Wichita Public Schools, Wichita, KS; **Barbara A. Grogan,** Teacher of Handicap-Special Education, Bayonne High School, Bayonne, NJ; **Jean Harrington,** Learning Support Teacher, Pleasant Hills Middle School, Pittsburgh, PA; **Pamela Kinzler,** Special Education Teacher, Penn Hills Senior High School, Pittsburgh, PA; **Donna Leonard,** Coordinator for SLD, School District of Hillsborough County, Tampa, FL; **Steve Little,** Special Education Teacher, Springfield Southeast High School, Springfield, IL; **Sandy Meents,** Special Education Curriculum Coordinator, Reddix Center, San Antonio, TX; **Gilda Meyers,** Special Education Specialist, E.D. Walker Special Education Center, Dallas, TX; **Niki Pennington,** SLD Teacher, Durant High School, Plant City, FL; **Berlyenn C. Poe,** Resource Teacher, Oak Ridge High School, Oak Ridge, TN; **Peter Saarimaki,** Math Consultant, Scarborough, ON, Canada; **Jim Steinwart,** Special Education Math Teacher, Springfield High School, Springfield, IL; **Gladys Uri,** Teacher, Foothills Adult Center, El Cajon, CA; **Joyce von Ehrenkrook,** Special Education Coordinator, Wichita Public Schools, Wichita, KS; **Dr. Bessie Watson Hampton,** Coordinator of Family and Consumer Sciences, Kansas City Missouri School District, Kansas City, MO; **Theodore S. Wiaterowski,** Special Needs Teacher, Mathematics, John S. Fine High School, Greater Nanticoke Area School District, Nanticoke, PA

Publisher's Project Staff

Director, Product Development: Karen Dahlen; Associate Director, Product Development: Teri Mathews; Editor: Jody Peterson; Development Assistant: Bev Johnson; Graphic Designer: Linda Rodriguez Nuñez; Design Manager: Nancy Condon; Purchasing Agent: Mary Kaye Kuzma; Marketing Manager/Curriculum: Brian Holl

Editorial and production services provided by Navta Associates, Inc. Publishing Services

Printed in the United States of America
ISBN 0-7854-2934-4
Product Number 93520
A 0 9 8 7 6 5 4

Contents

How to Use This Book: A Study Guide

Welcome to *Life Skills Math.* This book includes many of the math skills that you will need now and later in life. Why do you need these skills? Think about the world of mathematics around you. When you buy something, you use math to count money. When you measure something, you use numbers to calculate units of measurement. Most jobs require at least some sort of math. You will use the basic math skills in this book almost every day of your life at home, at school, and on the job.

As you read this book, notice how each lesson is organized. Information will appear at the beginning of each lesson. Read this information carefully. A sample problem with step-by-step instructions will follow. Use the instructions to learn how to solve a certain kind of problem. Once you know how to solve this kind of problem, you will have the chance to solve similar problems on your own. If you have trouble with a lesson, try reading it again.

Before you start to read this book, it is important that you understand how to use it. It is also important to know how to be successful in this course. This first section of the book is here to help you achieve these things.

How to Study

These tips can help you study more effectively:

◆ Plan a regular time to study.

◆ Choose a quiet desk or table where you will not be distracted. Find a spot that has good lighting.

◆ Gather all the books, pencils, paper, and other equipment you will need to complete your assignments.

◆ Decide on a goal. For example: "I will finish reading and taking notes on Chapter 1, Lesson 1, by 8:00."

◆ Take a five- to ten-minute break every hour to keep alert.

◆ If you start to feel sleepy, take a break and get some fresh air.

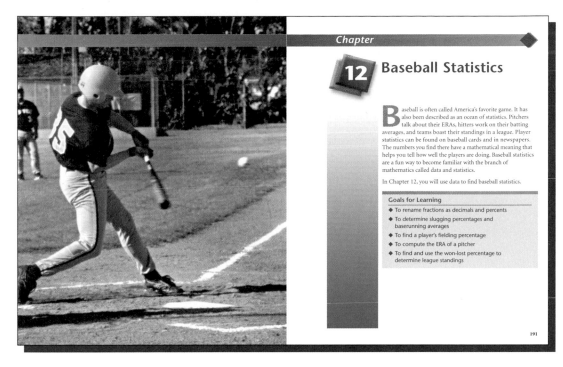

Before Beginning Each Chapter

◆ Read the chapter title and study the photograph.
What does the photo tell you about the chapter title?

◆ Read the opening paragraphs.

◆ Study the Goals for Learning. The Chapter Review and
tests will ask questions related to these goals.

◆ Look at the Chapter Review. The questions cover the
most important information in the chapter.

Note the Chapter Features

Application

A look at how a topic in the chapter relates to real life

Notes

Hints or reminders that point out
important information

> Look for this box
> for helpful tips!

Technology Connection
Use technology to
apply math skills

Try This
New ways to think about
problems and solve them

Writing About Mathematics
Opportunities to write about
problems and alternative solutions

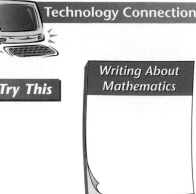

Before Beginning Each Lesson

Read the lesson title and
restate it in the form of
a question.

For example, write:
What are batting averages?

Look over the entire lesson,
noting the following:
◆ bold words
◆ text organization
◆ exercises
◆ notes in the margins
◆ photos

Lesson 1 Batting Averages

Batting average
A ratio of hits to at bats

Statistic
Fact collected and
arranged so as to show
certain information

Sacrifice out
Out made to advance
base runners

A baseball player's **batting average** is a **statistic** that measures
how well the player hits. The higher the batting average, the
better the player hits. A batting average is written as a decimal
rounded to three places. A player's batting average is found by
dividing the number of hits by the number of official at bats.
Walks and **sacrifice outs** do not count as official at bats.

EXAMPLE If a player has 26 hits for 72 at bats, then what is
the player's batting average?

$$\text{Batting Average} = \frac{\text{Number of Hits}}{\text{Number of Official at Bats}} = \frac{26}{72}$$

$$\begin{array}{r} 0.3611 \approx .361 \\ 72\overline{)26.0000} \\ -21\ 6 \\ \hline 4\ 40 \\ -4\ 32 \\ \hline 80 \\ -72 \\ \hline 80 \\ -72 \\ \hline 0 \end{array}$$

Exercise A Find the batting average for each player.

1. Ymato Ma 45 at bats 18 hits	**5.** Gil French 43 at bats 25 hits	**9.** Vic Salski 29 at bats 15 hits
2. Gail Wills 32 at bats 12 hits	**6.** Walt Jones 73 at bats 37 hits	**10.** Jake Shane 51 at bats 20 hits
3. Mike Speer 90 at bats 26 hits	**7.** Gwen Smith 28 at bats 9 hits	**11.** Tom Foster 28 at bats 10 hits
4. Sol Lausch 51 at bats 15 hits	**8.** Ben Cardin 63 at bats 35 hits	**12.** Robin Jay 22 at bats 6 hits

192   *Chapter 12 Baseball Statistics*

As You Read the Lesson

◆ Read the major headings.
◆ Read the subheads and paragraphs that follow.
◆ Read the content in the example boxes.
◆ Before moving on to the next lesson, see if you understand
  the concepts you read. If you do not, reread the lesson.
  If you are still unsure, ask for help.
◆ Practice what you learned by doing the exercises in
  each lesson.

Bold type

Words seen for the
first time will appear
in bold type

Glossary

Words listed in this
column are also found
in the glossary

Using the Bold Words

Knowing the meaning of all the boxed words in the left column
will help you understand what you read.

These words appear in **bold type** the first time they appear
in the book and are often defined in the paragraph.

> You can use **probability** to measure how likely an event
> is to happen.

All of the words in the left column are also defined in the **glossary**.

> **Probability** (prob ə bil´ ə tē) the chances that an outcome
> will happen (p. 53)

What to Do with a Word You Do Not Know

When you come to a word you do not know, ask yourself:

◆ **Is the word a compound word?**
Can you find two words within the word? This could
help you understand the meaning. For example: *rainfall.*

◆ **Does the word have a prefix at the beginning?**
For example: *improper.* The prefix *im-* means "not,"
so this word refers to something that is not proper.

◆ **Does the word have a suffix at the end?**
For example: *variable.* The suffix *-able* means "able to be,"
so this word refers to something that is able to be varied.

◆ **Can you identify the root word?**
Can you sound the word out in parts?
For example: *un known.*

◆ **Are there any clues in the sentence that will help you
understand the word?**

Look for the word in the margin box, glossary, or dictionary.

If you are still having trouble with a word, ask for help.

Using Tables to Solve Problems

Four tables can be found in the back of this book. There is one for each of the four main math operations: addition, subtraction, multiplication, and division. You are encouraged to memorize these tables or refer to them as needed. If you are allowed to use a calculator, you may choose to use it instead of these tables.

×	2	3	4	5	6	7	8	9	10	11	12
Multiplication Table											
2	4	6	8	10	12	14	16	18	20	22	24
3	6	9	12	15	18	21	24	27	30	33	36
4	8	12	16	20	24	28	32	36	40	44	48
5	10	15	20	25	30	35	40	45	50	55	60
6	12	18	24	30	36	42	48	54	60	66	72
7	14	21	28	35	42	49	56	63	70	77	84
8	16	24	32	40	48	56	64	72	80	88	96
9	18	27	36	45	54	63	72	81	90	99	108
10	20	30	40	50	60	70	80	90	100	110	120
11	22	33	44	55	66	77	88	99	110	121	132
12	24	36	48	60	72	84	96	108	120	132	144

360   *Multiplication Table*

Using the Chapter Reviews

◆ For each Chapter Review, answer the multiple-choice questions first.
◆ Answer the questions under the other parts of the Chapter Review.
◆ To help you take tests, read the Test-Taking Tips at the end of each Chapter Review.

Test-Taking Tip

When learning math vocabulary, make flash cards with words and abbreviations on one side and definitions on the other side. Draw pictures next to the words if possible. Then use the flash cards in a game to test your vocabulary skills.

Preparing for Tests

◆ Complete the exercises in each lesson. Make up similar problems to practice what you have learned. You may want to do this with a classmate and share your problems.
◆ Review your answers to lesson exercises and Chapter Reviews.
◆ Test yourself on vocabulary words and key ideas.
◆ Practice problem-solving strategies.

Problem-Solving Strategies

Following these steps will help you to solve math problems in this book:

1 ▶ Read

- ◆ Read the problem to discover what information you need.
- ◆ Make sure you understand the math concepts.
- ◆ Study the problem to decide if you have all the necessary information and if there is information you do not need.
- ◆ Begin thinking about the steps needed to solve the problem.

2 ▶ Plan

Think about the steps you will need to do to solve the problem. Decide if you will use mental math, paper and pencil, or a calculator. Will you need to draw a picture? Are measurements in the same units? Will you use a formula? Will you need to do more than one step?

These strategies may help you find a solution:

- ◆ Reword the problem.
- ◆ Draw a picture.
- ◆ Estimate your answer.
- ◆ Write an equation.
- ◆ Divide the problem into smaller parts.
- ◆ Make a chart or graph.
- ◆ Use a formula.
- ◆ Work backward.

3 ▶ Solve

- ◆ Follow your plan and do the calculations.
- ◆ Make sure to label your answer correctly.

4 ▶ Reflect

- ◆ Reread the problem.
- ◆ Does your answer make sense?
- ◆ Did you answer the question?
- ◆ Check your work to see if your answer is correct.

Counting Calories

Think of the last activity you did. It may have been reading a book, biking to school, or exercising in physical education class. No matter what the activity was, your body was using calories. When you eat food, you take in calories. When you count calories, you add and subtract whole numbers.

In Chapter 1, you will learn how to determine the number of calories you eat and use. You will also learn some of the ways charts and graphs can help you find information.

Goals for Learning

◆ To compute the total number of calories consumed

◆ To compute the total number of calories used by activities

◆ To read and interpret a nutrition label

◆ To read a graph to find information

Lesson 1 Adding Calories

Calorie
Unit of measure of the energy in food

Consume
To use; to eat or drink up

This chart shows that different foods have different amounts of **calories**.

Caloric Values of Common Foods	
Food	**Calories**
Hot dog with bun	280
Hamburger with bun	370
Relish, 1 tbsp	25
Cole slaw, $\frac{3}{4}$ cup	155
Skim milk, 1 cup	110
Cola, 1 cup	105
Frozen yogurt bar	105

You can find how many calories are in several foods by adding the calories in each food.

EXAMPLE Mike goes to a restaurant for lunch. He has a hot dog with a bun and one cola. How many calories does he **consume** in all? Use the chart of caloric values to find the calories in each food.

Solution Add to find the total.

Hot dog with bun	280	Calories
Cola	+105	Calories
	385	Total

The total number of calories Mike consumes is 385.

Exercise A Find the total number of calories of other customers' meals ordered at the same restaurant.

1. Misha asks for a hamburger and 1 cup of skim milk.

2. Maria orders a hamburger with relish and cole slaw.

3. José wants a hot dog, cole slaw, 1 cup of skim milk, and a frozen yogurt bar.

Caloric Values of Fruit Servings	
Fruit	**Calories**
Applesauce, 1 cup	230
Banana	120
Blackberries, 1 cup	85
Fruit cocktail, 1 cup	195
Orange	65
Peach	40
Pear	100
Plum	33
Raspberries, 1 cup	70

PROBLEM SOLVING

Exercise B Use the chart of Caloric Values of Fruit Servings. Find the answers to these questions by adding the calories.

1. Juan eats a banana, a peach, and an orange. How many calories does he consume?

2. Alan has three plums and a pear. How many calories are in the fruit?

3. Lee has a cup of applesauce and a cup of fruit cocktail for breakfast. How many calories does he eat?

4. How many calories are in 2 cups of applesauce?

5. How many calories are in two oranges and a pear?

6. Sue decides to make her own fruit cocktail for her friends. She uses one orange, one banana, two peaches, and 2 cups of raspberries. What is the total calorie count for this fruit cocktail?

7. How many calories are in two bananas, a peach, and two plums?

8. Aneka mixes 1 cup of blackberries with 1 cup of fruit cocktail. What is the total number of calories?

Here are the caloric values of some of the foods served at a local restaurant.

Food	Calories
Chicken, baked, 6 oz	190
Fish, breaded, 6 oz	200
Hamburger steak, 6 oz	270
Pot roast, 6 oz	320
Spaghetti, 1 cup	245
Beets, 1 cup	65
Black-eyed peas, 1 cup	220
Broccoli, 1 cup	50
Corn, creamed, 1 cup	210
Mixed vegetables, 1 cup	115
Potato, baked	95
Rice, 1 cup	201
Margarine, 1 tbsp	100
Milk, skim, 1 cup	110
Orange juice, 1 cup	50
Grapefruit juice, 1 cup	85
Apple juice, 1 cup	125

Most restaurant menus do not show the caloric values of food items. You may find it more difficult to count your calories when eating out.

PROBLEM SOLVING

Exercise C Use the caloric values chart from the local restaurant. Find the total caloric value of each person's meal by adding the calories.

1. Jimmy chooses chicken, creamed corn, rice, and 1 cup of grapefruit juice. How many calories are in his dinner?

2. Juanita enjoys breaded fish, 1 cup of broccoli, 1 cup of rice, and 1 cup of apple juice. How many calories are in her meal?

Fat calories

Calories that come from the fat in food

Writing About Mathematics

Make a list of the things you ate for breakfast today. Find out how many calories you consumed. Write about whether or not your breakfast was a healthy one.

Some calories have special names such as **fat calories**. These are calories that come from the fat content of the food. Most foods purchased in supermarkets have labels listing calories from fat.

Nutrition Facts

Serving Size 1/2 cup (120 mL)
Servings Per Container **3**

Amount Per Serving

Calories 130		Calories from Fat **30**	
Amount / serving	% Daily value	Amount / serving	% Daily value
Total Fat 3g	**5%**	**Total Carbohydrate** 23g	**8%**
Saturated Fat 0.5g	**3%**	Dietary Fiber 0.5g	**2%**
Cholesterol 0mg	**0%**	Sugars 6g	
Sodium 180mg	**7%**	**Protein** 2g	

This soup label shows 130 calories per serving with 3 servings. The soup also contains 30 calories per serving from fat.

EXAMPLES

Find the total number of calories in this can of soup.

$$
\begin{array}{r}
130 \\
3 \quad\quad 130 \\
\text{times} \ +130 \\
\hline
390
\end{array}
\quad
\begin{array}{l}
\\
\text{Calories per serving} \\
\\
\text{Total calories}
\end{array}
$$

$$
\text{or} \quad
\begin{array}{r}
130 \\
\times \ \ 3 \\
\hline
390
\end{array}
\quad
\begin{array}{l}
\text{Calories per serving} \\
\text{Number of servings} \\
\text{Total calories}
\end{array}
$$

Find the total number of fat calories in this can of soup.

$$
\begin{array}{r}
30 \\
30 \\
+ \ 30 \\
\hline
90
\end{array}
\quad
\begin{array}{l}
\text{Fat calories} \\
\text{per serving} \\
\\
\text{Total fat calories}
\end{array}
$$

$$
\text{or} \quad
\begin{array}{r}
30 \\
\times \ \ 3 \\
\hline
90
\end{array}
\quad
\begin{array}{l}
\text{Fat calories per serving} \\
\text{Number of servings} \\
\text{Total fat calories}
\end{array}
$$

Exercise D Use the labels to help you answer the questions.

Nutrition Facts

Serving Size 1/2 cup (130g)
Servings Per Container about 3.5

Amount Per Serving

Calories 160   Calories from Fat 10

% Daily Value

Total Fat 1g	**1%**
Saturated Fat 0g	**1%**
Polyunsaturated 0.5g	
Monounsaturated 0g	
Sodium 220mg	**9%**
Potassium 710mg	**20%**
Total Carbohydrate 31g	**10%**
Dietary Fiber 7g	**29%**
Sugars 8g	

Nutrition Facts

Serv. Size 1 cup (252g)
Servings about 2

Calories 260
Fat Cal. 100

* Percent Daily Values (DV) are based on a 2,000 calorie diet.

Amount/Serving	%DV*	Amount/Serving	%DV*
Total Fat 11g	**17%**	**Total Carb.** 31g	**10%**
Sat. Fat 5g	**25%**	Dietary Fiber 5g	**20%**
Cholest. 20mg	**7%**	Sugars 10g	
Sodium 1,150mg	**48%**	**Protein** 11g	

Vitamin A 10% • Vitamin C 2% • Calcium 4% • Iron 15%

8. Serving size equals _____.

9. Calories per serving is _____.

1. Fat calories per serving is _____.

2. Calories per serving is _____.

3. Serving size is _____.

Nutrition Facts

Serving Size 1/4 cup (60mL)
Servings Per Container about 5

Amount Per Serving

Calories 30   Calories from Fat 20

% Daily Value

Total Fat 2g	**3%**
Saturated Fat 1g	**5%**
Cholesterol Less Than 5mg	**1%**
Sodium 300mg	**13%**
Total Carbohydrate 4g	**1%**
Protein 1g	

4. How many calories per serving?

5. How many fat calories per serving?

6. How many servings?

7. Find the total calories from the label.

Nutrition Facts

Serving Size 1/2 cup (133g)
Servings Per Container about 3

Amount Per Serving

Calories 130   Calories from Fat 15

% Daily Value

Total Fat 1.5g	**2%**
Saturated Fat 1.5g	**8%**
Cholesterol 0mg	**0%**
Sodium 550mg	**23%**
Total Carbohydrate 24g	**8%**
Dietary Fiber 6g	**24%**
Sugars 4g	
Protein 6g	

Vitamin A 2%	•	Vitamin C 0%
Calcium 0%	•	Iron 6%

* Percent Daily Values are based on a 2,000 calorie diet.

10. How many calories per serving?

11. How many fat calories per serving?

12. How many servings?

13. Find the total calories from the label.

Lesson 2 Subtracting Calories

> Remember that when you subtract, you are looking for the *difference* between two numbers.

You can find the difference between calories consumed and calories used by subtracting.

EXAMPLE Ron consumes 2,700 calories on Monday. His body uses 548 calories by exercising for one hour. How many calories are not used? To find the answer, subtract the calories used from the calories consumed.

```
  2,700   Calories consumed
-   548   Calories used
  2,152   Calories not used (the difference)
```

PROBLEM SOLVING

Exercise A Find the answers to these questions by subtracting.

1. Fontana consumes an average of 2,200 calories per day. If her body uses 250 calories in 1 hour of walking, how many calories remain?

2. Derek consumes an average of 3,100 calories daily. His main activity is lying on the beach, listening to the waves. If his body burns 95 calories doing this, how many calories are left unused?

Exercise B Find the difference for each example.

1. 3,420 calories consumed
782 calories used

2. 3,641 calories consumed
395 calories used

3. 2,963 calories consumed
463 calories used

4. 2,460 calories consumed
568 calories used

Key words in a problem can help you figure out what to do. When you see the word *total*, you know that you should add.

Kyle is sixteen years old. He needs 3,000 calories each day to keep active and stay healthy.

The chart shows what Kyle eats for breakfast. It also shows the caloric value for each food.

Food	Calories
1 granola bar	150
2 apricots	25 each
2 slices bread	85 each
3 tbsp margarine	100 each
1 cup juice	54

EXAMPLE How many calories does Kyle consume at breakfast? Add to find the total.

150	Granola bar
25 25	Apricots
85 85	Bread
100 100 100	Margarine
+ 54	Juice
724	Total

Kyle consumes 724 calories at breakfast.

EXAMPLE How many more calories must Kyle consume during the day to reach the required 3,000 calories? Subtract to find the calories needed.

3,000   Calories required
− 724   Had at breakfast
2,276

Kyle needs to have 2,276 more calories during the day.

This is what Kyle eats during the rest of the day:

	Food	Calories	Food	Calories
Lunch:	Chicken, 2 slices	320	Bread, 2 slices	160
	Apple, 1 medium	80	Margarine, 1 tbsp	100
	Lemonade, 1 cup	100		
Snack:	Popcorn, 1 cup	55	Milkshake, 16 oz	420
Dinner:	Vegetable soup, 1 cup	120	Broccoli, 1 cup	50
	Mashed potatoes, 1 cup	220	Milk, 2 cups	248
	Roast beef, 9 oz	490	Chocolate pudding	185

Exercise A Answer the following questions by adding or subtracting.

1. How many calories does Kyle have at lunch?

2. How many calories are in his snack?

3. How many calories does Kyle have at dinner?

4. How many total calories does he have during the entire day including breakfast?

5. What is the difference between his total count and 3,000?

6. For his snack, suppose that Kyle drinks 1 cup of milk instead of a milkshake. By how much will he lower his calorie count?

7. If Kyle adds one more slice of chicken for lunch, how much higher will his calorie count be?

Try This

If Kyle eats 363 calories less than he should for the day, what can he add to his meals to bring his total calories up to 3,000? Include at least two different foods in your answer.

Increase

To make greater

Graph

A pictorial way to
display information

Vary

To differ in
characteristics

It is sometimes easy for people to **increase** their calories. The more they eat, the more calories they add. However, it can take more time and effort for your body to use calories.

The body gets a certain amount of energy from each calorie. The more active a person is, the faster he or she uses calories.

The **graph** shows the number of calories that are used in 1 hour of activity. The amounts shown may **vary** from person to person depending on age, weight, and gender.

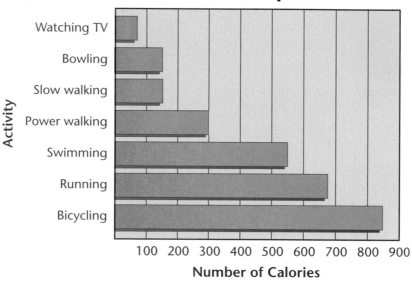

Calories Used per Hour

Technology Connection

A pedometer is a device that a person can wear while walking or running. It has features that tell you how many steps you take, how far you walk, and how many calories you use. How many steps do you think you take during a school day? Make a prediction. Borrow a pedometer from your physical education teacher to test your prediction. Share the results with your class.

Use the graph on page 10 to **estimate** needed information. The graph can help you estimate the number of calories used while walking slowly for 1 hour. The bar for slow walking reaches past the 100 line. Since the end of the bar is about halfway between 100 and 200, the estimate is 150 calories.

Exercise A Use the graph to estimate the number of calories used per hour for each of these activities.

1. Watching TV
2. Bicycling
3. Bowling
4. Running
5. Swimming
6. Power walking

Besides burning calories, jogging is good for a healthy heart and lungs.

The following table shows the number of calories different activities use in 1 hour.

Calories Used in 1 Hour	
Activity	**Calories**
Sitting in class	100
Studying	105
Eating	125
Playing a computer game	140
Raking a lawn	175
Playing volleyball	180
Playing table tennis	230
Lifting weights	500

EXAMPLE   Tomas consumes 3,385 calories in one day. Then he studies for 1 hour and lifts weights for 1 hour. Find the number of calories not used.

First, you add to find the calories used:

```
  105    Studying
+ 500    Lifting weights
  605    Calories used
```

Then, subtract the calories used from the calories consumed:

```
  3,385   Calories consumed
-   605   Calories used
  2,780   Calories not used
```

Exercise A Find the number of calories not used.

1. Jim consumes 2,935 calories. He spends 1 hour studying and 1 hour playing a computer game.

2. Katie's calorie consumption is 3,255. She sits in class for 1 hour and studies for 1 hour.

3. Mason consumes 2,892 calories. He plays a computer game for 1 hour and plays volleyball for 1 hour.

4. Jasmine lifts weights for 1 hour. Then she eats lunch for 1 hour. Her lunch totals 962 calories.

5. Lamont consumes 1,932 calories. He spends 1 hour each on raking a lawn, eating, and playing volleyball.

Calculator Practice

A calculator can help you add numbers. Key in each number carefully. Then check the number on the calculator display before you go on to the next number.

Calculator Exercise Add each list of calories to find each total.

1.
```
    265
    403
     80
+   219
```

2.
```
    281
    460
    290
+   310
```

3.
```
     71
     23
    125
+    62
```

4.
```
    923
  1,063
    103
+    98
```

A Healthy Plan

How do you know if you are consuming and using the right amount of calories each week? Think about a plan you can use.

David and Bridget wanted to find a way to make sure they ate healthy foods and consumed enough calories each day. They also wanted to be sure they used enough calories each day.

They decided to make a chart to record the calories they consume and use. Here is Bridget's chart for 1 week.

Day	Calories Consumed	Calories Used
Monday	2,560	2,490
Tuesday	2,320	1,900
Wednesday	3,100	2,805
Thursday	3,435	3,030
Friday	2,195	2,190
Saturday	2,800	3,300
Sunday	3,295	3,465

Exercises Use the chart to answer these questions.

1. On which day did Bridget consume the most calories?

2. On which day did Bridget consume the fewest calories?

3. On which day was there the greatest difference between the number of calories consumed and the number of calories used?

4. How can Bridget tell if she consumed more calories than she used for the week?

5. What is the difference between the total number of calories Bridget consumed and the total number of calories she used for the week?

6. Bridget spends a lot of time playing sports on the weekend. How does her chart show this?

Chapter 1 REVIEW

Food	Calories
Hot dog with bun	280
Hamburger with bun	370
French fries	290
Cola, 1 cup	105

Food	Calories
Skim milk, 1 cup	110
Pizza, 1 slice	450
Salad with dressing	250
Frozen yogurt bar	105

Write the letter of the best answer to each question. Use the charts above.

1. If Maureen has a hot dog with a bun, skim milk, and a salad for lunch, how many calories does she consume?

  A 620   **C** 655

  B 640   **D** 659

2. Devan orders two slices of pizza, one cola, and a frozen yogurt bar. She decides not to eat one slice of pizza. How many calories does Devan consume?

  A 640   **C** 650

  B 645   **D** 660

3. Sam has one slice of pizza, one cola, and French fries for lunch. Daniel has one slice of pizza, a salad, and one cola. What is the difference in how many calories they consume?

  A 40   **C** 50

  B 45   **D** 55

4. Darresha has a hot dog, French fries, and skim milk for lunch. She exercises for an hour and uses 452 calories. What is the difference between the calories consumed and the calories used?

  A 228   **C** 238

  B 229   **D** 239

5. If Emilio decides to order one of each item on the menu, how many calories will he consume?

  A 1,855   **C** 1,865

  B 1,860   **D** 1,870

Food	Calories
Hamburger	270
Lean steak, 6 oz	660
Vegetable soup	240
French fries	290
Cola, 1 cup	105
Skim milk, 1 cup	110

One-Hour Activity	Calories Used
Baseball	360
Basketball	500
Aerobics	300
Karate	480
Skateboarding	240

Use the information in the charts to find the answer to each problem.

6. Alvaro chooses a hamburger, French fries, and one cola for lunch. How many calories does he consume?

7. Evan has a lean steak, French fries, and 2 cups of skim milk. How many calories does he consume?

8. Cass needs 2,435 calories each day. She has vegetable soup, French fries, and a cup of skim milk. How many more calories does she need?

9. Marta has a hamburger and one cola. Sue has a lean steak and 1 cup of skim milk. Find the difference in how many calories the girls consume.

10. Joy plays baseball and basketball for 1 hour each. How many calories does she use?

11. Lance plays baseball for 1 hour and then does karate for 2 hours. Find the total calories he uses.

Find the number of calories not used.

12. 2,685 calories consumed; 1 hour of skateboarding

13. 3,230 calories consumed; 2 hours of baseball

14. 2,900 calories consumed; 3 hours of karate

15. 3,150 calories consumed; 3 hours of basketball

Use the information in the nutrition label to solve these problems.

16. How many servings are there?

17. Find the total fat calories in the container.

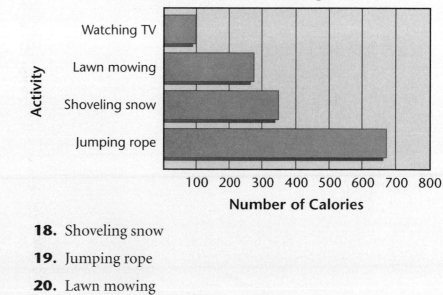

Nutrition Facts

Serving Size 5 crackers = 1 oz. (28.35g)
Servings Per Container 4

Amount Per Serving = 5 crackers
Calories = 116 Calories from Fat = 20

	% Daily Value
Total Fat 2.27g	**3%**
Saturated Fat 0.48g	**2%**
Cholesterol 0mg	**0%**
Sodium 213.55mg (0.21355g)	**9%**
Total Carbohydrate 19g	**6%**
Dietary Fiber 3.50g	**14%**
Sugars 2.28g	
Protein 4.61g	

Vitamin A	0%	•	Vitamin C	0%
Calcium	0%	•	Iron	6%

Use the graph to estimate the number of calories used per hour for each of these activities.

Calories Used per Hour

(bar graph showing, for Activity vs. Number of Calories (100–800): Watching TV, Lawn mowing, Shoveling snow, Jumping rope)

18. Shoveling snow

19. Jumping rope

20. Lawn mowing

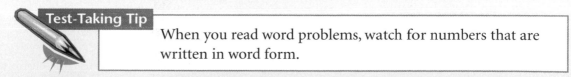

Test-Taking Tip

When you read word problems, watch for numbers that are written in word form.

2 Home Improvement

The Jung family supplements their income by buying an old house, making repairs, and then reselling the house. Typical repairs include installing new carpet, replacing old flooring, and repainting or wallpapering walls. The Jungs save money by watching for sales and by doing the work themselves. They use mathematics to determine how much carpet, how many rolls of wallpaper, or how many boxes of tiles they need to buy.

In Chapter 2, you will learn how to determine how many double rolls of wallpaper to buy for a project. You will find that there is sometimes a way to position carpet that is cheaper than another way.

Goals for Learning

◆ To compute the surface area of a room

◆ To find area in square yards when given the dimensions in feet

◆ To find the cost of tiling a room, given the dimensions of the room and cost of tiles

◆ To apply a rule for estimating the cost of wallpaper for a room

Area

Amount of space inside a shape

Length

The distance from end to end

Height

The distance from top to bottom

Unit

Any fixed amount, quantity, etc., used as a standard

When starting a project like painting walls, you will need to know the surface area of the walls before you can buy the paint. To find the **area**, multiply the **length** by the **height** of each wall to be painted. Remember to subtract the area of any doors or windows. Area is measured in square **units**.

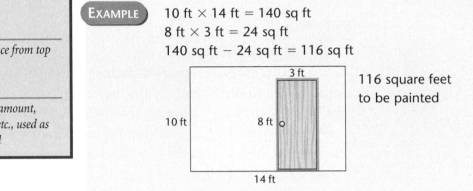

EXAMPLE   10 ft × 14 ft = 140 sq ft
8 ft × 3 ft = 24 sq ft
140 sq ft − 24 sq ft = 116 sq ft

116 square feet to be painted

Exercise A Find the surface area of each wall.

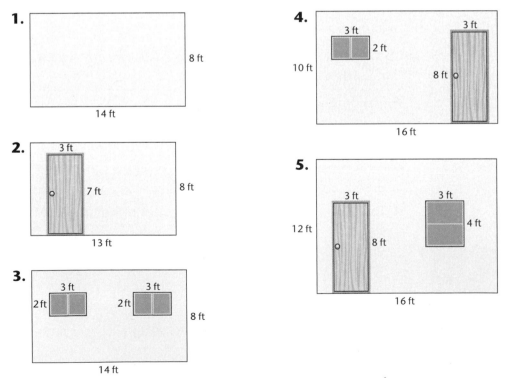

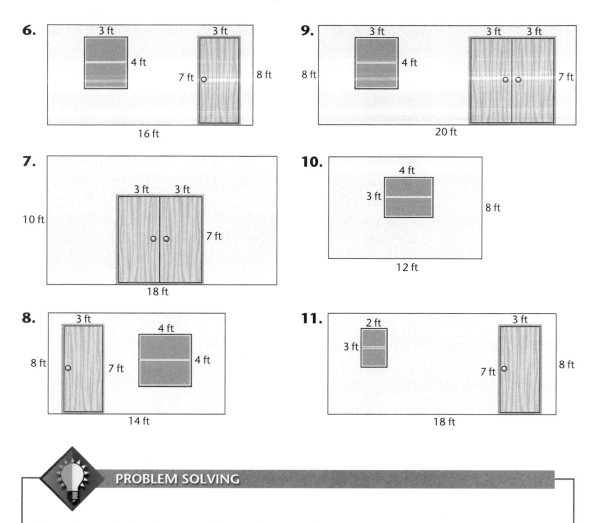

6. 3 ft · 3 ft · 4 ft · 7 ft · 8 ft · 16 ft

7. 3 ft · 3 ft · 10 ft · 7 ft · 18 ft

8. 3 ft · 4 ft · 8 ft · 7 ft · 4 ft · 14 ft

9. 3 ft · 3 ft · 3 ft · 4 ft · 8 ft · 7 ft · 20 ft

10. 4 ft · 3 ft · 8 ft · 12 ft

11. 2 ft · 3 ft · 3 ft · 3 ft · 7 ft · 8 ft · 18 ft

PROBLEM SOLVING

Exercise B Solve these problems about surface area.

1. What is the surface area of a wall that measures 8 feet by 12 feet? The wall has one window that measures 3 feet by 5 feet.

2. A wall measures 14 feet long and 8 feet high. There is a door that measures 3 feet by 7 feet. A window measures 3 feet by 4 feet. What is the surface area of the wall?

Technology Connection

Use the Internet to find information from local stores. What types of paints are available? What are typical costs per gallon? How many square feet of wall can each gallon cover?

An easy way to find the surface area of a room is to add the lengths of all walls. Then multiply the answer by the height of the room. Finally, subtract the area of any doors and windows.

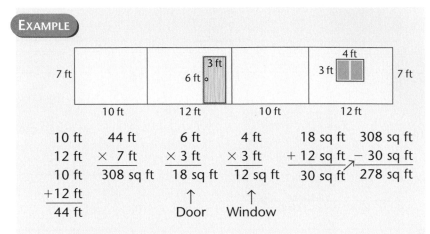

EXAMPLE

10 ft	44 ft	6 ft	4 ft	18 sq ft 308 sq ft
12 ft	× 7 ft	× 3 ft	× 3 ft	+ 12 sq ft − 30 sq ft
10 ft	308 sq ft	18 sq ft	12 sq ft	30 sq ft 278 sq ft
+12 ft		↑	↑	
44 ft		Door	Window	

The surface area is 278 sq ft.

Exercise C Find the surface area of each of these rooms.

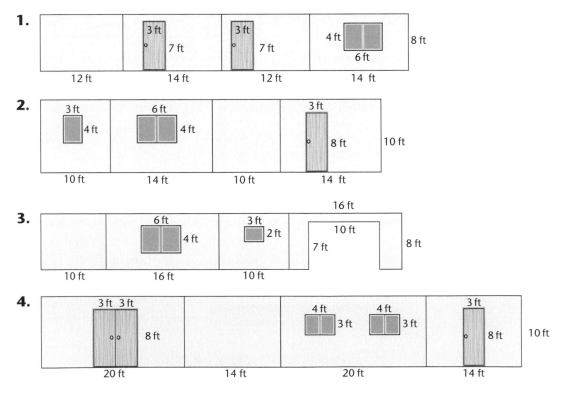

1.

2.

3.

4.

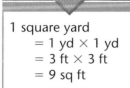

1 square yard
= 1 yd × 1 yd
= 3 ft × 3 ft
= 9 sq ft

Carpet is usually sold by the square yard in carpet stores. To find the number of square yards of carpet that you need, find the area of the floor in square feet. Divide this answer by 9. You divide by 9 because there are 9 square feet in 1 square yard.

EXAMPLE　**Step 1** 14 ft × 11 ft = 154 square feet

Step 2 $154 \div 9 = 17\frac{1}{9}$

There are $17\frac{1}{9}$ square yards.

Exercise A Find the number of square yards of carpet that are needed to carpet each floor.

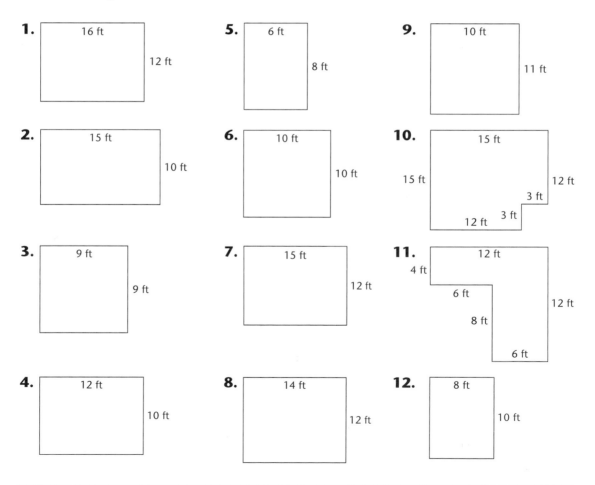

1. 16 ft / 12 ft

5. 6 ft / 8 ft

9. 10 ft / 11 ft

2. 15 ft / 10 ft

6. 10 ft / 10 ft

10. 15 ft / 15 ft / 12 ft / 3 ft / 3 ft / 12 ft

3. 9 ft / 9 ft

7. 15 ft / 12 ft

11. 12 ft / 4 ft / 6 ft / 12 ft / 8 ft / 6 ft

4. 12 ft / 10 ft

8. 14 ft / 12 ft

12. 8 ft / 10 ft

A **standard** size for carpet is 12 feet across. You buy the number of feet of carpet you need from a big roll of carpet. It may make a difference in the amount of carpet needed if you use the 12 feet in the wrong direction.

At least one dimension of the room must be 12 feet or less for the laid carpet to be one complete piece.

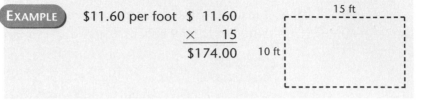

EXAMPLE $11.60 per foot
$$\begin{array}{r} \$\ 11.60 \\ \times\ \ \ \ \ 15 \\ \hline \$174.00 \end{array}$$

Exercise B Find the lowest price of carpet for each floor. The laid carpet must be one complete piece. Some carpet will need to be trimmed.

1. 12 ft / 8 ft — $11.45 per foot

3. 13 ft / 11 ft — $13.42 per foot

5. 9 ft / 8 ft — $11.32 per foot

2. 12 ft / 10 ft — $9.48 per foot

4. 10 ft / 11 ft — $13.89 per foot

6. 11 ft / 9 ft — $15.08 per foot

PROBLEM SOLVING

Exercise C Solve these problems.

1. A floor measures 11 feet by 15 feet. Jana bought a standard size carpet at $12.98 per foot. What did she pay?

2. A floor measures 12 feet by 16 feet. Gerald bought a standard size carpet at $14.46 per foot. What did he pay?

Width

The distance from side to side

Try This

In problem 6, find the cost if you can buy only whole cartons of tiles. Then find the cost if you can buy only single tiles. What is the difference in the costs?

Floor tiles are usually sold in cartons of 45. Each tile covers 1 square foot. To determine how many tiles you need, multiply the length by the **width** of the room. Divide that number by 45 to determine how many cartons you will need. Then multiply by the carton price to find a subtotal. Remember to multiply the remainder by the cost of a single tile to find the other subtotal. Then add the subtotals to find the total cost.

EXAMPLE   A carton costs $16.20. Each single tile costs $0.39. What is the cost to tile an 8 ft by 16 ft room?

An 8 ft by 16 ft room
$8 \times 16 = 128$ tiles
$128 \div 45 = 2$ cartons
  and 38 single tiles
$16.20 \times 2 = 32.40
$0.39 \times 38 = 14.82

$32.40	2 cartons
+14.82	38 singles
$47.22	Total cost

The cost is $47.22.

Exercise A If a carton of tiles costs $15.30 and a single tile costs $0.35, then find the cost of tiling each floor.

1. A room 12 ft by 14 ft
_____ cartons
_____ single tiles
_____ cost

4. A room 7 ft by 9 ft
_____ cartons
_____ single tiles
_____ cost

7. A room 10 ft by 10 ft
_____ cartons
_____ single tiles
_____ cost

2. A room 12 ft by 12 ft
_____ cartons
_____ single tiles
_____ cost

5. A room 10 ft by 12 ft
_____ cartons
_____ single tiles
_____ cost

8. A room 10 ft by 15 ft
_____ cartons
_____ single tiles
_____ cost

3. A room 9 ft by 14 ft
_____ cartons
_____ single tiles
_____ cost

6. A room 8 ft by 11 ft
_____ cartons
_____ single tiles
_____ cost

9. A room 10 ft by 16 ft
_____ cartons
_____ single tiles
_____ cost

Wallpaper is often sold by the **double roll**. You can estimate the amount of wallpaper that is needed to paper a room by using this rule:

Double roll

Wallpaper that covers twice the wall area of a single roll

Round up

To round to the next highest number

How to Measure for Wallpaper

Number of double rolls needed = distance around room × height of walls ÷ 60. Next, subtract one double roll for every four doors or windows. Always **round up** if you have a remainder after dividing by 60.

Writing About Mathematics

Describe an alternative method of finding the amount of wall space to be covered with wallpaper.

There are 60 square feet of wallpaper in a double roll.

EXAMPLE   One double roll of wallpaper costs $14.48.

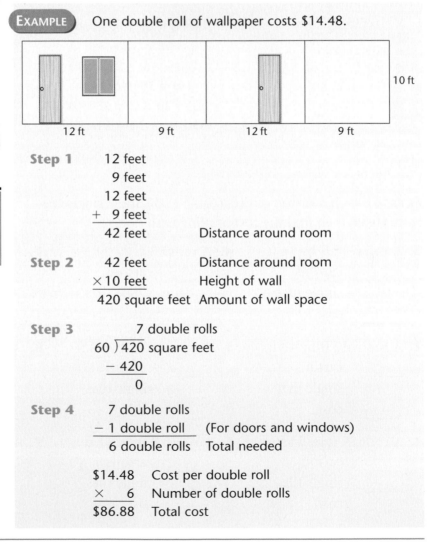

| 12 ft | 9 ft | 12 ft | 9 ft | 10 ft |

Step 1
```
   12 feet
    9 feet
   12 feet
 +  9 feet
   42 feet        Distance around room
```

Step 2
```
    42 feet        Distance around room
 × 10 feet         Height of wall
   420 square feet  Amount of wall space
```

Step 3
```
        7 double rolls
 60 ) 420 square feet
     − 420
        0
```

Step 4
```
    7 double rolls
  − 1 double roll    (For doors and windows)
    6 double rolls    Total needed
```

```
 $14.48    Cost per double roll
 ×     6   Number of double rolls
 $86.88    Total cost
```

Exercise A Find the cost of wallpapering each of these rooms.

1. One double roll of wallpaper costs $11.98.

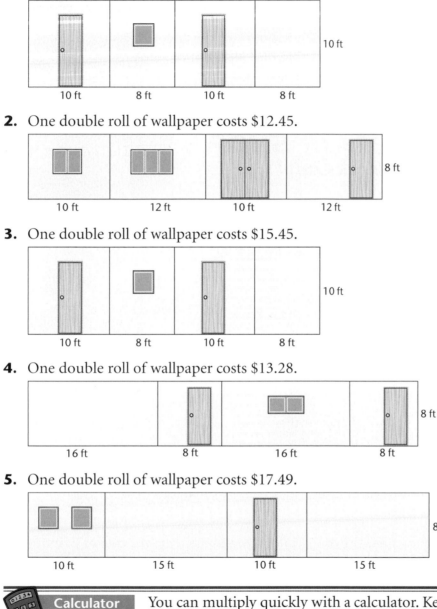

10 ft

10 ft   8 ft   10 ft   8 ft

2. One double roll of wallpaper costs $12.45.

8 ft

10 ft   12 ft   10 ft   12 ft

3. One double roll of wallpaper costs $15.45.

10 ft

10 ft   8 ft   10 ft   8 ft

4. One double roll of wallpaper costs $13.28.

8 ft

16 ft   8 ft   16 ft   8 ft

5. One double roll of wallpaper costs $17.49.

8 ft

10 ft   15 ft   10 ft   15 ft

Calculator Practice You can multiply quickly with a calculator. Key in each number. Check it on the calculator display before you key in the sign or the next number. Find the products of these numbers.

1. 12 × $14.53

2. 8 × $9.76

3. 10 × $12.53

4. 11 × $15.42

5. 9 × $17.67

6. 7 × $14.95

Fix It Up

Choose any room where you live. Your project is to measure the room for new carpet or new floor tiles, and for paint or wallpaper. Use the flyer below, or an ad you find in a newspaper, to determine prices for your choices.

HOME REPAIR SHOP

This Week Only!

Paint: Gallon of semigloss for $19.95
Covers 400 square feet. 15 colors available.

Wallpaper: $12.99 per double roll
12 styles available.

Tiles: Box of 45 for $30.00
Single tiles at $0.69 each. Choice of 8 styles.

Carpet: 12-ft widths at $15.75 per foot
Many colors available!

Exercises Do the activities and answer the questions.

1. Measure the floor of the room you have chosen. Will you be able to use a standard width carpet?

2. Compare the cost of buying carpet to the cost of buying tiles. Use the information from the flyer above, or a newspaper ad. Which will you choose for your room? Why?

3. Measure the walls of your room. Draw a sketch of the walls, including doors and windows.

4. Estimate the cost of wallpapering the walls. Estimate the cost of painting the room. Which will you choose? Why?

Chapter 2 REVIEW

Write the letter of the best answer to each question.

1. What is the surface area of the wall?

    A 83 sq ft

    B 99 sq ft

    C 104 sq ft

    D 120 sq ft

2. What is the surface area of this room?

    A 129 sq ft   **C** 336 sq ft

    B 297 sq ft   **D** 375 sq ft

3. How many square yards of carpet are needed?

    A 12

    B 36

    C 108

    D 972

4. If a carton of tiles costs $14.75 and a single tile costs $0.35, what is the cost of tiling the floor?

    A $29.50

    B $31.47

    C $31.60

    D $33.60

5. What is the cost of wallpapering the room if a double roll costs $14.95?

    A $29.90   **C** $83.72

    B $74.75   **D** $89.70

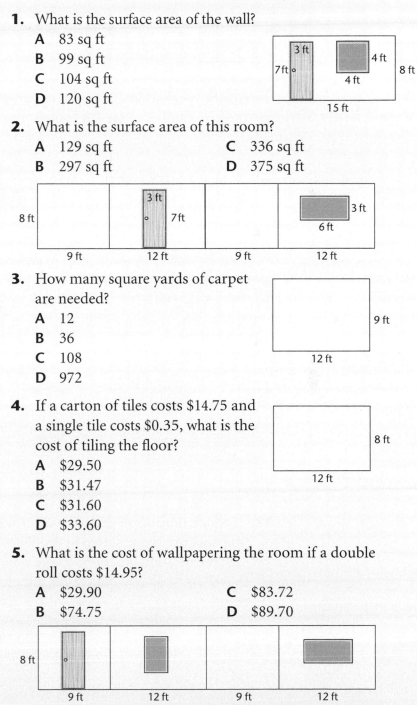

Find the answers.

6.　　346
　　　× 　7

9. 14) 639

12. 15) $34.95

7.　7) 5,292

10. 60) 4,740

13. $　154.32
　　　×　　　38

8.　　408
　　　× 　37

11.　　823
　　　× 226

Find the surface area of the walls drawn below. Subtract the area of any doors or windows.

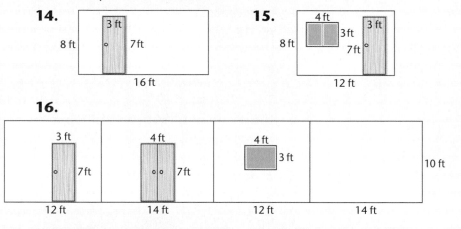

14.　3 ft　8 ft　7 ft　16 ft

15.　4 ft　3 ft　8 ft　3 ft　7 ft　12 ft

16.　3 ft　7 ft　12 ft　4 ft　7 ft　14 ft　4 ft　3 ft　12 ft　10 ft　14 ft

17. Find the number of double rolls of wallpaper needed to paper the room drawn in problem 16. Multiply the distance around the room by the wall height and divide by 60. Subtract one double roll for every four doors or windows.

Find the lowest cost of a carpet for each floor if 12-foot-wide carpeting costs $13.45 per foot.

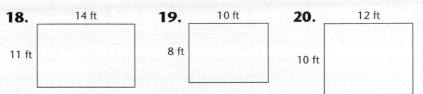

18. 14 ft / 11 ft

19. 10 ft / 8 ft

20. 12 ft / 10 ft

Find the number of square yards of carpet that are needed to carpet each floor.

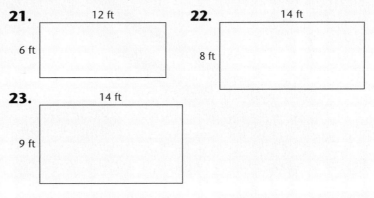

21. 12 ft / 6 ft

22. 14 ft / 8 ft

23. 14 ft / 9 ft

Find the lowest cost for tiling each floor described. Floor tiles that cover 1 square foot each are sold in cartons of 45 tiles for $17.00. Individual tiles cost $0.38 each.

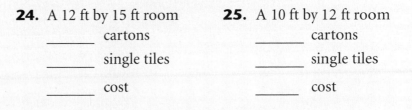

24. A 12 ft by 15 ft room

_____ cartons

_____ single tiles

_____ cost

25. A 10 ft by 12 ft room

_____ cartons

_____ single tiles

_____ cost

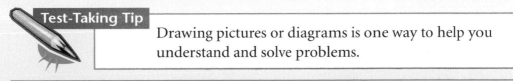

Test-Taking Tip

Drawing pictures or diagrams is one way to help you understand and solve problems.

3 Using Math in Sports

Whether you are a member of a sports team, or follow sports in the newspaper or on TV, you have experienced mathematics in sports. Baseball players keep track of batting averages, bowlers score their success, and Olympic records are broadcast on TV. Next time you think about numbers, think about sports! Adding, subtracting, multiplying, and dividing are some of the mathematics you'll discover there.

In Chapter 3, you will learn how to score spares and strikes in bowling. You will use your problem-solving skills as you explore the mathematics in weight lifting.

Goals for Learning

◆ To compute bowling scores

◆ To compute with whole numbers in the context of weight lifting

◆ To find average scores

Mathematics is used in scoring a bowling game. The score is usually kept by a computer, but you can keep score yourself. You add the number of pins knocked down by each ball.

The large rectangles on a score sheet are called **frames**. A bowler may roll two balls for each frame. The total number of pins you knock down with each roll is written in a small box in the frame.

Frame

In bowling, any of the divisions of a game in which all ten pins are set up anew

Add the pins from the two rolls to find the total pins knocked down in each frame.

EXAMPLES   Karen plays a 3-frame game. Look at her score sheet. Notice how the numbers are added.

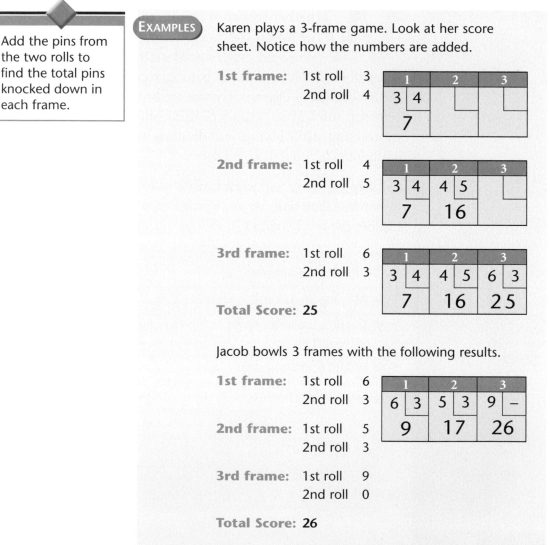

1st frame: 1st roll   3
          2nd roll   4

2nd frame: 1st roll   4
          2nd roll   5

3rd frame: 1st roll   6
          2nd roll   3

Total Score: 25

Jacob bowls 3 frames with the following results.

1st frame: 1st roll   6
          2nd roll   3

2nd frame: 1st roll   5
          2nd roll   3

3rd frame: 1st roll   9
          2nd roll   0

Total Score: 26

When Jacob hits no pins, he writes a dash in the box.

Exercise A On a separate sheet of paper, add to find the score for each frame.

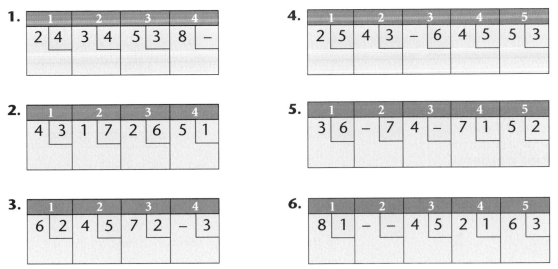

1.

1		2		3		4	
2	4	3	4	5	3	8	–

4.

1		2		3		4		5	
2	5	4	3	–	6	4	5	5	3

2.

1		2		3		4	
4	3	1	7	2	6	5	1

5.

1		2		3		4		5	
3	6	–	7	4	–	7	1	5	2

3.

1		2		3		4	
6	2	4	5	7	2	–	3

6.

1		2		3		4		5	
8	1	–	–	4	5	2	1	6	3

Exercise B Use the score sheet your teacher gives you. Fill in the frames with the scores for each game.

1. 1st frame: 1st roll 2
2nd roll 3

2nd frame: 1st roll 5
2nd roll 4

3rd frame: 1st roll 4
2nd roll 5

2. 1st frame: 1st roll 3
2nd roll 5

2nd frame: 1st roll 6
2nd roll 2

3rd frame: 1st roll 4
2nd roll 3

3. 1st frame: 1st roll 7
2nd roll 2

2nd frame: 1st roll 5
2nd roll 4

3rd frame: 1st roll 3
2nd roll 5

4. 1st frame: 1st roll 4
2nd roll 5

2nd frame: 1st roll 5
2nd roll 2

3rd frame: 1st roll 4
2nd roll 2

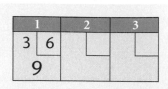

Spare

In bowling, knocking down all the pins with two rolls of the ball

◆

The number in the upper left corner of a frame tells how many pins were knocked down on the first roll.

Scoring a Spare With a little luck, you may knock down all ten pins with two rolls of the ball. When you do this, you score a **spare**. Getting a spare helps you to increase your score.

EXAMPLES

1st frame: 1st roll 3
             2nd roll 6

1		2	3
3	6		
9			

2nd frame: 1st roll 7
             2nd roll 3

1		2		3
3	6	7 /		
9				

The spare mark (/) means that ten pins are scored in the frame PLUS the number of pins on the first roll of the next frame.

3rd frame: 1st roll 4
             2nd roll 5

1		2		3	
3	6	7 /		4	5
9		23		32	

When a spare occurs in a frame, the total for that frame is the result of adding the previous frame total, plus ten, plus the number of pins knocked down on the first roll of the next frame.

1st frame: 1st roll 5
             2nd roll 3

1		2		3	
5	3	8 /		2	6
8		20		28	

2nd frame: 1st roll 8
             2nd roll 2

3rd frame: 1st roll 2
             2nd roll 6

Exercise C On a separate paper, write the number of pins that were knocked down on each roll.

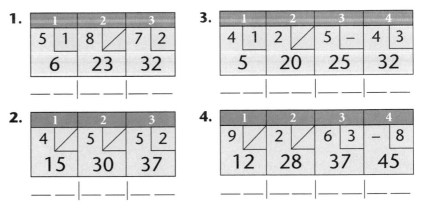

1.

1		2		3	
5	1	8	/	7	2
6		23		32	

— — | — — | — —

3.

1		2		3		4	
4	1	2	/	5	–	4	3
5		20		25		32	

— — | — — | — — | — —

2.

1		2		3	
4	/	5	/	5	2
15		30		37	

— — | — — | — —

4.

1		2		3		4	
9	/	2	/	6	3	–	8
12		28		37		45	

— — | — — | — — | — —

Exercise D Use the score sheet your teacher gives you. Fill in the scores for each frame.

1.
1st frame: 1st roll   4
             2nd roll   6

2nd frame: 1st roll   6
             2nd roll   2

3rd frame: 1st roll   5
             2nd roll   3

2.
1st frame: 1st roll   3
             2nd roll   7

2nd frame: 1st roll   4
             2nd roll   1

3rd frame: 1st roll   4
             2nd roll   6

4th frame: 1st roll   8
             2nd roll   0

5th frame: 1st roll   5
             2nd roll   2

Strike

In bowling, knocking down all ten pins on one roll of the ball

Scoring a Strike A **strike** occurs when a bowler knocks down all ten pins with the first roll of a frame.

The score for a strike is 10 plus the total number of pins the bowler knocks down with the next two rolls. A strike in the tenth frame gives the bowler two extra rolls.

1st frame: 1st roll 3
        2nd roll 5

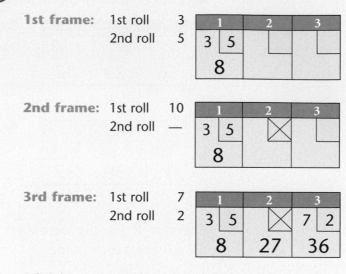

2nd frame: 1st roll 10
        2nd roll —

3rd frame: 1st roll 7
        2nd roll 2

Felicia's score is 96 for the sixth frame. Her game continues as shown.

7th frame: 1st roll 10
        2nd roll —

8th frame: 1st roll 3
        2nd roll 7

9th frame: 1st roll 6
        2nd roll 3

10th frame: 1st roll 10
        2nd roll —
1st extra roll   10
2nd extra roll   9

Exercise E On a separate sheet of paper, write the score for each frame.

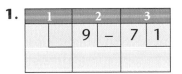

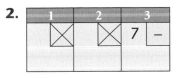

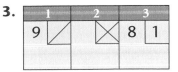

Exercise F Use the score sheet that your teacher gives you. Fill in the score for each frame.

1.

1		2		3		4		5		6		7		8		9		10	
6	3	5	2	8	1	✕		4	5	9	–	4	5	3	2	5	4	4	⟋	4

Try This

A perfect score for ten frames of bowling is 300. Using a blank score sheet, fill in the scores a bowler must get in each frame to reach 300.

2.

1st frame:	1st roll	5
	2nd roll	4
2nd frame:	1st roll	6
	2nd roll	2
3rd frame:	1st roll	4
	2nd roll	6
4th frame:	1st roll	3
	2nd roll	5
5th frame:	1st roll	8
	2nd roll	1
6th frame:	1st roll	2
	2nd roll	8
7th frame:	1st roll	4
	2nd roll	5
8th frame:	1st roll	3
	2nd roll	7
9th frame:	1st roll	6
	2nd roll	1
10th frame:	1st roll	10
	2nd roll	—
	1st extra roll	9
	2nd extra roll	1

3.

1st frame:	1st roll	8
	2nd roll	2
2nd frame:	1st roll	6
	2nd roll	4
3rd frame:	1st roll	10
	2nd roll	—
4th frame:	1st roll	9
	2nd roll	1
5th frame:	1st roll	8
	2nd roll	1
6th frame:	1st roll	6
	2nd roll	3
7th frame:	1st roll	8
	2nd roll	0
8th frame:	1st roll	8
	2nd roll	2
9th frame:	1st roll	10
	2nd roll	—
10th frame:	1st roll	10
	2nd roll	—
	1st extra roll	10
	2nd extra roll	10

Calculate

To find an answer by using mathematics

Compute

To calculate or figure out

When multiplying with zeros, check your answer to make sure it has the right number of zeros.

Weight lifting helps develop the muscles of the body and keeps a person physically fit. Mathematics is needed in weight lifting to **calculate** weight totals. When you use mathematics in weight lifting, you need to know how to **compute** with zeros.

EXAMPLES

Each member of the Martinsburg High School weight-lifting team lifts 300 pounds with barbells. Twenty-four members are on the team. What is the total weight the team lifts?

```
    300    Pounds each
×    24    Members
  1 200
+ 6 00
  7,200    Total pounds
```

Qui uses two 10-pound dumbbells to help build strength in his upper arms. Qui's exercise schedule requires 12 lifts with the dumbbells. What is the total weight each arm lifts after 12 lifts?

```
  12    Lifts
× 10    Pounds per lift
 120    Total pounds
```

Marcell lifts 150 pounds on his first attempt. He increases the weight by 24 pounds for his second lift. What is the total weight he lifts on the second lift?

```
  150    Pounds each
+  24    Pounds increased
  174    Total pounds
```

Writing About Mathematics

Computing with zeros comes in handy for more than just weight lifting. Write about a situation in your life when you can use this skill.

Exercise A Practice your skill with zeros. Find the answer to each problem.

1. 200
     − 15

3. 670
     − 568

5. 200
     − 156

7. 200
     − 198

2. 310
     − 182

4. 320
     − 196

6. 235
     − 220

8. 230
     − 62

9. 310 + 296 + 400

14. 806 + 209 + 10

10. 506 + 23 + 915

15. 101 + 310 + 1,091

11. 7,101 ÷ 9

16. 3,581 ÷ 10

12. 4,860 ÷ 12

17. 2,500 ÷ 25

13. 320 × 50

18. 4,700 × 70

PROBLEM SOLVING

Exercise B Solve these problems.

1. Sergio lifts a 95-pound barbell six times during his workout. What is the total weight that Sergio lifts?

2. Danielle lifts 55 pounds on her first attempt. She adds two 10-pound weights for the second lift. How many pounds does she lift on the second attempt?

3. Melissa's weight-lifting team lifts the following weights: 125, 90, 102, and 91 pounds. What is the total weight her team lifts?

4. José's new barbell set includes a 45-pound handle, two 10-pound plates, two 5-pound collars, and two $2\frac{1}{2}$-pound plates. How much does the set weigh in all?

Average

The number obtained by dividing the sum of two or more quantities by the number of quantities

When adding or dividing, be sure to line up the numbers carefully.

In comparing performances in sports, **average** scores are useful. An average is found by first adding all of the single scores and then dividing the sum by the number of single scores.

EXAMPLES The Silver Stingrays bowling team bowls 178, 183, 161, and 200. What is the team's average score?

Add.

$$
\left.\begin{array}{r} 178 \\ 183 \\ 161 \\ + 200 \\ \hline 722 \end{array}\right\} \text{Scores}
$$

Divide.

$$
180 \tfrac{2}{4} = 180 \tfrac{1}{2}
$$

$$
\begin{array}{r} 4 \overline{)722} \\ -4 \\ \hline 32 \\ -32 \\ \hline 02 \\ -0 \\ \hline 0 \end{array}
$$

The average score is $180 \tfrac{1}{2}$.

Cory lifts 112, 107, 103, 98, and 105 pounds during the weight-lifting finals. What is the average weight Cory lifts?

Add.

$$
\left.\begin{array}{r} 112 \\ 107 \\ 103 \\ 98 \\ +105 \\ \hline 525 \end{array}\right\} \text{Weights}
$$

Divide.

$$
\begin{array}{r} 105 \\ 5 \overline{)525} \\ -50 \\ \hline 25 \\ -25 \\ \hline 0 \end{array}
$$

The average weight is 105 pounds.

Exercise A Find the average for each set of numbers. Write remainders as fractions.

1. 26, 35, 20

2. 80, 83, 90

3. 180, 296, 121

4. 126, 103, 110

5. 165, 203, 175

6. 162, 200, 178

7. 202, 213, 185

8. 163, 200, 417, 831

PROBLEM SOLVING

Exercise B Solve these problems.

1. The Lapton High School bowling team bowls 178, 186, 275, and 190. What is the team's average score?

2. Ngoc's bowling scores are 263, 200, 217, 225, and 195. What is Ngoc's average score?

3. The first time that Anthony ever bowled, his scores were 79, 103, and 118. What was his average score?

4. Shanika lifts 125, 105, 150, 95, 150, 145, and 72 pounds during the weight-lifting finals. What is the average weight that Shanika lifts?

5. During the New Castle bowling tournament, spectators numbered 175, 180, 165, 180, 170, 175, and 192. What was the average attendance for spectators?

Technology Connection

Until a few years ago, bowlers kept their own scores, using score sheets and pencils. Today, computers automatically compute scores. Bowlers can use the computer system to figure out their average score per game. Some computers give the bowler suggestions for making tough shots. The next time you bowl, try to keep score using the computer system. How do you think this technology can help bowlers achieve higher scores?

Estimation Before you use a calculator to find an average, estimate the sum of the numbers.

EXAMPLE   Find the average of 275, 415, and 315.

Step 1   Estimate the sum first.

275	rounds to	300
415	rounds to	400
315	rounds to	+ 300
		1,000 Estimated sum

The exact sum on the calculator is 1,005. Since 1,005 is very close to the estimated sum, 1,005 is a reasonable answer.

Step 2   Estimate the average.
1,000 divided by 3 is about 333.

Step 3   Divide. $1005 \div 3 = 335$

The exact average on the calculator is 335. Since 335 is very close to 333, 335 is a reasonable answer.

The average of 275, 415, and 315 is 335.

You can find the average weight lifted. Just add all of the amounts lifted and divide by the number of lifts.

Calculator Exercise Use a calculator to find the average of each set of numbers. Estimate the sum of each set of numbers first. Use rounded numbers to estimate. Round your average to three decimal places. Write your answers on a separate sheet of paper.

	Numbers	Estimated Sum	Average	Exact Sum	Average
1.	26, 28, 20				
2.	38, 57, 31, 33				
3.	58, 42, 48				
4.	62, 69				
5.	32, 36, 51, 20				
6.	184, 108, 200, 190				
7.	260, 221, 315				
8.	3,001; 2,115; 2,815				
9.	516, 786, 912, 492, 758				
10.	9,984; 12,068; 11,496				

Try This

Use your calculator to find the average of these numbers: 128.35; 477.14; 588.432; 907.3; and 229.681. Estimate the sum first, using rounded numbers. Round your average to three decimal places.

Application

Using Statistics

The Richmond Rockets are one of the best high school basketball teams in the state. During their games, a student keeps a record of everything that happens. This record helps the players and coaches know what they do well and what they need to improve.

The coach needs to choose two new starters from the players listed on the record below. He will use the team's record, or statistics, to help make the decision.

Player	Cougars Game				Lions Game			
	Free throws	Assists	Rebounds	Points	Free throws	Assists	Rebounds	Points
David Michaels	3	4	8	15	2	1	7	12
Andre Jackson	4	2	3	20	3	4	4	17
Matt Clark	1	6	5	19	0	5	6	10
Malcolm Winters	4	2	6	18	5	5	6	15
Don Stevenson	2	2	4	12	5	6	2	17

Exercises Use the chart to answer these questions.

1. Which player averages the most free throws per game?

2. Which player has the highest point average per game? What is his point average?

3. Which player has the highest assist average per game? What is his assist average?

4. What is the total number of rebounds in both games? What is the average number of rebounds per game?

5. How can this information be helpful to the coach in choosing his new starters?

Chapter 3 R E V I E W

Write the letter of the best answer to each question.
Use the score sheet below.

1	2	3	4	5	6	7	8	9	10
5 | 2	8 | 1	5 | /	4 | 4	⊠	8 | –	⊠	2 | 4	3 | /	2 | / | 4
7	16	30	38	__	64	80	86	98	__

1. How many pins did the bowler knock down on the
second roll in the third frame?

   A 4

   B 5

   C 6

   D 7

2. What should be the total score for the fifth frame?

   A 54

   B 55

   C 56

   D 57

3. How many pins are knocked down in the sixth frame?

   A 0

   B 8

   C 9

   D 10

4. What is the total score for all ten frames?

   A 112

   B 114

   C 116

   D 118

5. How many pins are knocked down in the seventh frame?

   A 0

   B 8

   C 9

   D 10

Use the score sheet your teacher gives you. Fill in the frames.

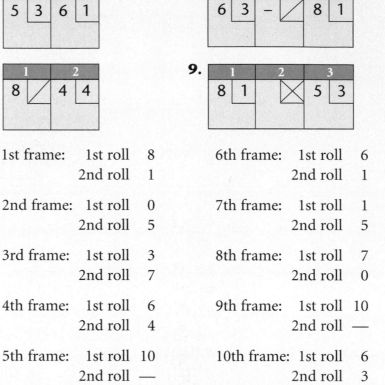

6.

1		2	
5	3	6	1

7.

1		2	
8	⟋	4	4

8.

1		2		3	
6	3	–	⟋	8	1

9.

1		2		3	
8	1	⊠		5	3

10.

| 1st frame: | 1st roll | 8 |
| | 2nd roll | 1 |

| 2nd frame: | 1st roll | 0 |
| | 2nd roll | 5 |

| 3rd frame: | 1st roll | 3 |
| | 2nd roll | 7 |

| 4th frame: | 1st roll | 6 |
| | 2nd roll | 4 |

| 5th frame: | 1st roll | 10 |
| | 2nd roll | — |

| 6th frame: | 1st roll | 6 |
| | 2nd roll | 1 |

| 7th frame: | 1st roll | 1 |
| | 2nd roll | 5 |

| 8th frame: | 1st roll | 7 |
| | 2nd roll | 0 |

| 9th frame: | 1st roll | 10 |
| | 2nd roll | — |

| 10th frame: | 1st roll | 6 |
| | 2nd roll | 3 |

11. Marco increases his 123-pound bench-press weight by 15 pounds. What is his new bench-press weight?

Find the averages.

12. 39, 42, 65

13. 72, 83, 91, 39, 36

14. Kenny bowls 216, 195, and 190. What is his average score?

15. Zakiya lifts these weights: 100, 80, 110, 140, 120, and 115 pounds. What is the average weight Zakiya lifts?

16. Jody lifts 132 pounds in 3 days. What is the average weight she lifts each day?

17. Sam lifts a 20-pound barbell 12 times. How many total pounds does he lift?

18. Peter wants to lift 1,000 pounds in 1 week. So far he has lifted 724 pounds. How many more pounds does Peter need to lift?

19. Jarrod can lift 117 pounds, using a bench press. Seth can lift 152 pounds. What is the difference?

20. Alena does 20 curls a day on each arm. She uses 10-pound weights. How many pounds does she curl in all?

Test-Taking Tip

Estimating answers to math problems is one way to check whether your answers on tests are reasonable.

Games of Chance

How many times have you played a game of cards or a board game? Did you wonder whether you could predict when you would beat your opponent? Mathematicians like you use probability to predict what will happen. Try it the next time you play a game with your friends. You will have them wondering what's your secret.

In Chapter 4, you will use coins, dice, and cards to explore probability. You will discover that experiments are done in mathematics, just as they are in science.

Goals for Learning

- ◆ To determine the total number of possible outcomes from flipping a coin
- ◆ To determine the probability of a given outcome when rolling one or two dice
- ◆ To use probability to predict the possibility of an event occurring
- ◆ To predict the probability of drawing a given card from a 52-card deck

Possible outcome

A result that can happen

Probability tree

A diagram showing all possible outcomes

When you flip a coin, there are only two **possible outcomes**. The coin will either land on heads or tails. We can use a **probability tree** to help us keep track of several flips of a coin.

EXAMPLE   What are the possible outcomes of flipping a coin three times?

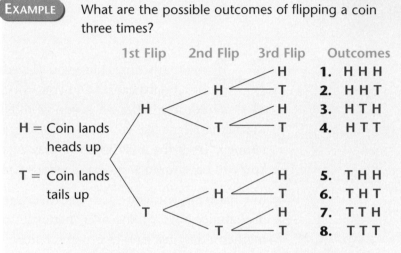

Eight different outcomes are possible.

PROBLEM SOLVING

Exercise A Use probability trees to answer these questions.

1. How many possible outcomes are there if you flip a coin two times?

2. If you flip a coin two times, how many outcomes give you a head and a tail?

3. Suppose you flip a coin four times. How many different possible outcomes are there?

4. With four coin flips, how many outcomes give two heads and two tails?

5. With four coin flips, how many outcomes give four tails?

6. With four coin flips, how many outcomes give three heads and one tail?

7. If you flip a coin five times, how many outcomes give three heads and two tails?

8. With five coin flips, how may outcomes give one tail and four heads?

Probability

The chances that an outcome will happen

Formula

A rule or method of doing something

Die

(plural: dice) small cube of bone, plastic, etc., marked on each side with from one to six spots and used usually in pairs

You can use **probability** to measure how likely an event is to happen. The probability of an event happening is the number of successful outcomes divided by the total number of possible outcomes. Probability is given in fractional form. In **formula** form, this is:

$$\text{Probability} = \frac{\text{Number of successful outcomes}}{\text{Total number of possible outcomes}}$$

As an example, consider the **die** (singular form of **dice**). A die has six faces. Each face is equally likely to appear when you roll the die.

What is the probability that you will roll a 5?

You can use probability to predict how many times an event is likely to happen.

EXAMPLE   If Sam rolls a die 24 times, how many times can he expect to roll a 5?

The probability of rolling a 5 with one roll is $\frac{1}{6}$

$\frac{1}{6} = \frac{\blacksquare}{24}$

Sam can expect to roll a 5 four times out of 24 rolls.

Exercise A Answer these questions about rolling one die. How many times can you expect to roll…

1. a 5 out of 18 rolls?

2. a 3 out of 24 rolls?

3. a 3 out of 30 rolls?

4. a 6 out of 30 rolls?

5. a 1 out of 12 rolls?

6. a 6 out of 54 rolls?

7. a 4 out of 36 rolls?

8. a 2 out of 48 rolls?

9. a 2 out of 42 rolls?

10. a 1 out of 72 rolls?

When you roll two dice, the likely outcomes are not equal. This is because there are different numbers of **possibilities** of rolling each **dice sum**. You can roll a 5 by rolling 1 and 4, 2 and 3, 3 and 2, and 4 and 1. You can roll a 4 by rolling 1 and 3, 2 and 2, and 3 and 1. You can roll a 5 four different ways, but you can roll a 4 only three different ways. Therefore, you will probably roll more 5s than 4s.

Writing About Mathematics

Describe what a probability tree looks like for rolling two dice.

This chart shows all of the possible outcomes of rolling two dice.

Exercise A Answer these questions about rolling two dice.

1. How many outcomes are possible?

2. What are all of the ways that you can roll a 6?

3. How many different ways are there to roll a 6?

4. What is the probability of rolling a 6?

5. What are all of the possible ways to roll a 9?

6. How many ways are there to roll a 9?

7. What is the probability of rolling a 9?

8. What is the least dice sum that you can roll with two dice?

9. What is the greatest dice sum that you can roll with two dice?

Try This

Use Exercise B. Find the probability of rolling a sum that is 9 or greater.

Exercise B Fill in this chart about the probability of rolling the given dice sum.

	Dice Sum	Probability of Rolling
1.	2	_____
2.	3	_____
3.	4	_____
4.	5	_____
5.	6	_____
6.	7	_____
7.	8	_____
8.	9	_____
9.	10	_____
10.	11	_____
11.	12	_____

Advance

To move forward

Many board games use the sum of two dice to determine how many spaces a player may **advance** on each turn. Below is the board for the game of *Journey*.

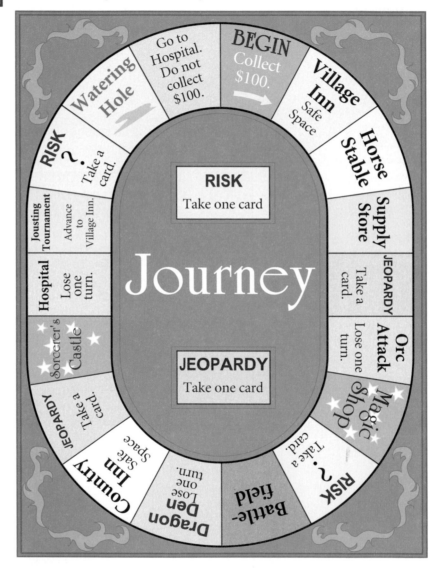

Clockwise

In the direction in which the hands of a clock rotate

When it is your turn in the game of *Journey*, you roll two dice. You find the sum of the dice, and then advance that number of spaces in a **clockwise** direction. You follow the directions printed in the space on which you land.

At each turn, you are more likely to land on some spaces than on others. This is because there are more ways to roll the number that will place you on those spaces.

 EXAMPLE   If you are on the BEGIN space, what is the probability that you will land on the Magic Shop on your next turn? This information will help you find a solution:

◆ Magic Shop is six spaces away.

◆ There are five different ways to roll a 6.

◆ There are 36 different outcomes of rolling two dice.

Therefore, the probability of landing on the Magic Shop is $\frac{5}{36}$.

PROBLEM SOLVING

Exercise A Answer these questions about probability. You may need to simplify fractions to simplest terms.

1. You are at BEGIN. What is the probability of landing on Orc Attack on your next turn?

2. You are at Battlefield. What is the probability of landing on Risk on your next turn?

3. What is the probability of landing on Supply Store from Village Inn?

4. What is the probability of landing on Country Inn from Magic Shop?

5. What is the probability of landing on Dragon Den from Village Inn?

More than one number on the dice roll might place you on the same square. For example, suppose that you are on Country Inn and you roll a 9. You would land on Village Inn. What would have happened if you had rolled a 4? You would have advanced to Jousting Tournament.

The directions there say, "Advance to Village Inn." The game has two events that would allow you to advance to Village Inn. Those events are: rolling a 4 or rolling a 9. To figure the probability of landing on Village Inn from Country Inn, you need to know the following:

Probability of Event A or Event B =
Probability of Event A + Probability of Event B

EXAMPLE Look at the board game on page 56. What is the probability of landing on Village Inn from Country Inn?

This information will help you find a solution:

◆ Could land on Village Inn by rolling a 4 or a 9

◆ Probability of rolling a 4 is $\frac{3}{36}$

◆ Probability of rolling a 9 is $\frac{4}{36}$

◆ Probability of rolling a 4 or a 9 is $\frac{3}{36} + \frac{4}{36}$, or $\frac{7}{36}$

Therefore, the probability of landing on Village Inn is $\frac{7}{36}$.

Exercise B Use the board game on page 56. Answer these questions about the probability of landing on a space from a given space. There may be more than one way of landing on the space, or there may be more than one of the spaces.

1. From Horse Stable to Dragon Den

2. From Dragon Den to Hospital

3. From Orc Attack to Risk

4. From Sorcerer's Castle to Village Inn

5. From Orc Attack to Village Inn

Expect

To look forward to

Experiment

A procedure used to test a theory

When you roll two dice, you can **expect** to roll a 7 six times out of 36 rolls, or one-sixth of the time. This is expected. This may or may not be what happens.

Try this **experiment**. Get two dice. Get a copy of the chart from your teacher. Each time that you roll the dice, make a mark on your chart next to the number that you rolled. Do this 36 times.

Remember that an experiment will not always result in the way you expect.

Dice Sum	Number of Times Rolled	Number of Times Expected
2		1
3		2
4		3
5		4
6		5
7		6
8		5
9		4
10		3
11		2
12		1

PROBLEM SOLVING

Exercise A Answer these questions about your chart.

1. Was the number of times rolled the same as the number of times expected for any of the dice sums?

2. Was the number of times rolled different from the number of times expected for any of the dice sums?

3. Why do you suppose the number of times that you rolled some numbers was different from the number of times that you expected to roll those numbers?

Predict

To state what will happen

You can determine how many times you can expect to roll a given number with two dice. The probability of rolling each number is different for each dice sum. You can **predict** how many times you can expect to roll a given number if you remember the formula for finding probability.

$$\text{Probability} = \frac{\text{Number of successful outcomes}}{\text{Total number of possible outcomes}}$$

EXAMPLES How many times can you expect to roll a 6 out of 72 rolls?

$$\frac{5}{36} = \frac{\blacksquare}{72}$$

You can expect to roll ten 6s.

How many times can you expect to roll a 4 out of 48 rolls?

3 chances out of 36, or
1 chance out of 12 $\frac{1}{12} = \frac{\blacksquare}{48}$

You can expect to roll four 4s.

Exercise A Answer these questions about rolling two dice. How many times can you expect to roll...

1. a 7 out of 24 rolls?

2. a 7 out of 18 rolls?

3. a 5 out of 36 rolls?

4. a 5 out of 18 rolls?

5. a 10 out of 60 rolls?

6. a 3 out of 54 rolls?

7. an 8 out of 108 rolls?

8. a 13 out of 24 rolls?

9. a 2 out of 36 rolls?

10. a 6 out of 36 rolls?

11. an 11 out of 54 rolls?

12. a 12 out of 72 rolls?

13. a 4 out of 72 rolls?

14. a 5 out of 63 rolls?

15. a 9 out of 27 rolls?

16. a 10 out of 48 rolls?

Suit

Any of the four sets of thirteen playing cards

Draw

To pick at random

Hearts and diamonds are red cards. Clubs and spades are black cards. The 13 cards in each suit are the ace, 2, 3, 4, 5, 6, 7, 8, 9, 10, jack, queen, and king.

A standard deck of playing cards has 52 cards in four **suits**: hearts, clubs, diamonds, and spades. Thirteen cards are in each suit.

Given that information, what is the probability that if you **draw** one card, it will be a 5?

$$\text{Probability} = \frac{\text{Number of successful outcomes}}{\text{Total number of possible outcomes}}$$

$$\text{Probability} = \frac{4}{52} = \frac{1}{13}$$

There are four 5s out of 52 possible cards, so the probability of drawing a 5 is $\frac{4}{52} = \frac{1}{13}$.

EXAMPLE What is the probability of drawing a black 8?

$$\text{Probability} = \frac{\text{Number of successful outcomes}}{\text{Total number of possible outcomes}}$$

$$\text{Probability} = \frac{2}{52} = \frac{1}{26}$$

There are only two black 8s: the 8 of clubs and the 8 of spades. Therefore, the probability of drawing a black 8 is $\frac{1}{26}$.

Exercise A Answer these questions about the probability of drawing certain cards. What is the probability of drawing…

1. a jack?

2. a black 3?

3. a club?

4. a 5 of hearts?

5. a red 8?

6. a king or a queen?

7. a black card?

8. a face card (king, queen, jack)?

9. a 10 of spades?

10. a card less than a 7? (Do not include aces.)

Rummy In the game of **rummy**, players are dealt seven cards. Then they draw cards and try to get three of a kind (such as three 7s) or a run in the same suit (such as the 3, 4, and 5 of spades). Because some of the 52 cards are already dealt, the probability of drawing a particular card is figured differently.

EXAMPLES   Study these seven-card hands:

What is the probability that this player will draw a 9?

52 cards − 7 = 45

Probability $= \frac{3}{45} = \frac{1}{15}$

(There are four 9s, but one is already in the player's hand.)

A 3 of clubs will give this player a run in the same suit (a 2, 3, 4, and 5 of clubs).

What is the probability that this player will draw a 3 of clubs?

Probability $= \frac{1}{45}$

(There is only one 3 of clubs.)

In both examples the total number of outcomes is 45 instead of 52 because seven cards are already in the hand (52 − 7 = 45).

Exercise B Answer these questions about the probability of drawing the card described. Remember to consider the cards that are already in the hand.

1. What is the probability of drawing a jack?

2. What is the probability of drawing a 7?

3. What is the probability of drawing the 6 of diamonds?

4. What is the probability of drawing a 2?

5. What is the probability of drawing a 4 or an 8?

6. What is the probability of drawing a queen?

7. What is the probability of drawing a 2, a 6, or a 7?

8. What is the probability of drawing the 6 of hearts or a 3?

9. What is the probability of drawing a club?

10. What is the probability of drawing a 3 or an ace?

Calculator Practice

Changing fractions to decimal equivalents can be easy when you use a calculator. Use the division function.

EXAMPLE Express $\frac{6}{13}$ as a decimal.

Solution Press these buttons in order:

$6 \div 13 =$

Answer 0.4615384

Calculator Exercise Use your calculator to change each fraction to a decimal.

1. $\frac{5}{8}$ _____

2. $\frac{3}{7}$ _____

3. $\frac{1}{6}$ _____

4. $\frac{3}{4}$ _____

5. $\frac{2}{9}$ _____

6. $\frac{1}{3}$ _____

7. $\frac{5}{6}$ _____

8. $\frac{4}{12}$ _____

9. $\frac{10}{11}$ _____

10. $\frac{15}{17}$ _____

11. $\frac{20}{21}$ _____

12. $\frac{18}{19}$ _____

13. $\frac{16}{17}$ _____

14. $\frac{28}{29}$ _____

15. $\frac{5}{13}$ _____

16. $\frac{3}{16}$ _____

Try This

You may not need a calculator to quickly change some fractions to decimals. Try these:

$\frac{1}{2}, \frac{5}{10}, \frac{12}{24}, \frac{3}{9}, \frac{17}{17}$

Use your answers to problems 1–16 to help you. Then use your calculator to check your answers.

Chances in Contests

Several businesses around town are holding contests.

Diner Deluxe

Drawing for free meal out of 5,000 customers entered.

BOOK SELLER

Free books! Five winners drawn from 500 entries.

THE ART STORE

Free oil painting for the winner. Drawn from 250 names entered.

MOVIE BONANZA

Free movie rental drawing! 200 customers entered.

Exercises Tonisha visited each of these businesses once. Find each probability.

1. Find the probability that Tonisha wins a free meal at Diner Deluxe.

2. Find the probability that Tonisha wins a free book from the Book Seller.

3. Find the probability that Tonisha wins the free oil painting from The Art Store if she entered the contest three times.

4. Find the probability that Tonisha wins a free movie rental from Movie Bonanza.

Technology Connection

Use a calculator to help you answer these questions about rolling six-sided dice.

1. How many outcomes are possible with one die?

2. How many outcomes are possible with two dice?

3. What is 6×6?

4. Suppose you have three dice. How do you think you could find the total number of outcomes?

5. Find the total number of possible outcomes if you roll three dice.

6. Explain the connection between the number of dice you roll and the number of possible outcomes.

7. Use the connection in problem 6 to find the total number of possible outcomes if five dice are rolled.

Chapter 4   R E V I E W

Write the letter of the best answer to each question.

1. When you roll a die, what is the probability of rolling a 6?

   A 6

   B 1

   C $\frac{1}{6}$

   D $\frac{6}{6}$

2. When you roll two dice, what is the probability of rolling an 8?

   A $\frac{5}{8}$

   B $\frac{5}{36}$

   C $\frac{8}{36}$

   D $\frac{5}{6}$

3. How many times would you expect to roll a 4 if you roll two dice 72 times?

   A 6

   B $\frac{3}{36}$

   C 3

   D 8

4. What is the probability of drawing a red card from a deck of 52 cards?

   A $\frac{1}{4}$

   B $\frac{1}{13}$

   C $\frac{2}{13}$

   D $\frac{1}{2}$

5. You draw the ace of spades for your first card. What is the probability that the next card you draw will also be an ace?

   A $\frac{1}{13}$

   B $\frac{3}{51}$

   C $\frac{4}{51}$

   D $\frac{3}{13}$

Write your answers in simplest form.

6. $\frac{15}{36} =$ **7.** $\frac{39}{52} =$

Fill in the missing numerator.

8. $\frac{5}{6} = \frac{\blacksquare}{42}$ **9.** $\frac{7}{36} = \frac{\blacksquare}{72}$

When you are rolling one die, how many times can you expect to roll…

10. a 4 out of 18 rolls?

11. a 2 out of 54 rolls?

12. a 5 out of 42 rolls?

When you are rolling two dice, how many times can you expect to roll…

13. a 4 out of 24 rolls?

14. a 9 out of 45 rolls?

When you are rolling two dice, what is the probability of…

15. rolling a 10?

16. rolling a 6?

This is part of a board game. Answer these questions about your next turn. For each question, start on the GO space.

For each turn, you roll two dice, advance the number of spaces that you rolled, and follow the directions on the space that you land on. The cards that you draw give you special favors, but do not tell you to move to any other spaces.

What is the probability that…

17. you will land on Battlefield?

18. you will land on Risk?

19. you will land on Dungeon?

A deck of 52 cards is shuffled. You draw one card. What is the probability that…

20. the card is a 6?

21. the card is a club?

22. the card is a king or a queen?

23. the card is a 4 or a red 6?

Answer these questions about playing rummy with a 52-card deck. Remember that seven cards are already in your hand.

24. What is the probability of drawing a 6?

25. What is the probability of drawing a 3?

Test-Taking Tip

If you are having trouble solving a problem on a test, then go on to the next problem and come back to any skipped problems.

5 Adjusting Recipes

C an you think of a time when you multiplied or divided with fractions and whole numbers? Maybe you were planning a menu and shopping list, or cooking and baking. Most recipes list ingredients as fractions or mixed numbers. Chefs in restaurants, bakers in factories, and cooks in their kitchens all multiply and divide with fractions to help them determine amounts of ingredients for their special recipes.

In Chapter 5, you will learn ways to increase recipes to feed more people and to reduce recipes to serve fewer.

Goals for Learning

◆ To rename an improper fraction to a mixed number in simplest form

◆ To convert measurement units to equivalent measurement units

◆ To adjust recipes by multiplying and dividing fractions and mixed numbers

Lesson 1 Equivalent Measurements

Recipe

Directions for making something

Equivalent

Equal to another in a particular way

Convert

To change to something of equal value

Ingredients in **recipes** are written many ways. It is helpful to know what the **equivalent** measurement is in case you need to adjust a recipe. Working with equivalent measurements can simplify many recipe adjustments. These equivalent measurements should be a part of a cook's working knowledge.

2 tablespoons = 1 ounce
3 teaspoons   = 1 tablespoon
16 tablespoons = 1 cup
2 cups   = 1 pint
2 pints   = 1 quart
4 quarts   = 1 gallon

Writing About Mathematics

Write a few sentences about why you might use equivalent measurements to adjust a recipe.

EXAMPLES   5 tablespoons = ■ teaspoons

Rule   When you **convert** large units to small units, you multiply.
From the table, 3 teaspoons = 1 tablespoon.

5 × 3 = 15 teaspoons

Solution 5 tablespoons = 15 teaspoons

3 gallons = ■ quarts
From the table, 4 quarts = 1 gallon.

3 × 4 = 12 quarts

Solution 3 gallons = 12 quarts

Exercise A Convert the larger units to smaller units. Multiply to find the answers.

1. 3 ounces = _____ tablespoons

2. 2 tablespoons = _____ teaspoons

3. 2 cups = _____ tablespoons

4. 5 pints = _____ cups

5. 2 gallons = _____ quarts

6. 3 quarts = _____ pints

7. 7 ounces = _____ tablespoons

8. 3 cups = _____ tablespoons

Divide to convert a smaller unit to a larger unit.

Try This

Choose a recipe from a cookbook or a food package such as a cereal box. List each ingredient and the measurements given. Then convert as many of the units as you can to equivalent units.

EXAMPLE  8 pints = ■ quarts

Rule When you convert small units to large units, you divide.
From the table, 2 pints = 1 quart.
8 ÷ 2 = 4 quarts

Solution 8 pints = 4 quarts

Exercise B Convert the smaller units to larger units. Divide to find the answers.

1. 8 tablespoons = _____ ounces

2. 6 teaspoons = _____ tablespoons

3. 64 tablespoons = _____ cups

4. 8 pints = _____ quarts

5. 16 quarts = _____ gallons

6. 6 tablespoons = _____ ounces

7. 20 quarts = _____ gallons

8. 10 tablespoons = _____ ounces

9. 12 teaspoons = _____ tablespoons

10. 8 cups = _____ pints

11. 36 tablespoons = _____ ounces

12. 16 pints = _____ quarts

Different measuring tools use different units.

Numerator

The part of a fraction that is above the line and that tells how many parts are used

Denominator

The part of the fraction that is below the line and that tells the number of parts in the whole

Factors

Numbers that when multiplied together form a product

Improper fraction

A fraction whose numerator is equal to or greater than its denominator

When using an improper fraction, divide the numerator by the denominator to find the factor you need.

Many recipes use fractions for the amounts of ingredients. A fraction has a **numerator** and a **denominator**. To increase a recipe, multiply the amount of each ingredient by the same **factor**. All mixed numbers must be expressed as **improper fractions** before multiplying.

Elsa's recipe for a frozen dessert will serve 4 people, but she wants to serve 8. What should she do?

EXAMPLE

Step 1 Divide the new number of servings by the old number of servings to find the conversion factor.

$$\text{New servings} = \frac{8}{4} = \frac{2}{1}$$
$$\text{Old servings}$$

The conversion factor is 2.

Step 2 Multiply each ingredient by the conversion factor.

Frozen Smoothie (Serves 4)	New Amount
$\frac{2}{3}$ cup mashed bananas	$\frac{2}{3} \times \frac{2}{1} = \frac{4}{3}$
$\frac{2}{3}$ cup low-fat milk	$\frac{2}{3} \times \frac{2}{1} = \frac{4}{3}$
2 cups orange sherbet	$2 \times 2 = 4$
$\frac{1}{2}$ teaspoon vanilla	$\frac{1}{2} \times \frac{2}{1} = 1$
$\frac{1}{4}$ cup chopped nuts	$\frac{1}{4} \times \frac{2}{1} = \frac{2}{4} = \frac{1}{2}$

Now let's take a closer look at the results of Elsa's multiplication.

New Adjusted Recipe
(Serves 8)

$\frac{4}{3}$ cups mashed bananas   1 teaspoon vanilla

$\frac{4}{3}$ cups low-fat milk $\frac{1}{2}$ cup chopped nuts

4 cups orange sherbet

Renaming Improper Fractions Elsa will have to simplify her fractions before she can begin to measure because some of the answers are improper fractions. They need to be **renamed**. To change an improper fraction to a **proper fraction**, divide the numerator by the denominator.

EXAMPLE Change $\frac{7}{5}$ to a proper fraction.

Numerator: $\dfrac{7}{5}$
Denominator:

$$5\overline{)7} \\ \underline{-5} \\ 2 \quad \text{Remainder}$$

$$1\frac{2}{5} \quad \frac{\text{Remainder}}{\text{Old denominator}}$$

Many recipes can be increased to serve more people. Multiply the amount of each ingredient by the same factor.

$$\frac{2}{4} = \frac{2 \div 2}{4 \div 2} = \frac{1}{2}$$

Simplifying Fractions to Simplest Form Think of the largest number that you can divide into both the numerator and the denominator with a zero remainder.

For example, to simplify $\frac{2}{4}$ to simplest form, the largest number that can be divided into both numbers is 2.

EXAMPLE Increase this recipe to serve 18 people.

Potatoes Royal (Serves 6)
6 baking potatoes
2 cups boiled cabbage
$\frac{1}{4}$ cup melted margarine
$\frac{1}{3}$ cup diced onions

Step 1 Divide the new number of servings by the old number of servings to find the conversion factor.

New servings = $\frac{18}{6}$ = $\frac{3}{1}$
Old servings

The conversion factor is 3.

Step 2 Multiply each ingredient by the conversion factor.

$6 \times 3 = 18$ baking potatoes

$2 \times 3 = 6$ cups boiled cabbage

$\frac{1}{4} \times 3 = \frac{3}{4}$ cup melted margarine

$\frac{1}{3} \times 3 = \frac{3}{3} = 1$ cup diced onions

Exercise A Increase these recipes to serve 12.

1. Polenta (Serves 6)

1 cup corn meal

3 cups water

$\frac{2}{3}$ tsp salt

$\frac{1}{3}$ cup grated cheese

1 tbsp margarine

2. Red Sauce (Serves 4)

1 diced onion

2 serrano chilies

$2\frac{1}{2}$ cups tomatoes

$\frac{1}{2}$ tsp cumin seed

$\frac{1}{3}$ tsp oregano

Exercise B Increase each recipe to serve the number of people shown.

1. Harry's Poppy-Seed Cake serves 8 people. Rewrite the recipe so it serves 24.

$\frac{1}{3}$ cup poppy seeds

$\frac{3}{4}$ cup milk

$\frac{3}{4}$ cup butter

$1\frac{1}{2}$ cups sugar

$1\frac{1}{2}$ tsp vanilla

2 cups flour

$2\frac{1}{2}$ tsp baking powder

$\frac{1}{4}$ tsp salt

4 egg whites, beaten

2. Lorena's favorite cookie recipe makes 4 dozen (48) cookies. Rewrite her recipe to make 12 dozen cookies (144).

1 cup granulated sugar

1 cup brown sugar

1 cup shortening

2 eggs, beaten

$2\frac{1}{2}$ cups flour

1 tsp baking soda

$\frac{1}{2}$ tsp baking powder

3 cups whole bran flakes cereal

3. Jason's Banana Enrolada (banana rolled in pastry) serves 4. Rewrite the recipe to serve 20.

$1\frac{1}{2}$ cups flour

2 tbsp granulated sugar

$\frac{1}{2}$ tsp salt

6 tbsp butter, softened but not melted

4 bananas

4. Bruno is preparing Escoveitch Fish (pickled fish) for a dinner party. The recipe serves 4. Rewrite it to serve 12.

2 lb fresh catfish

juice of 2 limes

$\frac{1}{2}$ tsp salt

1 tsp black pepper

2 onions, sliced

2 hot peppers

2 tbsp pimiento

1 cup vinegar

Exercise C Increase each ingredient by using the conversion factor given.

1. $\frac{3}{4}$ tablespoon sugar × 12

2. $2\frac{1}{2}$ cups shortening × 20

3. 9 teaspoons vanilla × 30

4. 12 whole apples × 10

5. 10 pounds ice × 3

6. 7 cups milk × 20

7. 8 cups flour × 10

8. $\frac{3}{4}$ cup flour × 20

9. $\frac{2}{3}$ cup brown sugar × 21

10. $3\frac{3}{4}$ cups sliced apples × 8

11. 5 tablespoons cream × 30

12. $\frac{2}{3}$ cup diced onions × 15

Exercise D Multiply these mixed and whole numbers.

1. $5\frac{4}{5} \times 10$

2. $20\frac{1}{2} \times 10$

3. $9\frac{4}{7} \times 14$

4. $12\frac{1}{2} \times 12$

5. $1\frac{2}{5} \times 15$

6. $22\frac{1}{3} \times 30$

7. $1\frac{5}{6} \times 18$

8. $3\frac{4}{7} \times 2$

9. $2\frac{4}{5} \times 15$

10. $1\frac{4}{9} \times 2$

11. $3\frac{1}{6} \times 24$

12. $4\frac{5}{6} \times 6$

13. $2\frac{3}{4} \times 8$

14. $10\frac{1}{6} \times 12$

15. $4\frac{5}{6} \times 18$

16. $10\frac{2}{5} \times 25$

17. $3\frac{6}{7} \times 21$

18. $22\frac{1}{7} \times 7$

Technology Connection

Computers have opened up a whole new world for finding, using, and saving recipes. Can't find an appealing recipe in a cookbook? Try the Internet. Just choose a search engine, type in your keywords, such as "salmon recipes," and see how many recipes are available. You can also find recipes on CD-ROM cookbooks. Many of these CD-ROMs contain thousands of recipes. Some of this software lets you save favorite recipes, modify them, and plan meals.

Writing About
Mathematics

Write about a
situation when you
would want to
decrease a recipe.

You may decrease a recipe by dividing the amount of each
ingredient by the same factor.

EXAMPLE Roland's recipe for vanilla pudding serves 8 people.
How can this recipe be adjusted so that it serves
only 4 people?

Step 1 Divide the old number of servings by the new
number of servings to find the conversion factor.

$$\frac{\text{Old servings}}{\text{New servings}} = \frac{8}{4} = \frac{2}{1}$$

The conversion factor is 2.

Step 2 Divide each of the ingredients by the conversion
factor. Roland's recipe calls for $2\frac{1}{2}$ cups milk.

$$2\frac{1}{2} \div \frac{2}{1} = \frac{5}{2} \div \frac{2}{1} = \frac{5}{2} \times \frac{1}{2} = \frac{5}{4} = 1\frac{1}{4}$$

$1\frac{1}{4}$ cups milk are needed for the adjusted recipe
to serve only 4 people.

Exercise A Practice dividing with mixed numbers.

1. $2\frac{1}{2} \div 4$

2. $3\frac{1}{2} \div 2$

3. $1\frac{1}{3} \div \frac{1}{2}$

4. $4\frac{1}{4} \div \frac{1}{2}$

5. $3\frac{2}{5} \div 5$

6. $2\frac{2}{3} \div \frac{1}{2}$

7. $4\frac{2}{3} \div 3$

8. $1\frac{1}{5} \div 1\frac{1}{2}$

9. $2\frac{3}{4} \div 2$

10. $5 \div 2\frac{1}{2}$

11. $1\frac{1}{6} \div \frac{2}{3}$

12. $2\frac{5}{6} \div 2\frac{1}{2}$

13. $3\frac{2}{5} \div 1\frac{1}{2}$

14. $1\frac{2}{3} \div 1\frac{1}{3}$

15. $5\frac{2}{5} \div 2\frac{1}{3}$

Exercise B Decrease these recipes to serve the number of people shown.

1. Decrease to serve 8:

Special Rolls (Makes 40)

5 pkg dry yeast

$3\frac{3}{4}$ cups warm water

$12\frac{1}{2}$ cups biscuit mix

5 tsp poultry seasoning

$2\frac{1}{2}$ tsp celery seed

2. Decrease to serve 6:

Best Green Beans (Serves 24)

$1\frac{1}{3}$ cups chopped onion

$5\frac{1}{3}$ tbsp salad oil

1 cup chili sauce

$1\frac{1}{3}$ tsp salt

8 cups green beans

3. Decrease to serve 8:

Super Meatballs (Serves 32)

6 lb ground beef

2 cups uncooked rice

4 tsp salt

1 tsp pepper

1 cup chopped onion

4 cans tomato soup

2 cups water

4. Decrease to serve 12:

Real Good Muffins (Makes 84)

$12\frac{1}{4}$ cups sifted flour

14 tbsp sugar

$17\frac{1}{2}$ tsp baking powder

$5\frac{1}{4}$ tsp salt

7 well-beaten eggs

$5\frac{1}{4}$ cups milk

$2\frac{1}{3}$ cups salad oil

5. Decrease to serve 8:

Nut-Orange Bread (Serves 56)

$15\frac{3}{4}$ cups sifted flour

$5\frac{1}{4}$ cups sugar

$15\frac{3}{4}$ tsp baking powder

$5\frac{1}{4}$ tsp salt

$1\frac{3}{4}$ tsp baking soda

$5\frac{1}{4}$ cups chopped nuts

7 tbsp grated orange peel

7 beaten eggs

$5\frac{1}{4}$ cups orange juice

14 tbsp salad oil

A calculator can help you **compare** fractions. First, calculate the decimal equivalent of each fraction. Then, compare the two decimals. Finally, write the correct **symbol** ($<$, $>$, or $=$). Remember that $<$ means "less than" and $>$ means "greater than."

Compare

To examine two numbers to determine which is larger

Symbol

A character that stands for something else

EXAMPLE Compare $\frac{8}{11}$ and $\frac{4}{7}$.

$$\frac{8}{11} \ \blacksquare \ \frac{4}{7}$$

$$8 \div 11 \ \blacksquare \ 4 \div 7$$

$$0.7272727 > 0.5714285$$

$$\frac{8}{11} > \frac{4}{7}$$

When finding an equivalent decimal for a fraction, divide the numerator by the denominator.

When comparing two decimal numbers, start by looking at the first digit to the right of the decimal point in both decimal numbers.

Calculator Exercise Use a calculator to help you compare the fractions in each set. Use $>$ or $<$ to show your comparison.

1. $\frac{5}{6}$ and $\frac{4}{9}$

2. $\frac{7}{10}$ and $\frac{6}{11}$

3. $\frac{15}{17}$ and $\frac{18}{23}$

4. $\frac{13}{15}$ and $\frac{3}{4}$

5. $\frac{6}{13}$ and $\frac{7}{15}$

6. $\frac{8}{13}$ and $\frac{7}{12}$

7. $\frac{2}{35}$ and $\frac{5}{72}$

8. $\frac{5}{19}$ and $\frac{2}{3}$

9. $\frac{34}{35}$ and $\frac{61}{62}$

10. $\frac{4}{5}$ and $\frac{7}{9}$

11. $\frac{10}{11}$ and $\frac{11}{12}$

12. $\frac{6}{17}$ and $\frac{5}{18}$

13. $\frac{9}{10}$ and $\frac{11}{12}$

14. $\frac{10}{13}$ and $\frac{12}{17}$

15. $\frac{6}{13}$ and $\frac{7}{17}$

16. $\frac{13}{15}$ and $\frac{8}{9}$

17. $\frac{15}{22}$ and $\frac{14}{23}$

18. $\frac{9}{20}$ and $\frac{8}{21}$

19. $\frac{11}{35}$ and $\frac{21}{35}$

20. $\frac{1}{20}$ and $\frac{2}{31}$

More Oatmeal Cookies

The students at Woodland Valley School are planning a bake sale for charity. Mr. Day's homeroom has been asked to bring in oatmeal cookies. Sandra shares her oatmeal cookie recipe. Sandra's recipe is for 2 dozen (24) cookies. Each student needs to make 4 dozen (48) cookies. Sandra started to make a chart showing how she would have to adjust the recipe.

Oatmeal Cookies	
2 dozen cookies	**4 dozen cookies**
1 egg	2 eggs
$1\frac{1}{8}$ cups flour	
$\frac{1}{2}$ tsp baking soda	1 tsp baking soda
$\frac{1}{2}$ tsp cinnamon	
$\frac{3}{8}$ cup granulated sugar	
$\frac{3}{8}$ cup brown sugar	
$\frac{1}{2}$ tsp vanilla	
$\frac{1}{2}$ cup butter	1 cup butter
$\frac{3}{4}$ cup oatmeal	$1\frac{1}{2}$ cups oatmeal
$\frac{1}{2}$ cup raisins	

Exercises Use Sandra's chart to answer these questions.

1. If $\frac{1}{2}$ teaspoon vanilla is needed for 2 dozen cookies, how much is needed for 4 dozen cookies?

2. How much brown sugar is needed for 4 dozen cookies?

3. How much flour is needed for 4 dozen cookies?

4. If there are 20 students in Mr. Day's homeroom and each student makes 4 dozen cookies, how many cookies will the class make?

5. If 20 students bake 4 dozen cookies, how many eggs are needed in all?

Chapter 5 R E V I E W

Write the letter of the best answer to each question.

1. After adjusting a recipe, Omar needs $\frac{8}{24}$ cup flour. Which is the simplest form of the fraction $\frac{8}{24}$?

   A $\frac{1}{8}$ C $\frac{1}{3}$

   B $\frac{1}{4}$ D $\frac{2}{6}$

2. Saritha's new cookie recipe calls for $2\frac{4}{12}$ cups sugar. Which is the simplest form of $2\frac{4}{12}$?

   A $2\frac{1}{12}$ C $2\frac{1}{3}$

   B $2\frac{1}{4}$ D $2\frac{1}{2}$

3. What is $\frac{1}{2}$ of $3\frac{1}{2}$ tablespoons diced peppers?

   A $1\frac{1}{2}$ tbsp   C $3\frac{1}{4}$ tbsp

   B $1\frac{3}{4}$ tbsp   D 7 tbsp

4. Julia needs $\frac{6}{4}$ cups of chicken stock for a soup recipe. Which of the following mixed numbers is equivalent to $\frac{6}{4}$?

   A $1\frac{1}{4}$ C $1\frac{3}{4}$

   B $1\frac{1}{2}$ D $1\frac{4}{4}$

5. A recipe calls for $1\frac{1}{2}$ cups peanut butter to make 24 peanut butter cookies. How much peanut butter is needed for 48 cookies?

   A 3 cups   C $3\frac{1}{2}$ cups

   B $3\frac{1}{4}$ cups   D $3\frac{3}{4}$ cups

Find the answers.

6. What is $\frac{2}{3}$ cup chopped nuts multiplied by 6?

7. Rename $\frac{5}{3}$ teaspoons cream as a mixed number.

8. How many cups are equal to 4 pints?

9. Neal's banana bread recipe calls for 4 bananas and serves 6 people. How many bananas does he need to serve 48?

10. Rename $\frac{8}{5}$ tablespoons butter as a mixed number.

11. Rename $2\frac{3}{4}$ cups milk as an improper fraction.

12. Sandra's spaghetti sauce recipe calls for $3\frac{1}{5}$ cups tomato paste to serve 8. How much tomato paste is needed to serve 16?

13. Convert 3 ounces of juice to tablespoons.

14. A recipe that serves 12 people calls for 4 cups of milk. How many cups of milk are needed for a recipe that serves 9 people?

15. How many pints are in 1 quart?

16. Convert 6 cups of water to pints.

17. Wanda plans to have a party for 12 people. She found a dessert recipe that calls for $4\frac{1}{2}$ cups of milk, but the recipe serves only 8 people. How many cups of milk will Wanda need if she makes that dessert?

18. Rename $3\frac{4}{5}$ cups flour as an improper fraction.

19. How many ounces do 8 tablespoons equal?

20. How many gallons do 8 quarts equal?

21. Lauren and Bruce's bread recipe calls for 6 cups sifted flour. How much flour will they need if they make only $\frac{2}{3}$ of the recipe?

22. Rick's cake recipe serves 6 people. It requires $2\frac{1}{4}$ cups flour. How much flour does he need to serve 18 people?

23. Jenna's cookie recipe requires $1\frac{1}{4}$ cups brown sugar to make 24 cookies. How much brown sugar is needed for 12 cookies?

24. How many quarts are in 1 gallon?

25. An Italian salad dressing recipe calls for $\frac{1}{4}$ cup vinegar to serve 8 people. How much vinegar is needed to serve 4 people?

Test-Taking Tip

Become familiar with where to locate tables and charts showing equivalent measurements. They can usually be found in the back of recipe books, dictionaries, and mathematics textbooks. Try to memorize the measurement conversions that are most commonly used.

Math and Crafts

What are your hobbies? Do they involve fabric, or string, or wood, or other materials? If they do, then you use mathematics to help you. Patterns often give important mathematical information about what materials are required. When you draw diagrams to help you build something, you use mathematics. Hobbies are only one example of where you can discover mathematics in your everyday life.

In Chapter 6, you will learn how to work with fractions to help you solve problems involving projects.

Goals for Learning

◆ To use a fabric guide to help find the amount of fabric a project requires

◆ To compute total lengths by adding fractional parts of a finished project

◆ To find the remaining lengths of materials by subtracting fractional parts of the amount used

◆ To use measurement involving fractions as it applies to repeating patterns

Fabric guide

Chart showing the amount of material needed to make garments

Wider widths allow more pieces to be cut out side by side rather than top to bottom. Less fabric is needed.

People who sew their own clothes can select the exact style and type of fabric. When they buy a pattern, a **fabric guide** on the back of the pattern tells them how much fabric they need. The amount of fabric depends on the width of the fabric.

Garment	Fabric Width in Inches	Misses Sizes 8	10	12	14	16	18
Top	36"	$1\frac{7}{8}$	$2\frac{1}{8}$	$2\frac{1}{8}$	$2\frac{1}{8}$	$2\frac{1}{8}$	$2\frac{1}{4}$ yd
	45"	$1\frac{1}{4}$	$1\frac{3}{8}$	$1\frac{3}{8}$	$1\frac{5}{8}$	$1\frac{5}{8}$	$1\frac{3}{4}$ yd
	60"	$1\frac{1}{8}$	$1\frac{1}{8}$	$1\frac{1}{8}$	$1\frac{1}{4}$	$1\frac{1}{4}$	$1\frac{1}{4}$ yd
Skirt	36"	$2\frac{5}{8}$	$2\frac{3}{4}$	$2\frac{3}{4}$	$2\frac{3}{4}$	$2\frac{3}{4}$	$2\frac{3}{4}$ yd
	45"	$2\frac{1}{8}$	$2\frac{3}{8}$	$2\frac{1}{2}$	$2\frac{3}{4}$	$2\frac{3}{4}$	$2\frac{3}{4}$ yd
	60"	$1\frac{7}{8}$	$1\frac{7}{8}$	2	2	2	2 yd
Pants	36"	$2\frac{1}{2}$	$2\frac{1}{2}$	$2\frac{5}{8}$	$2\frac{5}{8}$	$2\frac{5}{8}$	$2\frac{5}{8}$ yd
	45"	$2\frac{1}{4}$	$2\frac{3}{8}$	$2\frac{5}{8}$	$2\frac{5}{8}$	$2\frac{5}{8}$	$2\frac{5}{8}$ yd
	60"	$1\frac{3}{8}$	$1\frac{3}{8}$	$1\frac{1}{2}$	$1\frac{3}{4}$	$2\frac{1}{4}$	$2\frac{1}{4}$ yd
Jacket	36"	$2\frac{3}{8}$	$2\frac{3}{8}$	$2\frac{1}{2}$	$2\frac{1}{2}$	$2\frac{5}{8}$	$2\frac{3}{4}$ yd
	45"	$1\frac{7}{8}$	$1\frac{7}{8}$	$2\frac{1}{8}$	$2\frac{1}{8}$	$2\frac{1}{8}$	$2\frac{1}{4}$ yd
	60"	$1\frac{1}{2}$	$1\frac{1}{2}$	$1\frac{1}{2}$	$1\frac{5}{8}$	$1\frac{5}{8}$	$1\frac{5}{8}$ yd

How much 45″ fabric is needed to make a size 8 top and a size 10 skirt?

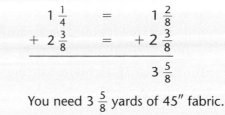

$$1\frac{1}{4} \quad = \quad 1\frac{2}{8}$$
$$+\ 2\frac{3}{8} \quad = \quad +\ 2\frac{3}{8}$$
$$\overline{\qquad\qquad\qquad 3\frac{5}{8}}$$

You need $3\frac{5}{8}$ yards of 45″ fabric.

Exercise A Use the fabric guide on page 88 to find the amount of fabric needed to make the garments listed. Remember to check for fabric width.

1. 45″ fabric
size 14 top
size 14 skirt

2. 60″ fabric
size 16 jacket
size 14 pants

3. 36″ fabric
size 18 top
size 16 pants

4. 45″ fabric
size 12 pants
size 10 jacket

5. 45″ fabric
size 16 top
size 18 skirt
size 16 jacket

6. 60″ fabric
size 12 top
size 10 pants
size 12 jacket

7. 60″ fabric
size 16 top
size 16 jacket
size 16 skirt

8. 45″ fabric
size 16 pants
size 14 top
size 14 jacket

9. 36″ fabric
size 14 top
size 14 jacket
size 16 pants
size 16 skirt

10. 60″ fabric
size 10 top
size 12 skirt
size 10 jacket
size 12 pants

11. 45″ fabric
size 10 top
size 10 skirt
size 10 jacket
size 10 pants

12. 36″ fabric
size 12 pants
size 14 top
size 12 skirt
size 14 jacket

Many people make decorative items by tying knots in **geometric** patterns. This is called **macramé**. Another craft is **beading**. Beads are strung on a cord, then made into jewelry or woven into a design. Careful measuring is needed for a successful and attractive project.

Exercise A Add the lengths to find the total length of each craft project.

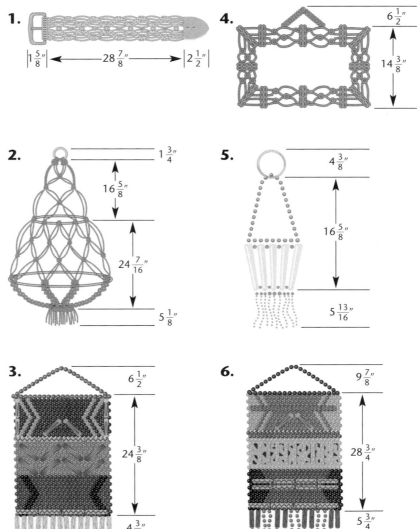

1. $1\frac{5}{8}''$ ← $28\frac{7}{8}''$ → $2\frac{1}{2}''$

4. $6\frac{1}{2}''$ $14\frac{3}{8}''$

2. $1\frac{3}{4}''$ $16\frac{5}{8}''$ $24\frac{7}{16}''$ $5\frac{1}{8}''$

5. $4\frac{3}{8}''$ $16\frac{5}{8}''$ $5\frac{13}{16}''$

3. $6\frac{1}{2}''$ $24\frac{3}{8}''$ $4\frac{3}{4}''$

6. $9\frac{7}{8}''$ $28\frac{3}{4}''$ $5\frac{3}{4}''$

You need to subtract mixed numbers for some craft or sewing projects. In subtraction, you must have like denominators.

EXAMPLES

$$12\frac{7}{8} - 3\frac{5}{8} = \blacksquare$$

$$\begin{array}{r} 12\frac{7}{8} \\ - 3\frac{5}{8} \\ \hline 9\frac{2}{8} \end{array} = 9\frac{1}{4} \text{ Difference}$$

$$14\frac{3}{4} - 6\frac{2}{3} = \blacksquare$$

$$\begin{array}{r} 14\frac{3}{4} = 14\frac{9}{12} \\ - 6\frac{2}{3} = - 6\frac{8}{12} \\ \hline 8\frac{1}{12} \text{ Difference} \end{array}$$

Macramé can be used to make rugs, plant hangers, and decorative wall hangings.

Exercise B Rewrite each problem in vertical form and find the difference. Write the answers in simplest form.

1. $4\frac{7}{8} - 1\frac{3}{4}$

2. $6\frac{2}{3} - 1\frac{1}{4}$

3. $15\frac{3}{8} - 7\frac{1}{16}$

4. $15\frac{15}{16} - 2\frac{3}{8}$

5. $6\frac{3}{4} - 2$

6. $15\frac{4}{5} - 8\frac{3}{10}$

7. $9\frac{2}{3} - 6\frac{1}{2}$

8. $29\frac{5}{6} - 3\frac{1}{3}$

9. $32\frac{4}{5} - \frac{1}{2}$

10. $23\frac{7}{8} - 16\frac{1}{6}$

PROBLEM SOLVING

Exercise C Solve these problems.

1. A wall hanging made with beading measures $12\frac{3}{4}$" long. If the main design in the center of the hanging is $8\frac{1}{2}$" long, what length remains for the two ends?

2. A macramé project is $15\frac{7}{8}$" long. It is made up of three sections. One section is $4\frac{3}{4}$" long, and another is $5\frac{1}{8}$" long. How long is the third section?

Regroup
To reorganize

After you have changed to common denominators, you may find that the top numerator is smaller than the bottom numerator. You must **regroup** before you subtract. Look at these examples.

EXAMPLES

$$25 \frac{2}{3} - 2 \frac{5}{6} = \blacksquare$$

$$
\begin{array}{ccccc}
25 \frac{2}{3} & = & 25 \frac{4}{6} & = & 24 \frac{10}{6} \\
- 2 \frac{5}{6} & = & - 2 \frac{5}{6} & = & - 2 \frac{5}{6} \\
\hline
& & & & 22 \frac{5}{6}
\end{array}
$$

$$28 - 4 \frac{3}{7} = \blacksquare$$

$$
\begin{array}{ccc}
28 & = & 27 \frac{7}{7} \\
- 4 \frac{3}{7} & = & - 4 \frac{3}{7} \\
\hline
& & 23 \frac{4}{7}
\end{array}
$$

Exercise D Find each difference. Write the answers in simplest form.

1. $13 \frac{1}{8}$
$- 9 \frac{1}{2}$

2. 15
$- 6 \frac{7}{12}$

3. $28 \frac{3}{4}$
$- 6 \frac{5}{6}$

4. $17 \frac{3}{8}$
$- 9 \frac{3}{4}$

5. $17 \frac{3}{5}$
$- 9$

6. $42 \frac{7}{16}$
$- 38 \frac{5}{8}$

7. $21 \frac{3}{4}$
$- 9 \frac{5}{6}$

8. 42
$- 17 \frac{5}{9}$

9. $32 \frac{3}{4}$
$- 17 \frac{5}{8}$

10. $21 \frac{1}{2}$
$- 17 \frac{7}{8}$

11. 48
$- 8 \frac{7}{9}$

12. $33 \frac{3}{5}$
$- 12 \frac{1}{2}$

13. $26 \frac{1}{8}$
$- 3 \frac{3}{4}$

14. $15 \frac{1}{3}$
$- 9 \frac{1}{2}$

15. 25
$- 14 \frac{7}{12}$

Allow the length to be the longer measurement.

When you work with fabric or wood, you have some scrap material left over. Careful placement of the pattern pieces may mean that the scraps will be large enough to use for some other project.

EXAMPLE Find the length and width of the two rectangular pieces of scrap material A and B.

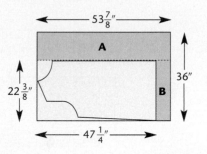

Piece A			Piece B		
36	=	$35\frac{8}{8}$	$53\frac{7}{8}$	=	$53\frac{7}{8}$
$-22\frac{3}{8}$	=	$-22\frac{3}{8}$	$-47\frac{1}{4}$	=	$-47\frac{2}{8}$
		$13\frac{5}{8}$			$6\frac{5}{8}$

Piece A

Length = $53\frac{7}{8}$"

Width = $13\frac{5}{8}$"

Piece B

Length = $22\frac{3}{8}$"

Width = $6\frac{5}{8}$"

In problem 3, what would be the length and width of the scraps if the piece was placed in a vertical position, rather than horizontal?

Exercise A Find the length and width of the two rectangular pieces of scrap material or wood in each of these patterns.

1.

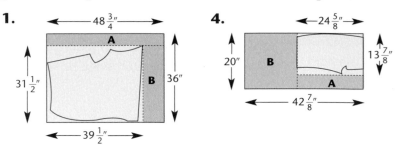

2.

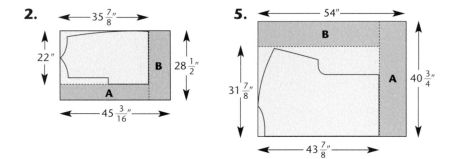

3.

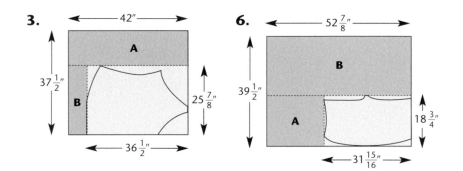

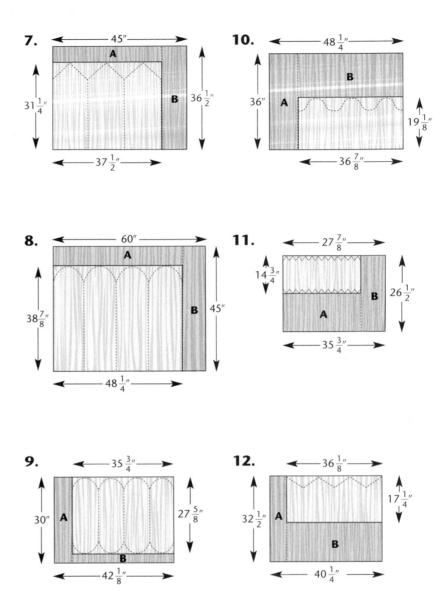

7.

45″

A

31 1/4″

36 1/2″

B

37 1/2″

10.

48 1/4″

B

36″

A

19 1/8″

36 7/8″

8.

60″

A

38 7/8″

45″

B

48 1/4″

11.

27 7/8″

14 3/4″

26 1/2″

B

A

35 3/4″

9.

35 3/4″

30″

A

27 5/8″

B

42 1/8″

12.

36 1/8″

17 1/4″

32 1/2″

A

B

40 1/4″

Lesson 4 Repeating Patterns

Repeat

Something that appears again

On some projects, the same design unit is repeated over and over. This design unit is called a **repeat**. The repeat is the same length throughout the design. A repeat is measured from one design to the same position on the next design.

Writing About Mathematics

Do you think the length of the pattern would change if you measured from the center of the scroll designs? Explain.

EXAMPLE   The pattern below repeats every $2\frac{1}{2}$ inches. How long will 20 repeats be?

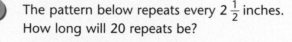

$$2\frac{1}{2} \times 20 = \frac{5}{2} \times \frac{20}{1} = 50''$$

Twenty repeats will be 50 inches long.

PROBLEM SOLVING

Exercise A Solve these problems.

1. A pattern repeats every $2\frac{3}{4}$ inches. How long are 16 repeats?

2. Another pattern repeats every $1\frac{7}{8}$ inches. How long are 20 repeats?

3. A belt is to have 18 repeats of $1\frac{3}{4}$ inches, plus $2\frac{3}{4}$ inches for a buckle. How long will the belt be?

4. The repeat in a pattern is $2\frac{1}{4}$ inches long. How many repeats are in 36 inches?

5. How many $1\frac{3}{8}$-inch repeats are there in $27\frac{1}{2}$ inches?

6. How long are 44 repeats if each is $\frac{7}{8}$ inches long?

7. How many $2\frac{3}{4}$-inch repeats are there in 33 inches?

Use your calculator to help you rename a mixed number as an improper fraction.

EXAMPLE Rename $18\frac{2}{3}$ as an improper fraction.

Step 1 Multiply the whole number by the denominator.

$18 \boxed{\times} 3 \boxed{=} 54$

Step 2 Add the product to the numerator.

$54 \boxed{+} 2 \boxed{=} 56$

Step 3 Write the sum, 56, as the new numerator, and use the original denominator.

Solution $18\frac{2}{3} = \frac{56}{3}$

Calculator Exercise A Write these mixed numbers as improper fractions. Use your calculator to help you.

1. $12\frac{11}{25}$
2. $9\frac{11}{34}$
3. $10\frac{6}{11}$
4. $20\frac{6}{13}$
5. $13\frac{5}{18}$
6. $57\frac{5}{14}$

7. $12\frac{11}{13}$
8. $16\frac{5}{11}$
9. $16\frac{15}{16}$
10. $24\frac{16}{17}$
11. $8\frac{6}{11}$
12. $8\frac{1}{15}$

13. $49\frac{12}{13}$
14. $15\frac{23}{34}$
15. $19\frac{2}{12}$
16. $7\frac{1}{10}$
17. $18\frac{11}{12}$
18. $4\frac{12}{15}$

Calculator Exercise B Write these mixed numbers as improper fractions. Use your calculator to help you.

1. $26\frac{2}{3}$
2. $15\frac{16}{19}$
3. $29\frac{6}{7}$
4. $11\frac{9}{10}$
5. $16\frac{10}{20}$
6. $12\frac{5}{11}$

7. $16\frac{13}{16}$
8. $12\frac{13}{14}$
9. $28\frac{5}{11}$
10. $39\frac{10}{13}$
11. $20\frac{10}{11}$
12. $19\frac{6}{7}$

13. $14\frac{12}{13}$
14. $22\frac{5}{7}$
15. $18\frac{10}{11}$
16. $18\frac{12}{13}$
17. $10\frac{11}{12}$
18. $18\frac{7}{8}$

Making Birdhouses

Bobbi has a piece of wood measuring 4 ft × 6 ft. She will cut out birdhouses from this wood. Each side of the birdhouse is a rectangle. Each birdhouse measures 8 in. × 6 in. × 8 in.

Exercises Answer these questions about Bobbi's birdhouse.

1. What is the length and width of the piece of wood in inches?

2. The birdhouse has six sides. Give the length and width of each side.

3. What is the surface area of the wood in inches?

4. What is the total surface area of each birdhouse?

5. Assuming no waste when the wood is cut, what is the total number of complete birdhouses that could be cut from the wood?

Technology Connection

Use the drawing feature of a computer to sketch the sides of the birdhouses on the piece of wood. Sketch the best layout for the greatest number of birdhouses.

Chapter 6   R E V I E W

Write the letter of the best choice for each problem.

1. A beading project has a main section that measures 12". It has two end sections that measure 3" each. What is the total length?

    A 4"

    B 8"

    C 16"

    D 18"

2. Find the length and width of scrap A.

    A $22\frac{7}{8}" \times 14\frac{1}{8}"$

    B $38\frac{1}{4}" \times 14\frac{1}{8}"$

    C $38\frac{3}{8}" \times 15\frac{3}{8}"$

    D $38\frac{7}{8}" \times 38\frac{1}{4}"$

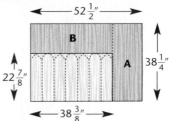

3. Find the length and width of scrap B.

    A $22\frac{7}{8}" \times 14\frac{1}{8}"$

    B $22\frac{7}{8}" \times 38\frac{1}{4}"$

    C $38\frac{3}{8}" \times 15\frac{3}{8}"$

    D $52\frac{1}{2}" \times 16\frac{3}{8}"$

4. Find the missing numerator. $15\frac{7}{8} = 14\frac{?}{8}$

    A 7

    B 8

    C 15

    D 127

5. Juanita is making a border that has a repeating pattern. The pattern repeats every $2\frac{5}{8}$ inches. The pattern repeats 20 times. There are two end pieces that measure $1\frac{3}{4}$ inches each. What is the total length of the border?

    A 49"

    B $52\frac{1}{2}"$

    C $54\frac{1}{4}"$

    D 56"

Find the answers and write them in simplest form.

6. $6\frac{3}{4}$
$+ 18\frac{1}{8}$

7. $9\frac{7}{8}$
$+ 4\frac{1}{2}$

8. $12\frac{3}{4}$
$- 5\frac{1}{3}$

9. $17\frac{3}{4}$
$- 11\frac{7}{8}$

Use this fabric guide to answer the questions.

Garment	Fabric Width in Inches	8	10	12	14	16	18
				Misses Sizes			
Top	36"	$1\frac{3}{4}$	$1\frac{7}{8}$	$1\frac{7}{8}$	$2\frac{1}{8}$	$2\frac{1}{8}$	$2\frac{1}{4}$ yd
	45"	$1\frac{1}{4}$	$1\frac{3}{8}$	$1\frac{3}{8}$	$1\frac{5}{8}$	$1\frac{5}{8}$	$1\frac{3}{4}$ yd
	60"	$1\frac{1}{8}$	$1\frac{1}{8}$	$1\frac{1}{8}$	$1\frac{1}{4}$	$1\frac{1}{4}$	$1\frac{1}{4}$ yd
Skirt	36"	$2\frac{5}{8}$	$2\frac{3}{4}$	$2\frac{3}{4}$	$2\frac{3}{4}$	$2\frac{3}{4}$	$2\frac{3}{4}$ yd
	45"	$2\frac{1}{8}$	$2\frac{3}{8}$	$2\frac{1}{2}$	$2\frac{3}{4}$	$2\frac{3}{4}$	$2\frac{3}{4}$ yd
	60"	$1\frac{7}{8}$	$1\frac{7}{8}$	2	2	2	2 yd

How many yards of fabric are needed for each project?

10. 45" fabric
size 12 top
size 12 skirt

12. 36" fabric
size 8 top
size 10 skirt

14. 36" fabric
size 8 top
size 8 skirt

11. 60" fabric
size 10 top
size 10 skirt

13. 60" fabric
size 12 top
size 14 skirt

Find the total length of each craft project.

15. $|1\frac{7}{8}''|$ ←—— $29\frac{3}{4}''$ ——→ $|2\frac{3}{8}''|$

16.

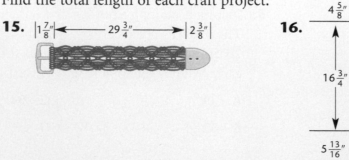

$4\frac{5}{8}''$

$16\frac{3}{4}''$

$5\frac{13}{16}''$

Find the length and width of these pieces of scrap material A and B.

17.

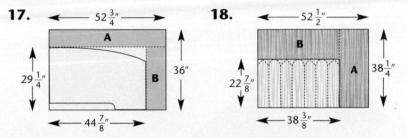

18.

Answer these questions about repeating patterns.

19. Anna is making a border that has a repeating pattern. The pattern repeats every $1\frac{3}{4}$ inches. How long are 14 repeats?

20. Carlo's belt is to have 15 repeats of $1\frac{7}{8}$ inches plus $3\frac{5}{8}$ inches for the buckle. How long will the finished belt be?

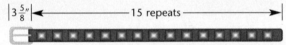

21. Diane is making a camera strap that is to be 38 inches long. It will have 12 repeats of $2\frac{3}{4}$ inches each with equal borders at each end. How long will each of the two borders be?

22. How long are 23 repeats if each is $3\frac{1}{8}$ inches long?

Find the missing numerators.

23. $14\frac{5}{8} = 13\frac{\blacksquare}{8}$ **24.** $25\frac{3}{4} = 24\frac{\blacksquare}{8}$ **25.** $8 = 7\frac{\blacksquare}{3}$

Test-Taking Tip

Drawing a picture or diagram can help you solve a problem.

Fractions in the Home

Recycling scraps of fabric can show your creative abilities. Scrap quilts were ways that early settlers first recycled cloth. They cut and sewed together old socks, leftover bedding, and scraps from dressmaking to make colorful, warm quilts. They used math, especially fractions, to make the different patterns in the quilts. Next time you work on a project, think of how you might use mathematics to conserve your materials and challenge your creativity!

In Chapter 7, you will explore some of the many ways we use measurement with fractions in our daily lives.

Goals for Learning

◆ To add fractions to find totals

◆ To subtract fractions to find amounts of leftover materials

◆ To multiply fractions to find area

◆ To divide mixed numbers and fractions

To add fractions with unlike denominators, find the least common denominator and rewrite each fraction with the least common denominator.

When you are finding the total measurement of two or more items, you may have to add fractions. Be careful to keep the same unit of measure within the same problem.

EXAMPLES   Lisa wants to combine $3\frac{1}{2}$ cups of flour and 1 pint of milk. How many cups in all does that make? Remember, 1 pint equals 2 cups.

$$
\begin{array}{rclcrl}
3\frac{1}{2} & \text{cups of flour} & = & & 3\frac{1}{2} & \text{cups of flour} \\
+\,1 & \text{pint of milk} & = & + & 2 & \text{cups of milk} \\
\hline
& & & & 5\frac{1}{2} & \text{cups}
\end{array}
$$

Answer: $5\frac{1}{2}$ cups in all

Lynette buys $2\frac{1}{4}$ yards of green material and $4\frac{2}{3}$ yards of red material. How many yards of material does Lynette buy?

$$
\begin{array}{rclcrl}
2\frac{1}{4} & \text{yards} & = & & 2\frac{3}{12} & \text{yards} \\
+\,4\frac{2}{3} & \text{yards} & = & + & 4\frac{8}{12} & \text{yards} \\
\hline
& & & & 6\frac{11}{12} & \text{yards}
\end{array}
$$

Answer: $6\frac{11}{12}$ yards

Exercise A Find the least common denominator for each set of fractions.

1. $\frac{1}{2}$ and $\frac{1}{3}$ 4. $\frac{6}{7}$ and $\frac{1}{21}$ 7. $\frac{4}{9}$ and $\frac{1}{6}$

2. $\frac{3}{8}$ and $\frac{1}{6}$ 5. $\frac{3}{11}$ and $\frac{7}{8}$ 8. $\frac{3}{14}$ and $\frac{3}{12}$

3. $\frac{2}{7}$ and $\frac{10}{12}$ 6. $\frac{8}{18}$ and $\frac{1}{3}$ 9. $\frac{16}{20}$ and $\frac{3}{5}$

Exercise B Practice adding fractions. Write your answers in simplest form.

1. $2\frac{3}{4}$
$+\ 1\frac{1}{5}$

4. 2
$+\ 9\frac{1}{8}$

7. 5
$+\ 3\frac{7}{8}$

2. $5\frac{2}{5}$
$+\ 1\frac{4}{6}$

5. 12
$+\ 2\frac{5}{6}$

8. $3\frac{1}{8}$
$+\ 5\frac{1}{6}$

3. $4\frac{3}{7}$
$+\ 2\frac{5}{6}$

6. 8
$+\ 3\frac{1}{4}$

9. $6\frac{1}{3}$
$+\ 4\frac{4}{6}$

PROBLEM SOLVING

Exercise C Solve these problems. Include the units in your answers.

1. $2\frac{1}{3}$ yards $+\ 1\frac{1}{2}$ ft

2. $2\frac{1}{2}$ pints $+\ 3\frac{3}{4}$ cups

3. Carlos buys $6\frac{1}{2}$ feet of blue webbing and $3\frac{4}{5}$ feet of yellow webbing to fix his lawn chairs. How many feet of webbing does he buy in all?

4. Tess's notebook paper measures $7\frac{15}{16}$ inches wide and $10\frac{7}{8}$ inches long. Find the perimeter of Tess's notebook paper.

5. Find the perimeter of Jacob's patio shown below. (The perimeter equals the sum of the sides.)

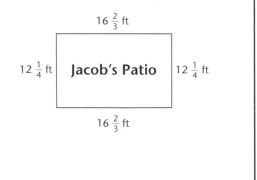

When you measure items, you may need to subtract quantities with fractions.

EXAMPLES

Maria buys a quart jar of mayonnaise. She uses $1\frac{1}{4}$ cups in a salad. How many cups of mayonnaise are left? (1 quart = 4 cups)

$$
\begin{array}{rll}
4 \text{ cups} & = & 3\frac{4}{4} \text{ cups} \\
-1\frac{1}{4} \text{ cups} & = & -1\frac{1}{4} \text{ cups} \\
\hline
& & 2\frac{3}{4} \text{ cups}
\end{array}
\qquad
\begin{array}{l}
4 = 3 + 1 \\
 = 3 + \frac{4}{4} \\
 = 3\frac{4}{4}
\end{array}
$$

Answer: $2\frac{3}{4}$ cups of mayonnaise are left.

Warren uses $5\frac{3}{4}$ feet of a $12\frac{1}{8}$-foot board. How much of the board is left?

$$
\begin{array}{rlllll}
12\frac{1}{8} \text{ feet} & = & 12\frac{1}{8} \text{ feet} & = & 11\frac{9}{8} \text{ feet} \\
-5\frac{3}{4} \text{ feet} & = & -5\frac{6}{8} \text{ feet} & = & -5\frac{6}{8} \text{ feet} \\
\hline
& & & & 6\frac{3}{8} \text{ feet}
\end{array}
\qquad
\begin{array}{l}
12\frac{1}{8} = 11 + 1 + \frac{1}{8} \\
\phantom{12\frac{1}{8}} = 11 + \frac{8}{8} + \frac{1}{8} \\
\phantom{12\frac{1}{8}} = 11 + \frac{9}{8} \\
\phantom{12\frac{1}{8}} = 11\frac{9}{8}
\end{array}
$$

Answer: $6\frac{3}{8}$ feet are left.

Lumber is generally sold in standard lengths. When you plan a building project, double-check your addition and subtraction so that you purchase the right amount of materials.

Exercise A Practice subtracting fractions. Write your answers in simplest form.

1. 13
$-5\frac{2}{3}$

2. $6\frac{5}{8}$
$-2\frac{1}{3}$

3. $3\frac{1}{6}$
$-2\frac{3}{8}$

4. $18\frac{5}{6}$
$-2\frac{4}{11}$

5. $4\frac{6}{11}$
$-\frac{3}{4}$

6. 15
$-2\frac{1}{10}$

7. $5\frac{2}{3}$
$-\frac{8}{9}$

8. $13\frac{2}{7}$
$-3\frac{13}{14}$

PROBLEM SOLVING

Exercise B Solve these problems. Include the units in your answers.

1. 1 yard $-16\frac{1}{4}$ inches

2. 2 quarts $-5\frac{1}{2}$ cups

3. Seamus uses $2\frac{5}{8}$ yards of a 6-yard piece of canvas to patch his tent. How many yards are left?

4. Lelia needs a shade for a window that is $48\frac{3}{4}$ inches long. She finds a shade that is 72 inches long. How much longer is the shade than the window?

5. Micah has $6\frac{3}{4}$ gallons of white paint and 7 quarts of green paint. How much more white paint than green paint does he have?

6. Russ buys 6 feet of picture wire. He uses $29\frac{1}{2}$ inches to hang a mirror. How much does he have left?

Frequently you need to use measurements in home projects. If one measurement is repeated many times, then you can multiply to find the total length.

EXAMPLE   Miranda wants to make a bookcase with 4 shelves to fit between two windows. Each shelf is to be $21\frac{1}{4}$ inches long. How many inches of shelving does she need? To find the total length of shelving needed, she can multiply $21\frac{1}{4}$" by 4.

$$21\frac{1}{4} \times 4 = \blacksquare$$

Write mixed numbers as improper fractions.

$$\frac{85}{4} \times \frac{4}{1} = \blacksquare$$

$$\frac{85}{1} = 85 \text{ inches of shelving}$$

Exercise A Find the length of shelving needed for each project. Give your answers in inches.

1. $16\frac{1}{4}" \times 7$

2. $13\frac{3}{4}" \times 4$

3. $24\frac{7}{8}" \times 6$

4. $28\frac{1}{4}" \times 16$

5. $13\frac{1}{2}" \times 5$

6. $16\frac{7}{8}" \times 3$

7. $30\frac{4}{5}" \times 2$

8. $6\frac{1}{8}" \times 22$

Try This

Assume that the length of one wall in a classroom is $496\frac{1}{3}"$. If the length of all four walls in the classroom is exactly the same, what is the total length of the classroom walls? Give your answer in inches.

Finding the Area To find the area of a surface, you can multiply length by width.

EXAMPLE Charlie's hobby is gardening. He is getting ready to plant flowers in a flower bed that is $14 \frac{1}{2}$ feet long and $8 \frac{3}{4}$ feet wide. What is the area? Remember, area equals the length times the width. Write your answer in square feet.

Length × Width = Area

$$14 \frac{1}{2} \times 8 \frac{3}{4} = \blacksquare$$

$$\frac{29}{2} \times \frac{35}{4} = \frac{1{,}015}{8} = 126 \frac{7}{8} \text{ square feet}$$

Exercise B Find the area of each. Write your answer in square units.

1. $2 \frac{1}{3}$ ft × 3 ft

2. $2 \frac{3}{5}$ in. × 20 in.

3. $\frac{4}{7}$ miles × 5 miles

4. $4 \frac{2}{3}$ yd × 30 yd

5. $1 \frac{1}{2}$ ft × $2 \frac{5}{6}$ ft

6. 3 miles × $\frac{3}{4}$ miles

7. $5 \frac{3}{8}$ in. × $5 \frac{2}{3}$ in.

8. $3 \frac{7}{8}$ yd × $\frac{4}{5}$ yd

9. 8 yd × $16 \frac{2}{9}$ yd

10. $6 \frac{3}{4}$ in. × 12 in.

11. 14 in. × $5 \frac{4}{7}$ in.

12. $13 \frac{4}{9}$ yd × $\frac{5}{8}$ yd

13. $9 \frac{1}{2}$ ft × 6 ft

14. $8 \frac{1}{3}$ miles × $2 \frac{1}{2}$ miles

15. $6 \frac{3}{4}$ in. × $2 \frac{1}{2}$ in.

16. $3 \frac{1}{9}$ yd × 9 yd

17. $4 \frac{3}{5}$ ft × 10 ft

18. 12 miles × $5 \frac{1}{3}$ miles

19. $7 \frac{5}{8}$ in. × $3 \frac{1}{4}$ in.

20. $15 \frac{1}{2}$ ft × $8 \frac{1}{10}$ ft

***Exercise* C** Practice multiplying with fractions. Find these lengths. Write your answers in the units given.

1. $3\frac{1}{2}$ ft $\times$ 3

2. $6\frac{2}{3}$ in. $\times \frac{1}{2}$

3. $2\frac{3}{4}$ yd $\times$ 5

4. $1\frac{1}{5}$ yd $\times$ 6

5. $1\frac{2}{5}$ in. $\times 1\frac{1}{2}$

6. $5\frac{2}{5}$ ft $\times 1\frac{1}{3}$

7. 21 in. $\times \frac{2}{3}$

8. $3\frac{2}{9}$ in. $\times 2\frac{1}{12}$

9. $1\frac{1}{3}$ ft $\times 1\frac{1}{5}$

10. $2\frac{1}{6}$ yd $\times 1\frac{1}{6}$

11. $2\frac{3}{4}$ in. $\times 1\frac{1}{2}$

12. $7\frac{2}{5}$ ft $\times 2\frac{2}{3}$

 PROBLEM SOLVING

***Exercise* D** Solve these problems.

1. Diego's gravy recipe calls for $2\frac{1}{2}$ tablespoons cornstarch. How much will he need if he makes only $\frac{2}{3}$ of the recipe?

2. Helena's bookshelf plan calls for 5 shelves, each measuring $25\frac{1}{2}$ inches. Find the total length of shelving in inches.

3. Mr. Ellis is installing wall-to-wall carpeting in his family room. If the room measures 13 by $14\frac{1}{2}$ feet, how many square feet of carpeting will he need?

4. Tehron's kitchen measures 16 by $12\frac{1}{4}$ feet. If she is installing 1-square-foot tiles, how many tiles will she need?

5. Brian purchases $20\frac{1}{2}$ feet of hall carpet and has $\frac{2}{3}$ of it left. How many feet does he have left?

Invert

To reverse in postition

When a fraction is inverted, the numerator and the denominator are switched.

To divide a mixed number, first change the mixed number to a fraction. Then **invert** the divisor and multiply.

EXAMPLES Eve buys $22\frac{1}{3}$ feet of shelf paper. How many 5-foot shelves can she cover with the paper? Eve can use division to solve this problem.

$$22\frac{1}{3} \div 5 = \blacksquare$$

$$\frac{67}{3} \div \frac{5}{1} = \blacksquare$$

$$\frac{67}{3} \times \frac{1}{5} = \frac{67}{15} = 4\frac{7}{15}$$

Eve can cover 4 shelves. The remainder of $\frac{7}{15}$ is not enough to cover a complete shelf.

Tony's apartment has a balcony that is $2\frac{2}{3}$ yards wide. Its area is $13\frac{1}{3}$ square yards. What is the length of the balcony?

Area	÷	Width	=	Length
$13\frac{1}{3}$	÷	$2\frac{2}{3}$	=	$\blacksquare$
$\frac{40}{3}$	÷	$\frac{8}{3}$	=	$\blacksquare$

$$\overset{5}{\underset{1}{\frac{40}{3}}} \times \overset{1}{\underset{1}{\frac{3}{8}}} = \frac{5}{1} = 5 \text{ yards}$$

The balcony is 5 yards long.

Knowing the length, width, and area of your balcony will help you plan for outdoor furniture. You may even have room for a gas grill!

Exercise A Practice dividing with fractions and mixed numbers.

1. $\frac{5}{6} \div \frac{2}{3}$

2. $\frac{4}{5} \div 8$

3. $2\frac{3}{4} \div \frac{6}{7}$

4. $5\frac{1}{7} \div \frac{2}{5}$

5. $6\frac{2}{5} \div 1\frac{1}{2}$

6. $5\frac{1}{4} \div \frac{5}{6}$

7. $7\frac{1}{7} \div 10$

8. $5 \div \frac{2}{5}$

9. $3\frac{4}{5} \div 3\frac{1}{8}$

10. $4\frac{1}{3} \div 1\frac{1}{2}$

PROBLEM SOLVING

Exercise B Solve these problems.

1. If the area of a cabinet top is $3\frac{1}{2}$ square feet, and the length is $1\frac{1}{4}$ feet, then what is the width?

2. Jeff's recipe for barbecue sauce calls for $2\frac{1}{3}$ tablespoons vinegar. How much vinegar will he use if he divides the recipe by 4?

3. Hai needs $15\frac{1}{3}$ feet of rope for a project. If the rope is divided into 4 equal pieces, how long is each piece?

4. Bo is cutting rubber floor mats for the basement. He has $25\frac{1}{4}$ feet of matting. Each mat is to be $5\frac{1}{4}$ feet long. How many mats can he cut?

Technology Connection

Does your home need a makeover? Are you wondering what kind of changes you can make for the money you have? There are several different software programs available that can help you plan a home remodeling project. You can use this software to design everything from a closet to an entire house. You can have fun using this software to design your "dream home," too! Ask your school resource center specialist or librarian if there is such software that you can try.

You can use a calculator to help you express improper fractions as mixed numbers.

EXAMPLE Write $\frac{235}{15}$ as a mixed number.

Step 1 Divide the numerator by the denominator.

$235 \;\boxed{\div}\; 15 \;\boxed{=}\; 15.666666$

Step 2 Multiply the whole number portion, 15, by the denominator, 15.

$15 \;\boxed{\times}\; 15 \;\boxed{=}\; 225$

Step 3 Subtract the product, 225, from 235 for the new numerator.

$235 \;\boxed{-}\; 225 \;\boxed{=}\; 10$

Solution $\frac{235}{15} = 15\frac{10}{15} = 15\frac{2}{3}$

Calculator Exercise A Express these improper fractions as mixed numbers in simplest form. Use your calculator.

1. $\frac{18}{3}$ **4.** $\frac{42}{13}$ **7.** $\frac{20}{8}$ **10.** $\frac{45}{9}$

2. $\frac{93}{35}$ **5.** $\frac{89}{5}$ **8.** $\frac{30}{11}$ **11.** $\frac{80}{21}$

3. $\frac{23}{4}$ **6.** $\frac{109}{10}$ **9.** $\frac{34}{17}$ **12.** $\frac{66}{30}$

Calculator Exercise B Express these improper fractions as mixed numbers in simplest form. Use your calculator.

1. $\frac{128}{15}$ **7.** $\frac{132}{34}$ **13.** $\frac{103}{15}$

2. $\frac{135}{17}$ **8.** $\frac{27}{8}$ **14.** $\frac{216}{3}$

3. $\frac{253}{51}$ **9.** $\frac{18}{5}$ **15.** $\frac{129}{15}$

4. $\frac{47}{5}$ **10.** $\frac{178}{10}$ **16.** $\frac{623}{45}$

5. $\frac{63}{8}$ **11.** $\frac{75}{6}$ **17.** $\frac{400}{18}$

6. $\frac{72}{7}$ **12.** $\frac{291}{28}$ **18.** $\frac{273}{14}$

How Much Shelving to Buy

Shandra is going to redecorate her bedroom. She wants to hang some shelves on the walls. Before going to the hardware store for materials, Shandra measures the length of each wall in inches. She also decides how long she wants each shelf to be on each wall. Here are the measurements:

Wall Measurements		
Wall	**Wall Length**	**Shelf Length**
North	$125\frac{1}{2}''$	$72\frac{1}{4}''$
South	$125\frac{1}{2}''$	$72\frac{1}{4}''$
East	$150\frac{1}{4}''$	$85\frac{1}{2}''$
West	$150\frac{1}{4}''$	$85\frac{1}{2}''$

Exercises Use the chart to answer these questions.

1. The west wall is $150\frac{1}{4}$ inches long. The shelf for that wall will be $85\frac{1}{2}$ inches long. What is the difference between the two measurements?

2. The shelves on the north and south walls are each $72\frac{1}{4}$ inches long. What is the total length for both shelves?

3. What is the perimeter of Shandra's bedroom? Give your answer in inches.

4. Shandra decides to divide the wood for the east wall into three parts to make three shelves. How long is each shelf?

5. How much wood does Shandra need to buy to make all of the shelves for her bedroom?

Chapter 7   R E V I E W

Write the letter of the best answer for each problem.

1. $15\frac{3}{8}$
   $+\ 7\frac{5}{6}$

    A $22\frac{5}{24}$ **C** $24\frac{5}{24}$

    B $23\frac{5}{24}$ **D** $25\frac{5}{24}$

2. $2\frac{5}{6}$
   $+12\frac{1}{4}$

    A $15\frac{1}{24}$ **C** $16\frac{1}{24}$

    B $15\frac{1}{12}$ **D** $16\frac{1}{12}$

3. $5\frac{9}{11}$
   $-\ 3\frac{1}{3}$

    A $1\frac{16}{33}$ **C** $2\frac{16}{33}$

    B $1\frac{20}{33}$ **D** $2\frac{20}{33}$

4. Jane and Sam are helping their dad build a deck in their yard. Their dad sends them to the store to buy 12 boards of wood that are each $12\frac{1}{8}$ feet long. How many feet of wood do they buy in all?

    A 143 ft   **C** 145 ft

    B $144\frac{1}{2}$ ft   **D** $145\frac{1}{2}$ ft

5. Julie is weaving a rug. Two sides of the rug are $42\frac{1}{2}$ inches long, and two sides are $20\frac{1}{4}$ inches long. What is the perimeter of the rug?

    A $120\frac{1}{2}$ in.   **C** $125\frac{1}{2}$ in.

    B $122\frac{1}{2}$ in.   **D** $127\frac{1}{2}$ in.

Perform the following operations. Write your answers in simplest form.

6. $12\frac{4}{5}$ **7.** 16 **8.** $8\frac{12}{15}$ **9.** $9\frac{2}{7}$

$+ \, 4\frac{2}{3}$ $- \, 3\frac{2}{5}$ $- \, 5\frac{1}{5}$ $- \, 3\frac{4}{9}$

Find the answers.

10. $5\frac{1}{5}$ ft $\times$ $1\frac{1}{2}$ ft $=$

11. 7 ft $\div$ $1\frac{2}{5}$ ft $=$

Solve these problems. Write your answers in simplest form. Include the units of measure in your answers.

12. Marco uses $\frac{3}{4}$ of an old shelf that is 22 inches long. How much is left over?

13. Fran measures the distance around her desk. The measurements are 26 inches, $30\frac{1}{2}$ inches, 26 inches, and $30\frac{1}{2}$ inches. Find the perimeter of Fran's desk.

14. Otto has a board $6\frac{1}{2}$ feet long. If he divides the board into shelves $\frac{2}{3}$ foot long, how many shelves can he cut?

15. Cara's kitchen has a length of $12\frac{1}{2}$ feet and a width of 10 feet. What is the area of her kitchen?

16. If Bridget's room is 11 feet by $8\frac{3}{4}$ feet, then how many square feet of flooring should she buy?

17. Sun Li needs curtains for her window. She buys curtains that are 60 inches long. How much should she shorten them if her window is $49\frac{7}{8}$ inches long?

18. Satha buys $1\frac{5}{8}$ yards of braid trim and $\frac{3}{8}$ yard of lace trim. How many yards of trim does she buy?

19. Matthew is digging a flower bed around three sides of his patio. If one side of the patio is $8\frac{3}{4}$ feet, and the other two sides are each $5\frac{7}{8}$ feet, then how many feet long will his new flower bed be?

20. Kyle plans to cover his kitchen shelves. He buys a roll of shelf paper that is $25\frac{1}{2}$ feet long. How many shelves can he fully cover if each shelf is 4 feet long?

Test-Taking Tip

Review your corrected tests. You can learn from previous mistakes.

Spending Money

As consumers, we spend money for goods and services. A smart shopper knows how much a purchase will be, finds the better buy, and calculates what amount of change is due. But money is not always expressed as whole numbers, or dollars. Why? Because our money system has parts of dollars called *cents*. You'll save your pennies when you know how to apply mathematics to decimals, such as money.

In Chapter 8, you will learn how to add and subtract with money and other decimals.

Goals for Learning

◆ To compare decimals

◆ To read prices and write them in decimal form

◆ To find the total amount of a purchase of several items

◆ To compute the amount of change due

Decimal

A whole number followed by a point and places to the right; the numbers to the point's right equal less than one

Decimal place

Position to the right of the decimal point

Add hundredths, then tenths, then ones, then tens.

When you add **decimals**, keeping the **decimal places** in the same column is important so that you will not add tenths to hundredths. You can do this easily if you place the decimals in vertical form and line up the decimal points. For example, to add 3.4 + 0.07 + 6, you would write in a column. Placing the zeros will help keep numbers in the correct column.

EXAMPLES Add 3.4 + 0.07 + 6   Add 8 + 0.02 + 0.6

$$
\begin{array}{r} 3.4 \\ 0.07 \\ + 6 \\ \hline \end{array} \quad OR \quad
\begin{array}{r} 3.40 \\ 0.07 \\ + 6.00 \\ \hline 9.47 \end{array} \qquad
\begin{array}{r} 8 \\ 0.02 \\ + 0.6 \\ \hline \end{array} \quad OR \quad
\begin{array}{r} 8.00 \\ 0.02 \\ + 0.60 \\ \hline 8.62 \end{array}
$$

Exercise A Write these problems in vertical form, then add. Remember to line up the decimal points.

1. 6 + 0.35 + 2.6

2. 5.8 + 16 + 0.45

3. 15.61 + 1.2 + 9

4. 2 + 0.008 + 0.25

5. 3.6 + 8 + 2.35

6. 14.1 + 2 + 0.506

7. 8.2 + 0.07 + 11

8. 13.62 + 1.2 + 0.309

Adding Prices Stavros goes shopping for a camping trip and buys the following items. How much money does he spend for them? Remember to add decimal points if needed.

EXAMPLE

Stavros's List	Price Shown	Actual Price
Baked beans	45¢	$0.45
Dry cereal	1.95	$1.95
Beef stew	2.50	$2.50
Tomatoes	95¢	$0.95
Fruit juice	4.58	+ $4.58
		$10.43

Stavros spends $10.43 for the items.

Writing About Mathematics

Suppose you only want one can of green beans. What do you think the store would charge? Why?

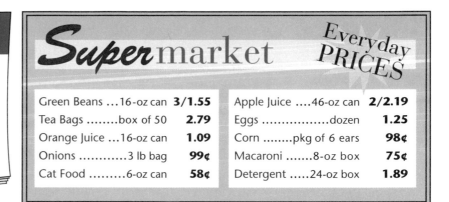

Try This

Find the greatest number of each item you could buy with $10. Do not include tax.

Exercise B Add the prices to find the total for each order.

1. 3 cans of green beans
   1 package of corn
   3 pounds of onions

2. 1 dozen eggs
   1 box of detergent
   1 box of tea bags
   2 cans of apple juice

3. 1 box of detergent
   1 box of tea bags
   3 cans of green beans
   1 can of cat food

4. 1 box of macaroni
   3 pounds of onions
   1 dozen eggs
   1 can of orange juice

To compare decimal numbers, compare the greatest place value of each.

EXAMPLE   True or False: $8.93 < 9.78$
Compare the ones: $8 < 9$. True

Exercise C Write *True* or *False* for each comparison.

1. $7.41 > 0.97$

2. $0.12 < 0.12$

3. $5.9 < 6.09$

4. $0.81 > 0.094$

5. $4.16 < 4.06$

6. $4.02 > 7.420$

When you add decimals on a calculator, remember to include any decimal points. Press the ⊞ button after each addend except the last one. Press the ⊟ button after the last addend.

> **EXAMPLE**   Add 3.7 + 8 + 0.006.
>
> 3.7 ⊞ 8 ⊞ $.006$ ⊟ 11.706

Calculator Exercise   Add these numbers on your calculator.

1.   235.06
      1,238.091
      462.923
      2,630.105
  +   62.188

2.   2.23402
      0.081152
      1.120803
      0.18165
  +   3.5176

3.   1.60606
      0.234
      1.5678
      92.4
      5.8
  +   348.59

4.   936.4
      2.49
      2,417.68
      3.017
      5,234.1
  +   0.74

5.   50.638
      1.1093
      175.2063
      361.189
  + 201.892

6.   0.136
      1.4892
      12.6
      9.82
  +   0.965

7.   530.61
      15.8
      9.004
      0.005
      6.8
      14.50963
  + 368.523

8.   5.243
      0.006
      9.2
      67.03
      1.3956
  +   86.4

Adding zeros to the right of the decimal point does not change the value of the number.
$100 = $100.00

When you subtract decimals, first line up the decimal points. You may need to write zeros before you can subtract.

EXAMPLE   Ms. Lawson buys a jacket for $92.49. How much change will she receive if she gives the salesclerk $100?

$$
\begin{array}{r}
\$\,100 \\
-\ 92.49 \\
\end{array}
\qquad
\begin{array}{r}
\$100.00 \\
-\ 92.49 \\
\hline
\$\ \ 7.51 \\
\end{array}
$$

Write a decimal point and two zeros here.

Ms. Lawson will receive $7.51 change.

Exercise A Write these subtraction problems in vertical form, then subtract. Remember to line up the decimal points. Add any zeros that are needed.

1. $23 − $2.67

2. 4 − 2.09

3. 2.1 − 0.92

4. 6 − 0.721

5. 1 − 0.34

6. 2.4 − 0.024

7. 5.03 − 0.223

8. 89.1 − 0.2

9. $50 − $1.93

10. 3 − 0.04

11. 24.93 − 3.4

12. 9.2 − 0.334

13. 56 − 2.33

14. 1.1 − 0.11

15. 30 − 0.093

16. 0.234 − 0.092

17. 2.03 − 0.8

18. 67.9 − 0.341

19. 1 − 0.3

20. 4 − 0.4

21. 12.5 − 3.4

22. 107 − 0.51

23. 7.1 − 0.77

24. 2.4 − 1.34

Exercise B Find the amount of change due for each purchase.

	Cost	Paid With			Cost	Paid With
1.	$79.60	$100		**13.**	$0.54	$20
2.	$18.75	$20		**14.**	$39	$50
3.	$42.50	$50		**15.**	$567.09	$1,000
4.	$39.36	$40		**16.**	$73.15	$100
5.	$1.59	$2		**17.**	$15.65	$75
6.	$42.70	$50		**18.**	$4.76	$10.76
7.	$11.95	$20		**19.**	$1.23	$2
8.	$11.76	$20		**20.**	$2.41	$10.01
9.	$17.36	$20.01		**21.**	$39.23	$50.03
10.	$9.78	$50		**22.**	$1.11	$20
11.	$11.90	$40		**23.**	$203	$500
12.	$4.02	$10.02		**24.**	$8.98	$20

Adding and Subtracting Money Both addition and subtraction with money take place when you buy more than one item at a time.

Check your answer by subtracting the purchases one at a time.

EXAMPLE Amy buys a shirt for $12.45, a skirt for $19.50, and socks for $3.99. If she gives the salesclerk $50, how much change will she receive?

First you add the items together. Then you subtract to find the amount of change due.

Step 1 Add to find the total.
$12.45
 19.50
+ 3.99
$35.94 ◄— total

Step 2 Subtract to find the change due.
$ 50.00
−35.94
$ 14.06 ◄— change due

***Exercise* C** Find the amount of change due for each purchase.

	Items Bought	Paid With
1.	DVD Player, $89.95 2 DVDs, $28.99	$150
2.	Shirt, $19.99 Coat, $92.00	$200
3.	Radio, $29.95 Earphones, $12.00	$50
4.	Iron, $21.50 Toaster, $12.50 Slow Cooker, $44.99 Blender, $16.00	$100
5.	Shorts, $24.80 Shirt, $48.75 Socks, $6.00 Shoes, $69.10	$200

PROBLEM SOLVING

***Exercise* D** Solve each problem.

1. Byron bought a belt for $26.50 and a pair of pants for $49.00. What change did he receive from $100?

2. Crystal bought a VHS movie for $19.50 and a DVD for $23.90. She bought labels for $3.50 and a CD stand for $25.99. What change did Crystal receive from $100?

Shopping for Best Buys

You are sent to the store to buy 6 cans of green beans, 12 pounds of apples, and 48 ounces of peanut butter.

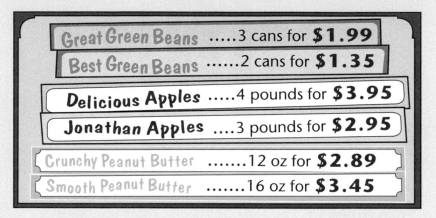

Great Green Beans .....3 cans for **$1.99**

Best Green Beans ......2 cans for **$1.35**

Delicious Apples .....4 pounds for **$3.95**

Jonathan Apples ....3 pounds for **$2.95**

Crunchy Peanut Butter ....12 oz for **$2.89**

Smooth Peanut Butter ....16 oz for **$3.45**

Exercises Use the signs above to answer these questions.

1. Find the cost for 6 cans of green beans for each brand. Which brand will cost less?

2. Find the cost of 12 pounds of apples for each kind. Which kind will cost less?

3. Find the cost of 48 ounces of each type of peanut butter. Which type will cost less?

4. Find the least cost for all of your purchases.

Technology Connection

Suppose you are given $25 for the purchases in the Application.

Use a spreadsheet to enter the following.

In C1: $25.00

In A2: Green Beans	In B2: (enter the cost)	In C2: Enter the formula = C1–B2
In A3: Apples	In B3: (enter the cost)	In C3: Enter the formula = C2–B3
In A4: Peanut Butter	In B4: (enter the cost)	In C4: Enter the formula = C3–B4

What is your result?

Chapter 8 REVIEW

Write the letter of the best answer to each question.

1. Which statement is correct?
   a. $0.34 < 0.341$ b. $10.8 > 10.9$ c. $5.9 < 5.95$
   A   a only
   B   a and b
   C   a and c
   D   c only

2. Which of the following shows 89¢ written in decimal form?
   A $0.89
   B   0.89
   C $89
   D $8.90

3. Add $3.87 + 4 + 0.096$.
   A   7.896
   B   7.966
   C   8.83
   D   8.966

4. Subtract $8.69 - 2.407$.
   A   6.22
   B   6.283
   C   6.297
   D   11.097

5. Find the change from $50 for purchases of $25.98 and $15.56.
   A $8.46
   B $24.02
   C $34.44
   D $41.54

Ten-thousands	Thousands	Hundreds	Tens	Ones		Tenths	Hundredths	Thousandths	Ten-thousandths
0	0	0	0	0	.	0	0	0	0

What is the place value of each underlined digit?

6. $\underline{2}1.65$

7. $3.\underline{0}15$

8. $0.3\underline{5}$

9. $1.603\underline{5}$

10. $26.7\underline{2}$

11. $2\underline{3}1.72$

12. $12.0\underline{9}6$

13. $36.2\underline{1}$

Write *True* or *False* for each of these comparisons.

14. 0.091 > 1.1

15. 0.035 < 0.10

16. 0.01 > 0.0098

Write these prices correctly with decimal points.

17. Tomatoes, can   2/87¢

18. Peanut butter, jar   179¢

Find the total amount of each purchase.

19. Cooking oil $1.75
Baked beans   45¢
10 lb potatoes $2.79

20. Frozen dinner $1.59
Canned corn   55¢
Lettuce   75¢

Find the amount of change due.

21. Coat, $29.95—Paid $50

22. Shoes, $49.11—Paid $50

Add or subtract.

23. $2.50 + $0.85 + $30

24. 5.6 + 0.28 + 5 + 0.6

25. $29 − $0.89

26. 1.1 − 0.063

Find the total cost and the amount of change due for each set of purchases.

	Items Bought	Paid With
27.	Hat, $49.00 Gloves, $29.95 Shoes, $88.95	$200
28.	Slippers, $35.00 Shirt, $31.99 Ribbon, $6.00	$100
29.	Art Print, $55.60 Vase, $32.00 Lamp, $22.00	$150
30.	Software, $250.00 Added memory, $42.00 CDs, $19.00	$400

Test-Taking Tip

Look over a test before you begin answering questions. See how many parts there are. See what you are being asked to do in each part.

Earning Money

How are people paid for the work they do? Are they paid a weekly or yearly salary? Are their paychecks based upon an hourly wage? When you read advertisements for jobs, it is important to know how to convert the pay that is offered to the amount you can expect in your paycheck. Let mathematics help you!

In Chapter 9, you will learn how to multiply and divide with whole numbers and decimals.

Goals for Learning

◆ To multiply to find gross pay

◆ To divide to find hourly pay if the weekly pay is known

◆ To divide to find weekly salary if the yearly salary is known

◆ To compute overtime pay

We multiply decimals to compute the **gross pay** that a worker who is paid by the hour earns.

Gross pay

Pay before deductions

Per

For each; for every

When multiplying with money, be careful where you place the decimal point in the product.

EXAMPLES

Lin works part time as a bricklayer's helper and earns $9.75 **per** hour. If he works 35 hours during a 1-week period, how much is his gross pay for that week?

Multiply the hourly wage by the number of hours worked.

$\begin{array}{r} \$\quad 9.75 \leftarrow 2 \text{ decimal places} \\ \times \quad\quad 35 \leftarrow 0 \text{ decimal places} \\ \hline 48\ 75 \\ +\ 292\ 5 \\ \hline \$\ 341.25 \leftarrow 2 + 0 \text{ decimal places} = 2 \text{ decimal places} \end{array}$

Since two decimal places are in the factors, count off two decimal places in the product.

Lin's gross pay is $341.25.

Marti earns $10.50 per hour at her part-time job after school. If she works 6 hours during a 1-week period, how much does she earn?

$\begin{array}{r} \$\ 10.50 \\ \times \quad\quad 6 \\ \hline \$\ 63.00 \end{array}$

The total number of places to the right of a decimal determines the number of places in the answer.

Marti earns $63.00.

Exercise A Find the gross pay for these workers.

1. 32 hours at $6.75 per hour

2. 17 hours at $7.19 per hour

3. 22 hours at $6.85 per hour

4. 18 hours at $6.78 per hour

5. 23 hours at $7.10 per hour

6. 27 hours at $8.89 per hour

Exercise B Find the answers by multiplying.

1. Heather works part time as a shoe salesclerk and earns $6.80 per hour. She works an 11-hour week. Find her weekly gross earnings.

2. Nelson works 8 hours per week as a carpenter's helper and earns $6.90 per hour. What is Nelson's gross pay each week?

3. Cammy's part-time job earns her $6.75 per hour as a stock clerk. How much does Cammy earn if she works 22 hours?

4. The Super Food Market pays $6.90 per hour for a person to stock shelves. How much will a person earn at this job, working 15 hours?

5. Jamal tutors after school and earns $9.75 per hour. If he works 6 hours a week, how much does Jamal earn per week?

Exercise C Find the gross pay.

1. 30 hours at $8.50 per hour

2. 22 hours at $7.60 per hour

3. 15 hours at $7.75 per hour

4. 28 hours at $9.50 per hour

5. 16 hours at $8.00 per hour

6. 19 hours at $8.65 per hour

7. 23 hours at $7.75 per hour

8. 36 hours at $8.25 per hour

9. 12 hours at $10.95 per hour

10. 17 hours at $12.00 per hour

11. 11 hours at $9.65 per hour

12. 28 hours at $7.16 per hour

13. 32 hours at $7.00 per hour

14. 23 hours at $9.95 per hour

15. 31 hours at $7.18 per hour

16. 42 hours at $7.25 per hour

17. 25 hours at $8.25 per hour

18. 16 hours at $9.50 per hour

19. 15 hours at $7.50 per hour

20. 8 hours at $8.60 per hour

21. 5 hours at $12.20 per hour

22. 38 hours at $6.90 per hour

23. 36 hours at $7.60 per hour

24. 40 hours at $8.00 per hour

Multiplying Decimals by Decimals When you multiply decimals, lining up the decimal points is not necessary. The total number of places to the right of the decimal point in each factor determines the placement of the decimal point in the answer.

EXAMPLES

When you see this:
4.35 × 1.7 =

Write this:

```
      4.3 5 ◄—2 places
   ×     1.7 ◄—1 place
      3 0 4 5
   + 4 3 5
      7.3 9 5 ◄—3 places
```

When you see this:
0.204 × 0.06 =

Write this:

```
      .204 ◄—3 places
   × .06 ◄—2 places
      .01224 ◄—5 places
```

Exercise D Multiply these decimals. Count the decimal places in each factor before you place the decimal point in the answer.

1.
```
$  3.25
×   1.5
```

2.
```
$  4.20
×   16
```

3.
```
$  1.95
×   .28
```

4.
```
   5.56
×   3.2
```

5.
```
   .063
×   2.9
```

6.
```
   1.03
×   .99
```

7.
```
$  2.06
×   1.5
```

8.
```
   .68
×   2.5
```

9.
```
   735
×   5.2
```

10.
```
   1.69
×   13
```

11.
```
   52.33
×   2.3
```

12.
```
   .263
×   .09
```

13.
```
   .087
×   .06
```

14.
```
   7.31
×   1.06
```

15.
```
   .2106
×   .35
```

16.
```
   .0528
×   .003
```

17.
```
   .002
×   .03
```

18.
```
   1.006
×  1.07
```

19.
```
   3.15
×   .16
```

20.
```
   .819
×   23
```

21.
```
   5.1
×  .06
```

22.
```
   .205
×   .01
```

23.
```
   2.68
×   10
```

24.
```
$  4.78
×  100
```

Multiplying With Decimal Parts of an Hour

The number of hours an employee works may not always be a whole number. The worker may get paid for $\frac{1}{4}$, $\frac{1}{2}$, or $\frac{3}{4}$ of an hour.

 EXAMPLES

Nilor works $11\frac{1}{2}$ hours after school, earning $8.25 per hour. How much is his gross pay? (Remember: $11\frac{1}{2} = 11.5$)

$$
\begin{array}{r}
\$\quad 8.25 \quad \longleftarrow 2 \text{ places} \\
\times \quad 11.5 \quad \longleftarrow 1 \text{ place} \\
\hline
4\ 125 \\
8\ 25 \\
+\ 82\ 5 \\
\hline
\$\ 94.875 \quad \longleftarrow 3 \text{ places}
\end{array}
$$

Since only two decimal places are needed for money, round the gross pay to the nearest cent. Nilor's gross pay is $94.88.

Alicia works as a server and earns $8.57 per hour. If she works $12\frac{1}{4}$ hours for 1 week, how much is her gross pay? (Remember: $12\frac{1}{4} = 12.25$)

$$
\begin{array}{rl}
12.25 & \text{Hours} \\
\times \quad \$8.57 & \text{Per hour} \\
\hline
85\ 75 & \\
6\ 12\ 5 & \\
+\ 98\ 00 & \\
\hline
\$104.98\ 25 & \text{Gross pay}
\end{array}
$$

Remember, only two decimal places are used for money. $104.9825 \approx $104.98

Alicia's gross pay is $104.98.

When rounding, if the digit you are looking at is greater than or equal to 5, round up. If the digit is less than or equal to 4, round down.

Writing About Mathematics

Explain a way to keep track of the number of hours you work each week and how much gross pay you earn.

EXAMPLE An employee works $10\frac{1}{4}$ hours for an hourly pay of $8.59. Find the gross pay. (Remember: $10\frac{1}{4} = 10.25$)

$$\begin{array}{r} 10.25 \leftarrow \text{2 decimal places} \\ \times \quad \$8.59 \leftarrow \text{2 decimal places} \\ \hline 92\ 25 \\ 5\ 12\ 5 \\ + 82\ 00 \\ \hline \$\ 88.04\ 75 \approx \$88.05 \end{array}$$

The employee's gross pay is $88.05.

PROBLEM SOLVING

Exercise E Find the gross pay. Round your answers to the nearest cent.

1. Anthony works $11\frac{1}{2}$ hours earning $7.25 per hour. Find Anthony's gross pay.

2 José earns $10.00 per hour as a tutor after school. Find his gross pay if he works $9\frac{1}{4}$ hours.

3. Kim is an assistant clerk at a hospital. She earns $6.80 an hour. She works $36\frac{3}{4}$ hours in 1 week. How much is her gross pay?

4. Mandy works as a carpenter's helper. She earns $10.25 per hour. If she works $28\frac{3}{4}$ hours in 1 week, how much is her gross pay?

5. Keiko earns $7.25 per hour with a baby-sitting service. Find her gross pay if she works 17 hours.

6. Casey worked 7 hours on Friday and $7\frac{1}{2}$ hours on Saturday as a part-time housecleaner. What is her gross pay if she earns $6.75 per hour?

Exercise F Find the gross pay. Round your answers to the nearest cent.

1. $30\frac{1}{2}$ hours at $7.65 per hour

2. $15\frac{1}{2}$ hours at $6.92 per hour

3. $6\frac{3}{4}$ hours at $7.25 per hour

4. $12\frac{1}{2}$ hours at $6.82 per hour

5. $13\frac{1}{2}$ hours at $6.75 per hour

6. $10\frac{3}{4}$ hours at $7.00 per hour

7. 5 hours at $6.83 per hour

8. $27\frac{1}{2}$ hours at $6.78 per hour

9. $4\frac{3}{4}$ hours at $6.90 per hour

10. $15\frac{1}{2}$ hours at $8.70 per hour

11. $23\frac{1}{2}$ hours at $8.36 per hour

12. $26\frac{1}{2}$ hours at $6.90 per hour

13. $39\frac{1}{4}$ hours at $6.75 per hour

14. $25\frac{3}{4}$ hours at $7.62 per hour

15. $10\frac{1}{4}$ hours at $7.93 per hour

16. $22\frac{1}{2}$ hours at $6.80 per hour

Try This

Pat works $16\frac{1}{2}$ hours a week in a child-care center. She earns $10.25 per hour. How much is her gross pay for 1 week? How much is her gross pay for 1 year (52 weeks)? If Pat earns a raise of $0.25 per hour, how much is her weekly gross pay? How much is her yearly gross pay?

Child care can be a part-time job or a full-time profession for people who want to work with children.

Overtime

Time beyond the estimated limit

Time and a half

Payment of 1.5 times the hourly rate for work

Double time

Payment of 2 times the hourly rate

Writing About Mathematics

Write a paragraph explaining the difference between time-and-a-half and double-time pay.

Overtime Pay Workers earn more than their hourly rate of pay when their employer asks them to work longer than the agreed-upon, or "straight," time. **Overtime** may be paid at the rate of **time and a half** or **double time.**

 EXAMPLE Gary works 43 hours at $6.79 per hour with time and a half for all time worked over 40 hours. What is his gross pay?

Step 1 Separate straight time from overtime.

$$\begin{array}{r} 43 \\ -\ 40 \\ \hline 3 \end{array}$$

43   Total time
− 40   Agreed straight time
3   Overtime

Step 2 Convert 3 hours to time and a half. To do so, multiply by 1.5.

1.5 $1.5 = 1\frac{1}{2}$
× 3   Hours to be converted
4.5   Time and a half

Step 3 Add straight time to time and a half.

40.0
+ 4.5
44.5   Time used to compute gross pay

Step 4 Multiply the total time by the rate per hour.

44.5   Hours
× $6.79   Rate per hour
$302.155   ≈ $302.16

Gary's gross pay is $302.16.

Try This

Joe works 47 hours every week for 1 year. He gets paid $8.50 per hour, and time-and-a-half pay for time over 40 hours. What is his gross pay for 1 year? How much more does he make per year by working overtime than he would if he just worked 40 hours per week?

Exercise A Find the gross pay, including time and a half.

1. Carol works 44 hours at $7.20 per hour with time and a half for all time over 40 hours. Find Carol's gross pay.

2. Ricardo works 44 hours at $10.00 per hour with time and a half for all time over 40 hours. Find Ricardo's gross pay.

3. Alexandra works 9 hours at $7.25 per hour with time and a half for all time over 8 hours. Find Alexandra's gross pay.

4. Compute the gross pay for Cindy's 46-hour workweek if she gets $9.60 per hour and time and a half for all time over 40 hours.

5. Twelve hours at $7.50 per hour with time and a half after 8 hours.

6. Forty-five hours at $7.00 per hour with time and a half after 40 hours.

7. Fifteen hours at $6.75 per hour with time and a half after 8 hours.

8. Thirty-seven hours at $7.00 per hour with time and a half after 3 hours.

9. Forty-one and one-half hours at $6.80 per hour with time and a half after 40 hours.

10. Forty-two and three-fourths hours at $7.50 per hour with time and a half after 40 hours.

11. Twelve hours at $11.75 per hour with time and a half after 8 hours.

12. Sixteen hours at $9.50 per hour with time and a half after 10 hours.

13. Forty-three hours at $14.00 per hour with time and a half after 40 hours.

14. Eighteen hours at $6.75 per hour with time and a half after 16 hours.

15. Forty-three hours at $8.60 per hour with time and a half after 40 hours.

Working overtime is often necessary to get a job done on time.

Double-Time Earnings

To find double-time earnings, first multiply the overtime hours by 2.

EXAMPLE

Hatsue works 48 hours at a rate of $8.29 per hour for 1 week. She is paid straight time for 40 hours and double time for the time over 40 hours. What is her gross pay?

Step 1 Separate straight time from double time.

$$
\begin{array}{rl}
48 & \text{Total time} \\
-\,40 & \text{Agreed straight time} \\
\hline
8 & \text{Hours at the double-time rate}
\end{array}
$$

Step 2 Convert 8 hours to double time. To double, multiply by 2.

$$
\begin{array}{rl}
8 & \text{Hours to be converted} \\
\times\,2 & \\
\hline
16 & \text{Hours double time}
\end{array}
$$

Step 3 Add straight time to double time.

$$
\begin{array}{rl}
40 & \text{Hours straight time} \\
+\,16 & \text{Hours double time} \\
\hline
56 & \text{Total hours}
\end{array}
$$

Step 4 Multiply the rate per hour and the total.

$$
\begin{array}{rl}
\$\ \ 8.29 & \text{Per hour} \\
\times\ \ \ \ \ 56 & \text{Total hours} \\
\hline
\$464.24 & \text{Gross pay}
\end{array}
$$

Hatsue's gross pay is $464.24.

Technology Connection

How can the latest technology help you manage your money? There are several software programs available that are designed to help people manage their money. You can try one out at your school or neighborhood library. These programs have checkbook registers to keep track of your deposits and withdrawals. They can remind you when monthly bills are due. They can help you keep track of investments. They can even make graphs to show how you are spending your money. Think about how these programs can help a family plan a budget and save for the future.

Exercise B Find the gross pay, including double time.

1. Find Luke's pay for 48 hours if he earns $8.20 per hour with double time for any hours over 40.

2. Marconi, a plumber's helper, works 45 hours in 1 week. He earns $6.78 an hour, with 5 of the 45 hours at double time. Find Marconi's gross pay.

3. Pam earns $6.75 an hour baby-sitting. If she works 16 hours per week and charges double time for any time over 10 hours, then how much is her gross pay?

4. Thirteen hours at $6.76 per hour with double time over 10 hours.

5. Eighteen hours at $7.30 per hour with double time over 10 hours.

6. Forty-seven hours at $6.80 per hour with double time over 40 hours.

7. Nine and one-half hours at $8.00 per hour with double time over 8 hours.

8. Forty and one-half hours at $10.50 per hour with double time over 40 hours.

9. Ten and one-half hours at $9.00 per hour with double time over 8 hours.

10. Thirteen and one-half hours at $10.25 per hour with double time over 8 hours.

11. Forty-eight hours at $10.75 per hour with double time after 40 hours.

12. Ten hours at $8.67 per hour with double time after 8 hours.

13. Eleven hours at $6.75 per hour with double time after 8 hours.

When you divide a decimal by a whole number, you divide as though you were dividing whole numbers. After you have found the quotient, you bring the decimal point straight up into the quotient.

EXAMPLE $291.60 ÷ 30 = ■

$$
\begin{array}{r}
\$9.72 \\
30\ \overline{)\ \$291.60} \\
-270 \\
\hline
21\ 6 \\
-\ 21\ 0 \\
\hline
60 \\
-\ 60 \\
\hline
0
\end{array}
$$

If the divisor is a decimal, then follow these steps:

Step 1   Move the decimal point in the divisor to the right of the number.

Step 2   Move the decimal point in the dividend the same number of places to the right.

Step 3   Divide and bring the decimal point up into the quotient.

$0.0855 ÷ 1.5 =$

$$
\begin{array}{r}
0.057 \\
1.5\overline{)\ 0.0.855} \\
-\ 75 \\
\hline
105 \\
-\ 105 \\
\hline
0
\end{array}
$$

Exercise A Find the quotients.

1. $157.5 \div 42$ **7.** $0.00558 \div 0.06$

2. $35.28 \div 18$ **8.** $0.00736 \div 0.008$

3. $11.256 \div 2.8$ **9.** $156.4 \div 34$

4. $88 \div 3.2$ **10.** $0.01943 \div 0.67$

5. $0.08052 \div 0.61$ **11.** $5.848 \div 8.5$

6. $0.23427 \div 0.57$ **12.** $15.75 \div 0.35$

Exercise B Find the quotients.

1. $0.045 \div 9$ **7.** $81.6 \div 0.03$

2. $160.5 \div 3$ **8.** $0.316 \div 5$

3. $821 \div 2.5$ **9.** $18 \div 2.4$

4. $0.015 \div 2$ **10.** $6,004 \div 0.32$

5. $1.25 \div 0.25$ **11.** $0.0185 \div 0.05$

6. $6.615 \div 6$ **12.** $16.58 \div 0.25$

Calculator Practice   You can use a calculator to divide decimals by whole numbers.

EXAMPLE $5.85 \div 7 = \blacksquare$

$5.85 \div 7 = 0.8357142$

Calculator Exercise Find the quotients. Use a calculator.

1. $0.0016 \div 43$ **6.** $1.57 \div 89$

2. $117.3 \div 5$ **7.** $456.98 \div 796$

3. $88.556 \div 19$ **8.** $24.153 \div 55$

4. $1,111 \div 523$ **9.** $0.341 \div 7$

5. $12,039 \div 4,000$ **10.** $3.41 \div 70$

Remember to line up the digits carefully when solving long division problems.

Dividing the Yearly Salary Sometimes the yearly **salary** for a job is mentioned in a want ad or in a job description. To find the weekly salary, divide the yearly salary by the number of weeks worked.

EXAMPLE Monica is paid $18,832 per year working as a word processor. Find Monica's weekly salary if she works 52 weeks per year.

$$\$362.153 \approx \$362.15$$

$$
\begin{array}{r}
52 \overline{)\,\$18{,}832.000} \\
-15\,6 \\
\hline
3\,23 \\
-3\,12 \\
\hline
112 \\
-104 \\
\hline
80 \\
-52 \\
\hline
280 \\
-260 \\
\hline
200 \\
-156 \\
\hline
44
\end{array}
$$

Divide to three decimal places and round to the nearest cent. Monica works 52 weeks a year. She is paid $362.15 per week.

People who work for large companies may be paid a yearly salary.

In a division problem, you can add zeros to the dividend until you have no remainder or until the digits in the quotient begin to repeat.

Exercise C For each yearly salary below, find the amount paid weekly. There are 52 weeks in a year. Round your answers to the nearest cent.

1. $22,938

2. $19,850

3. $25,652

4. $20,084

5. $21,372

6. $36,744

7. $24,482

8. $20,920

9. $29,100

10. $18,981

11. $29,777

12. $30,868

13. $25,226

14. $26,412

15. $21,856

16. $32,750

17. $25,655

18. $20,852

19. $31,672

20. $24,312

21. $22,880

22. $33,670

23. $27,151

24. $27,524

25. $24,222

26. $20,000

27. $33,468

28. $45,575

29. $28,710

30. $29,623

31. $33,405

32. $24,260

33. $35,486

34. $26,810

35. $40,676

36. $28,582

Exercise D For each yearly salary below, find the amount paid monthly. There are 12 months in a year.

1. $19,164

2. $26,028

3. $35,556

4. $22,800

5. $58,224

6. $47,472

7. $27,672

8. $37,224

Remember to round
each quotient to
the nearest cent.

Dividing Gross Pay You can find the hourly rate when you
know the gross pay. Divide the gross pay by the number of
hours worked.

EXAMPLE Vernon's weekly gross pay is $494. If he works
40 hours, then what is his hourly rate?

$$
\begin{array}{r}
\$12.35 \\
40\,\overline{)\,\$494.00} \\
-\ 40 \\
\hline
94 \\
-\ 80 \\
\hline
14\ 0 \\
-\ 12\ 0 \\
\hline
2\ 00 \\
-\ 2\ 00 \\
\hline
0
\end{array}
$$

Vernon's hourly rate is $12.35.

Exercise E Find the hourly rates. Round your answers to the
nearest cent.

	Gross Pay	Hours Worked	Hourly Rate		Gross Pay	Hours Worked	Hourly Rate
1.	$220.00	30	_____	**13.**	$98.54	14	_____
2.	$56.40	8	_____	**14.**	$220.00	32	_____
3.	$55.00	8	_____	**15.**	$85.98	11	_____
4.	$105.00	15	_____	**16.**	$165.28	24	_____
5.	$77.00	11	_____	**17.**	$55.60	8	_____
6.	$131.25	15	_____	**18.**	$152.64	12	_____
7.	$112.25	15	_____	**19.**	$444.99	11	_____
8.	$74.16	9	_____	**20.**	$65.44	8	_____
9.	$138.40	20	_____	**21.**	$107.40	15	_____
10.	$112.80	16	_____	**22.**	$88.00	12	_____
11.	$85.68	12	_____	**23.**	$116.80	16	_____
12.	$103.75	15	_____	**24.**	$89.20	12	_____

Exercise F Find the hourly rates. Round your answers to the
nearest cent

	Gross Pay	Hours Worked	Hourly Rate		Gross Pay	Hours Worked	Hourly Rate
1.	$78.50	10	_____	**7.**	$145.20	20	_____
2.	$77.00	7	_____	**8.**	$104.00	14	_____
3.	$67.26	9	_____	**9.**	$174.80	19	_____
4.	$133.65	19	_____	**10.**	$46.80	6	_____
5.	$39.60	5	_____	**11.**	$43.20	6	_____
6.	$81.00	12	_____	**12.**	$95.85	13	_____

Calculator Practice You can use a calculator to help you convert a weekly salary to a yearly salary.

Writing About Mathematics

How can you use mathematics to help you figure out if your weekly paycheck is correct?

EXAMPLE $535 weekly for 52 weeks = ■ yearly salary

$535 \times 52 = 27820$ or **$27,820.00** yearly salary

Calculator Exercise Convert each weekly salary to a yearly salary. Use a calculator.

1. $455.00   **7.** $550.00

2. $389.50   **8.** $379.00

3. $405.00   **9.** $401.00

4. $370.00   **10.** $558.00

5. $456.79   **11.** $599.96

6. $373.39   **12.** $423.35

Which Job Is Best?

Maria recently graduated from college with a degree in computer programming. She has been offered two similar jobs, and she must decide which job to take. Both jobs seem very interesting and challenging, so she will choose the job that has the best pay.

Company A is offering Maria an annual salary of $58,800. She will get the same pay regardless of the number of hours she works each week. Company B is offering $22.00 per hour. Maria is expected to work 42 hours per week, with 2 of those hours paid at time and a half.

Exercises Use the information about each job to answer the questions below.

1. If Maria works for Company A, what will be her weekly pay?

2. What will be the hourly pay if Maria works for Company A and works 40 hours per week?

3. What will be Maria's weekly pay if she works for Company B?

4. What will be Maria's yearly salary if she works for Company B?

5. Which company is offering Maria the best pay?

Chapter 9 R E V I E W

Write the letter of the best answer to each question.

1. James works part-time at an animal shelter. He works 12 hours a week and gets paid $9.81 an hour. What is his weekly pay?
   A $107.72
   B $117.72
   C $127.72
   D $137.72

2. Michael works 13 hours a week and earns $151.00. How much is his hourly pay?
   A $11.60
   B $11.61
   C $11.62
   D $11.63

3. Tito's after school job is in a clothing store. He works 15 hours a week with time and a half after 10 hours. His hourly pay is $8.75. What is his weekly pay?
   A $153.13
   B $154.00
   C $155.13
   D $156.00

4. Madison earns $322.68 per week. How much does she earn in one year?
   A $15,779.36
   B $16,779.36
   C $17,773.36
   D $18,773.36

5. Corrina earns $32,487 a year working as a dental hygienist. What is her weekly gross pay?
   A $611.75
   B $622.75
   C $623.75
   D $624.75

Find the products.

6. 2.78 × 0.36

7. 0.076 × 0.09

8. 2.9 × 0.19

Find the gross pay.

9. Thirty-five hours at $9.25 per hour.

10. Six hours at $8.75 per hour.

11. Three hours at $8.15 per hour.

12. Ten and one-fourth hours at $6.75 per hour.

13. Twelve and one-half hours at $7.20 per hour.

14. Eighteen and three-fourths hours at $9.10 per hour.

15. Forty-four hours at $7.10 an hour with time and a half after 40 hours.

16. Forty-five hours at $7.25 per hour with time and a half after 40 hours.

17. Eighteen hours at $15.00 per hour with double time after 40 hours.

18. Forty-six hours at $8.90 an hour with double time after 40 hours.

Divide. Round the quotient to the nearest hundredth.

19. 72.96 ÷ 48

20. 0.1152 ÷ 6.4

21. 0.00144 ÷ 0.08

22. 5.0587 ÷ 5.2

Convert each yearly salary to a weekly salary. Round your answer to the nearest cent.

23. $20,083

24. $21,215.50

25. $52,981

26. $46,418

Convert each weekly gross pay to an hourly rate. Round your answer to the nearest cent.

27. $142.20 for 18 hours

28. $161.85 for 15 hours

29. $541.00 for 40 hours

30. $276.31 for 19 hours

Test-Taking Tip

When you are asked to compute numbers, always check the problem to find decimal numbers. Then, double-check your placement of the decimal point in your answer.

10 Traveling

People travel on vacation. Businesspeople travel for work. Students travel to social events and school. There will be times in your life when you will be glad that you know how to use mathematics in your travels. Reading maps, determining mileage, even booking a cruise—all use mathematics in ways you may not have considered until now.

In Chapter 10, you will learn how decimals are used in traveling and discover how mathematics can make decimals work for you.

Goals for Learning

◆ To compute mileage with the aid of an odometer
◆ To compute the cost of a rental car
◆ To use a map to compute mileage
◆ To multiply with a conversion factor to convert currency
◆ To compute costs of hotel stays and cruises

An **odometer** measures how far a car has traveled. It measures this distance in tenths of a mile. The odometer is found on the **speedometer** of the car.

Odometer

An instrument for measuring the distance traveled by a vehicle

Speedometer

An instrument that measures how fast a car is traveling

EXAMPLE At the beginning of the trip, the odometer reads

At the end of the trip, the odometer reads

Subtract to find how many miles have been driven.

$$\begin{array}{r} 44{,}015.2 \\ -\ 43{,}877.5 \\ \hline 137.7 \end{array}$$

The total distance traveled is 137.7 miles.

The position on the odometer that measures tenths of a mile is usually a different color.

Calculator Practice

Calculator Exercise Use your calculator to help you find the miles traveled. Write your answers on a separate sheet of paper.

	Trip Begins With	Trip Ends With	Miles Traveled
1.	72155.7	72389.2	_____
2.	69016.1	69143.0	_____
3.	28823.8	29002.0	_____
4.	31057.8	33850.4	_____
5.	89163.1	90014.3	_____
6.	30062.5	32145.9	_____
7.	29915.1	31304.5	_____

Exercise A Answer these questions about odometer readings.

1. At the beginning of Susan's vacation, she notices that the odometer in her car reads

.

When she returns, the odometer reads

.

How far has she driven?

2. When Sam changes his oil, his odometer reads

.

It reads

at the next oil change. How far has he driven between oil changes?

3. While driving, Kabuo sees a sign that reads "Dallas—189 miles." He glances at his odometer and sees that it reads

.

What will it read when Kabuo gets to Dallas?

4. Todd is going to the beach for the day. The beach is 48.7 miles away. If the odometer reads

when he leaves, what will it read when Todd arrives at the beach?

5. When Barbara leaves for work in the morning, her odometer reads

.

It reads

when she arrives. How far has she driven to work?

6. Cathy takes her car to a mechanic for a tune-up every 15,000 miles she drives. If her odometer reads

,

how many more miles will Cathy drive before her car gets its next tune-up?

Gas mileage is usually better when a car is driven on the open roads than when it is driven in cities. Stop-and-go traffic in cities lowers gas mileage.

You can use your odometer to help compute your gas mileage. This is the number of miles that you can expect to travel on one gallon of gas.

EXAMPLE To compute your gas mileage, follow these steps:

Step 1 Fill your gas tank and record the odometer reading.

Step 2 The next time that you buy gas, fill the tank again. Record the number of gallons of gas that you bought and the odometer reading.

Step 3 Subtract the two odometer readings to find the number of miles driven.

Step 4 Divide this answer by the number of gallons of gas that you just bought. Round your answer to the nearest whole number.

$$\begin{array}{r} 27{,}873.7 \\ -\ 27{,}675.2 \\ \hline 198.5 \end{array}$$ Reading at second filling
Reading at first filling

You buy 8.1 gallons of gas.

$$\frac{24.5}{8.1\,\overline{)198.5}} \approx 25 \text{ miles per gallon or 25 mpg}$$

Small cars usually get better gas mileage than larger cars.

Exercise A Compute the gas mileage each driver gets. Round your answers to the nearest whole number. Write your answers on a separate sheet of paper.

	Reading at First Fill-Up	Gallons of Gas Bought	Reading at Second Fill-Up	Gas Mileage
1.	43872.5	6.2	44075.2	_____
2.	39989.6	9.2	40230.3	_____
3.	56035.3	10.3	56398.5	_____
4.	87392.7	8.4	87631.6	_____
5.	21981.3	7.6	22160.1	_____
6.	70384.3	9.3	70699.2	_____
7.	06721.9	8.9	06997.9	_____
8.	13297.2	7.2	13491.6	_____
9.	00428.4	8.4	00779.6	_____
10.	66879.2	8.1	67041.0	_____

The display on a gas pump shows the amount of gas you purchased. You can use this information to calculate your gas mileage.

Gas station A usually sells gasoline 3¢ per gallon cheaper than gas station B across the street. Would it matter to you which gas station you went to? Why?

The cost of an automobile trip can be found by multiplying the number of gallons of gasoline used by the cost per gallon. Round the cost to the nearest cent.

EXAMPLE Find the total cost of 12.6 gallons of gasoline used at $1.43 per gallon.

$$
\begin{array}{r}
\$\quad 1.4\,3 \quad \text{Cost per gallon} \\
\times \quad\;\; 1\,2.6 \quad \text{Number of gallons used} \\
\hline
8\,5\,8 \\
2\,8\,6\;\; \\
+\,1\,4\,3\;\;\;\; \\
\hline
\$\,18.0\,1\,8 \approx \$18.02
\end{array}
$$

$18.02 is the total cost.

Exercise A Find the total cost of gasoline. Round to the nearest cent.

1. 1.6 gallons at $1.85
2. 25.1 gallons at $1.25
3. 1.1 gallons at $1.24
4. 80 gallons at $2.04
5. 26.7 gallons at $1.35
6. 3.3 gallons at $1.25
7. 18.4 gallons at $1.35
8. 27.5 gallons at $1.28
9. 27.4 gallons at $1.11
10. 52.5 gallons at $1.19
11. 3.5 gallons at $1.32
12. 39 gallons at $1.67
13. 3.2 gallons at $1.28

14. 50 gallons at $1.25
15. 42.9 gallons at $2.01
16. 31.5 gallons at $1.28
17. 43.2 gallons at $1.86
18. 4.6 gallons at $1.26
19. 37.7 gallons at $1.33
20. 42.9 gallons at $1.24
21. 2.9 gallons at $1.16
22. 31.4 gallons at $1.55
23. 17.5 gallons at $1.17
24. 10.8 gallons at $1.28
25. 1.6 gallons at $1.29
26. 12.3 gallons at $1.22

Some travelers need to rent a car. Rental rates differ for different types of cars.

Type of Car	Per Day	Per Week	Plus per Mile
Subcompact	$19.95	$99.95	24¢
Compact	$29.95	$150.00	26¢
Midsize	$35.00	$209.95	28¢
Large	$39.95	$259.95	30¢
Van	$45.50	$300.50	32¢

PROBLEM SOLVING

Exercise A Use the chart of car rental rates to help you answer these questions.

1. How much does renting a midsize car for 1 day cost if you drive it 127 miles?

2. Hilary rents a compact car for 1 week. She drives it 628 miles. What is the cost?

3. Audrey rents a van for 4 days. What is the charge if she drives the car 473 miles?

4. How much would Audrey pay if she rents a compact car instead of the van?

5. How much would Audrey save if she rents the compact car instead of the van?

6. What does Bob pay to rent a large car for 2 weeks if he drives 473 miles?

7. Kim rents a subcompact car for 4 days. She drives 608 miles. How much does Kim pay?

8. Juan drives the midsize car that he rents 462 miles. How much does Juan pay if he rents the car for 3 days?

Using a map to compute distances traveled often requires the use of basic mathematical operations.

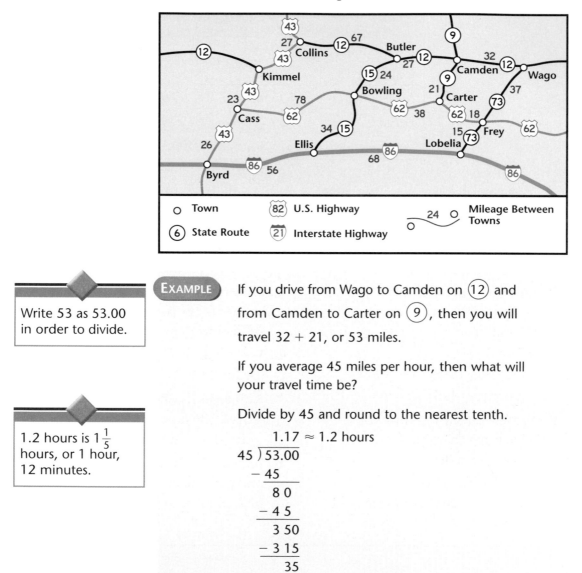

| Town | (82) U.S. Highway | 24 O Mileage Between Towns |
| (6) State Route | (21) Interstate Highway | |

EXAMPLE

Write 53 as 53.00 in order to divide.

If you drive from Wago to Camden on (12) and from Camden to Carter on (9), then you will travel 32 + 21, or 53 miles.

If you average 45 miles per hour, then what will your travel time be?

1.2 hours is $1\frac{1}{5}$ hours, or 1 hour, 12 minutes.

Divide by 45 and round to the nearest tenth.

$$
\begin{array}{r}
1.17 \approx 1.2 \text{ hours} \\
45 \overline{)53.00} \\
-45 \\
\hline
8\,0 \\
-4\,5 \\
\hline
3\,50 \\
-3\,15 \\
\hline
35
\end{array}
$$

Exercise A Use the road map on page 160 to answer these questions. Round your answers to the nearest tenth.

1. How far will you drive if you go from Butler to Cass along (15) and (62)?

2. If you average 42 miles per hour, then how long will this trip take?

3. You drive from Lobelia to Bowling along (86) and (15). How far will you travel?

4. If the trip from Lobelia to Bowling takes 2.3 hours, then what is the average rate of speed?

5. What is the distance from Byrd to Frey along (86) and (73)?

6. If you average 52 miles per hour, then how long will it take you to make this trip?

7. How far is it from Camden to Cass along (9) and (62)?

8. How far is it from Camden to Cass along (12) and (43)?

9. If you go from Camden to Cass along (9) and (62), then you can average 37 miles per hour. If you use (12) and (43), then you can average 42 miles per hour. Which route takes less time?

10. How far is it from Kimmel to Lobelia along (43) and (86)?

Try This

In question 9, about how many minutes of time will you save?

Technology Connection

Use map Web sites on a computer to plan a trip from your school to a nearby city. Check the map, the driving route given, the estimated miles to drive, and the estimated time. Compute the cost if a car averages 25 mpg, and gas costs $1.39 per gallon.

Gas mileage is found by dividing the distance traveled by the gallons of gas used. If you know the number of miles that you get per gallon of gas, you can predict the amount of gas that you will use to drive a given distance. You divide the distance by the miles per gallon.

EXAMPLE Pedro drove 314 miles and got 32 miles per gallon. How many gallons of gas were used?

$$
\begin{array}{r}
9.81 \approx 9.8 \text{ gallons of gas} \\
32 \overline{)314.00} \\
-\ 288 \\
\hline
26\ 0 \\
-\ 25\ 6 \\
\hline
40 \\
-\ 32 \\
\hline
8
\end{array}
$$

About 9.8 gallons of gas were used.

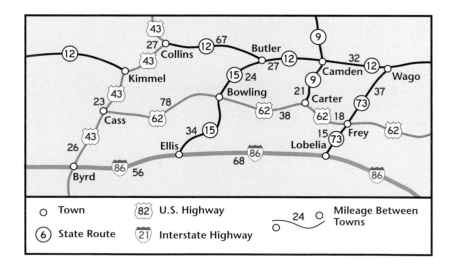

○ Town	⬡82 U.S. Highway	24 ○ Mileage Between Towns
⬡6 State Route	⬡21 Interstate Highway	

Exercise A Use the map on page 162 to help you answer these questions about gasoline consumption. Round your answers to the nearest tenth.

1. You use 3.2 gallons of gas to go from Collins to Carter along ⑫ and ⑨. What is your gas mileage?

2. You drive from Ellis to Wago along ⑧⑥ and ⑦③. If your car gets 31 miles per gallon of gas, how many gallons do you use?

3. You use 5.2 gallons of gas to drive from Cass to Lobelia along ⑥②ʼ and ⑦③. What is your gas mileage?

4. You use 3.9 gallons of gas to drive from Carter to Byrd along ⑥②, ⑮, and ⑧⑥. What is your gas mileage?

5. How many gallons of gas will you use to drive from Bowling to Collins along ⑮ and ⑫ if your car gets 34 miles per gallon?

6. You drive from Frey to Cass along ⑥②. How many gallons of gas do you use if your car gets 28 miles per gallon?

7. You use 3.5 gallons of gas to drive from Camden to Ellis along ⑨, ⑥②, and ⑮. What is your gas mileage?

8. Your car gets 36 miles per gallon. How many gallons of gas will you use to drive from Collins to Frey along ⑫, ⑮, and ⑥②?

Try This

Your car gets 21 miles per gallon. How many gallons of gas will you save if you travel from Byrd to Wago by ⑧⑥ and ⑦③ rather than ④③ and ⑫? Round your answer to the nearest tenth.

Hotel rates are given as the cost for each person.

Hotel Length of Stay	Room Type	Single	Extra Night	Double Cost for Each	Extra Night
Seaside Inn					
3 Nights	Standard	$179.25	$49.25	$79.25	$25.25
	Deluxe	269.25	59.25	99.25	30.25
7 Nights	Standard	379.25	49.25	159.25	40.25
	Deluxe	550.25	57.25	209.25	55.25
Bay Hotel					
3 Nights	Superior	259.30	69.30	139.80	99.80
7 Nights	Superior	500.30	69.30	239.80	99.80
Forest Lodge					
3 Nights	Standard	309.35	115.35	140.35	109.35
7 Nights	Standard	400.35	115.35	240.35	109.35

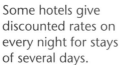

Some hotels give discounted rates on every night for stays of several days.

EXAMPLES

Mr. and Mrs. Mendez are spending 7 nights at the Seaside Inn in a deluxe double room.

The cost is 2 × $209.25, or $418.50.

Carl spends Friday, Saturday, Sunday, and Monday night in a superior single room at the Bay Hotel.

The cost is $259.30 + $69.30 = $328.60.

Wong spends 7 nights in a standard single room at the Seaside Inn. Rachelle and Gary spend 8 nights at the Forest Lodge in a standard double room.

Rachelle and Gary will have to pay for 1 additional night beyond the 7-night rate.

The cost is $379.25 + (2 × $240.35) + (2 × $109.35) = $1,078.65.

Exercise A Use the hotel rate chart on page 164 to answer these questions.

1. How much will Elise pay to spend 7 nights at the Forest Lodge in a single room?

2. Yuneng and Miranda are going to spend 7 nights in a standard room at the Seaside Inn. What will they pay if they share a double room?

3. How much will 4 nights cost in a single room at the Bay Hotel?

4. How much will Pat and Lee pay to stay for 8 nights in a double room at the Bay Hotel?

5. A travel agent arranges for a group of 38 people to stay for 3 nights. They are all staying in double rooms. Twelve people are staying at the Seaside Inn in deluxe rooms; 16 at the Forest Lodge; and 10 at the Bay Hotel. What is the total bill?

Often the difference between a standard and a deluxe room at a seaside resort is a view of the ocean from your window.

Currency

Money

Conversion factor

A number you multiply a measurement by to obtain an equivalent measurement

If you are traveling outside of the United States, you will need to change from U.S. **currency** to another country's currency. To do this, multiply by the **conversion factor**. To change from another country's currency to U.S. currency, divide by the conversion factor. The exchange rates for currency often change daily. Before taking a trip to another country, be sure to check the exchange rate on the Internet or at a local bank.

Writing About Mathematics

How do you know when a foreign currency dollar is worth less than a U.S. dollar?

EXAMPLES Change 40 U.S. dollars to Barbados currency. Use the currency conversion chart.

$$
\begin{array}{r}
1.98 \\
\times\ \ 40 \\
\hline
79.20
\end{array}
$$

40 United States dollars = 79.20 Barbados dollars.

Change 99 Barbados dollars to U.S. currency.

$$
\begin{array}{r}
50 \\
1.98.\overline{)99.00.} \\
-99\ 0 \\
\hline
00
\end{array}
$$

99 Barbados dollars = 50 United States dollars.

Place	Currency	Conversion Factor 1 U.S. Dollar =
Barbados	Barbados dollar = 100 cents	1.98 BDD
Bermuda	Bermudan dollar = 100 cents	1.00 BED
Cayman Islands	Cayman Is. dollar = 100 cents	0.82 CID
Haiti	Gourde = 100 centimes	25.50 GOU
Jamaica	Jamaican dollar = 100 cents	47.05 JAD
Trinidad	Trinidad dollar = 100 cents	6.12 TTD
West Indies	East Carib dollar = 100 cents	2.70 ECD

Exercise A Use the conversion chart on page 166 to help you make these currency conversions. Round any remainders to two decimal places.

1. Change 43 United States dollars to Haitian currency.

2. Change 36 Cayman Islands dollars to United States currency.

3. Change 30 East Carib dollars to United States currency.

4. Change 85 United States dollars to Trinidad dollars.

5. Change 78 Jamaican dollars to United States currency.

6. Change 75 gourdes to United States currency.

7. Change $46.76 in Bermudan currency to United States currency.

8. Change $8.52 in Cayman Islands currency to United States currency.

9. Change $35.00 in United States currency to Barbados currency.

10. Change 14 gourdes and 75 centimes to United States currency.

11. Change $42.56 in United States currency to West Indies currency.

How are these currencies similar? How are they different?

You can purchase a package tour for a cruise from a travel agent. This offers the air flight and the sea cruise for one basic price. The price that you pay depends on the city from which you fly and the size of your room on the ship.

Room Size	Cruise Only Rates per Person	Flight/Cruise Package Rates			
		New York	Washington	Detroit	St. Louis
Small	$975.59	$1,160.02	$1,170.48	$1,210.62	$1,240.32
Medium	$1,005.48	$1,189.91	$1,200.37	$1,240.51	$1,270.21
Large	$1,160.56	$1,344.99	$1,355.45	$1,395.59	$1,425.29
Suite	$1,390.73	$1,575.16	$1,585.62	$1,625.76	$1,655.46
Child Under 12	$250.45	$434.88	$445.34	$485.48	$515.18

Single Occupant Pays 1.5 Times the Cruise-Only Rate.
All rates are for one person and are for double occupancy.

Cruise ships sail to exotic locations throughout the world.

> **EXAMPLE** If two people fly from St. Louis and stay in a suite, then they will pay 2 × $1,655.46, or $3,310.92.

PROBLEM SOLVING

Exercise A Use the rate chart on page 168 to help you find the total cost.

1. Carlos and Juditha have a suite on the ship. What is the cost of their trip if they fly from New York?

2. Christie and Alphonse are taking their 8-year-old grandson on a cruise. They are leaving from St. Louis and staying in a small room on the ship. What is the total cost of their trip?

3. The plane fare is the difference between the cruise-only rate and the flight/cruise rate. What is the plane fare from Washington?

4. What is the plane fare from New York?

5. Greg wants to fly from Detroit and stay in large a room by himself on the ship. How much will this trip cost? Remember to include his plane fare.

6. Fred and Dottie are flying from Washington. How much will their trip cost if they stay in a small room on the ship?

7. Beth and Hank are taking 2-year-old Sally along. They are staying in a suite on the ship. What will it cost them if they leave from St. Louis?

8. Julio and Dee fly from New York and stay in a medium-size room on the ship. How much does their trip cost?

9. Inez and Irv are staying in a small room on the ship. How much is their trip if they leave from Detroit?

10. Jim and Janice are traveling with Mary and Eli. They leave from St. Louis and stay in a medium-size room on the ship. What is the total cost of the four travelers' trip?

Vacation Costs

You live in Martin Park and are planning a three-day weekend in Oglesby with a friend. You will return home by way of Johnson City.

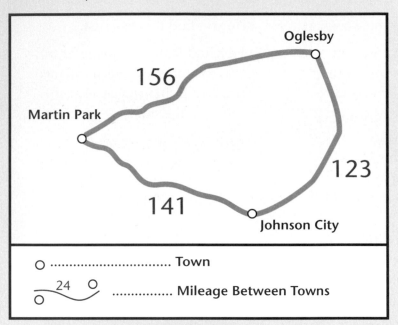

O .... Town

24 O .... Mileage Between Towns

Exercises Use the map and the hotel sign above to answer these questions.

1. If your car averages 20 miles per gallon of gas, how much gas will you use?

2. Find the cost of the gas used if the current gas price is $1.48 per gallon.

3. You and your friend will share a hotel room. Find the cost for a three-night stay.

4. You have allowed $10 per meal and $9 for a movie, per person. Find the cost for three days of meals and for the movie.

Chapter 10 R E V I E W

Write the letter of the best answer to each question.

1. While driving, Pierre sees a sign that reads "Boston—126 miles." His odometer currently reads 101246.3. What will it read when Pierre gets to Boston?
   A 101120.3
   B 101272.3
   C 101362.3
   D 101372.3

2. Find the gas mileage if the odometer reading at the first fill-up is 87421.7, and at the second fill-up it is 88026.4. You used 22.6 gallons to fill the tank.
   A 26 mpg
   B 27 mpg
   C 28 mpg
   D 604.7

3. Scott rents a car for $34.85 per day. He drives 820 miles in 3 days at 28¢ per mile. How much does Scott pay?
   A $104.55
   B $229.60
   C $264.45
   D $334.15

4. Maria drives 432 miles and uses 21.6 gallons of gas. What gas mileage did Maria's car get?
   A 2 mpg
   B 20 mpg
   C 196 mpg
   D 9,331.2

5. Mr. and Mrs. Bender want to rent a hotel room for 3 nights. The double cost for each person is $81.75. What is their total cost?
   A $163.50
   B $245.25
   C $408.75
   D $490.50

Find the answers.

6. $48.6 - 5.324$

7. 4.023×0.93

8. $9.048 \div 2.6$

9. $36.83 + 9.284 + 52$

Answer these word problems.

10. Tom drives to the beach for the day. When he leaves the house, his odometer reads 0 1 6 8 3 2 5 .

When he arrives at the beach, it reads 0 1 6 9 0 9 4 . How far is it to the beach?

11. While driving, Mike sees a sign that reads "Portland– 187 miles." Mike looks at his odometer and sees that it reads 0 3 7 0 4 2 5 . What does Mike's odometer read when he gets to Portland?

12. Find the total cost of 12.2 gallons of gasoline at $1.50 per gallon.

13. Will rents a midsize car for 4 days. He pays $32.95 per day plus 28¢ per mile. How much does Will pay if he drives the car 482 miles?

14. One U.S. dollar equals 0.82 Cayman Islands dollar. What is 40 U.S. dollars in Cayman Islands currency?

15. One U.S. dollar equals 47.05 Jamaican dollars. What is 62 Jamaican dollars in U.S. currency? Round to two decimal places.

16. How much will 11.5 gallons of gasoline cost at $1.75 per gallon?

17. Bob rents a compact car for $29.95 per day plus 26¢ per mile. Bob drove 382 miles in 2 days. How much does he pay?

Find the gas mileage.

Reading at First Fill-Up	Gallons of Gas Bought	Reading at Second Fill-Up	Gas Mileage
18. 48537.2	9.3	48835.8	_____
19. 10736.5	5.8	10872.8	_____

Use this road map to help you answer the questions.

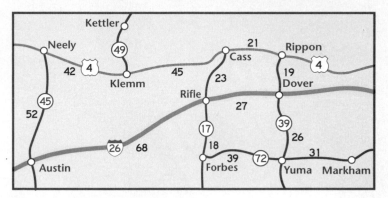

20. How far will you drive if you go from Dover to Klemm along (39) and (12)?

21. This trip takes 1.7 hours. What is your average rate of speed?

22. You drive from Austin to Cass along (45) and (12). How far do you drive?

23. You use 5.2 gallons of gas to make this trip. What is your gas mileage rounded to one decimal place?

24. You drive from Yuma to Cass along (72) and (17). How far do you drive?

25. How much shorter would the trip be if you drive along (39) and (12)?

Test-Taking Tip

When you read a mathematics problem, decide whether multiple steps are required to solve the problem.

11 Watching the Clock

H ere's a riddle for you to solve—What may have hands but cannot wave? If you guessed a clock, you're right! Clocks come in many styles. Some have hands, some are digital, and others have Roman numerals. Some clocks may have no numbers at all. Knowing how to tell time and compute with hours and minutes helps you at home and in school. When you understand time, you can make better decisions and choices in scheduling your activities.

In Chapter 11, you will explore time, using clocks with faces and digital clocks. You will also discover ways to use time to help you predict arrivals and calculate parking fees.

Goals for Learning

◆ To tell time, using clocks with faces and digital clocks

◆ To find elapsed time

◆ To use time skills to interpret television programming schedules

◆ To compute fees for parking meters

◆ To use a schedule of times to calculate elapsed time

Elapsed time is the amount of time that has passed from one time to another. Find the amount of elapsed time by subtracting the earlier time from the later time. If you must rename, then remember that 1 hour is the same as 60 minutes.

EXAMPLES How much time has **elapsed** from the time shown on Clock A to the time shown on Clock B?

Clock A Clock B

Clock A shows 3:28 P.M.   Clock B shows 7:52 P.M.

$$
\begin{array}{r}
7:52 \\
- 3:28 \\
\hline
4:24
\end{array}
$$

4 hours and 24 minutes have elapsed.

Clock A  Clock B

Clock A shows 2:42 P.M.   Clock B shows 7:21 P.M.

$$
\begin{array}{r}
7:21 \\
- 2:42 \\
\end{array}
$$
← Rename 1 hour to 60 minutes →
$$
\begin{array}{r}
6:81 \\
- 2:42 \\
\hline
4:39
\end{array}
$$

4 hours and 39 minutes have elapsed.

Clock A  Clock B

Clock A shows 11:26 A.M.   Clock B shows 4:33 P.M.

$$
\begin{array}{r}
4:33 \\
- 11:26 \\
\end{array}
$$
← Add 12 hours →
$$
\begin{array}{r}
16:33 \\
- 11:26 \\
\hline
5:07
\end{array}
$$

5 hours and 7 minutes have elapsed.

Writing About Mathematics

Write about a way you can figure out elapsed time without subtracting.

Exercise A Subtract to find how much time has elapsed from the time shown on Clock A to the time shown on Clock B.

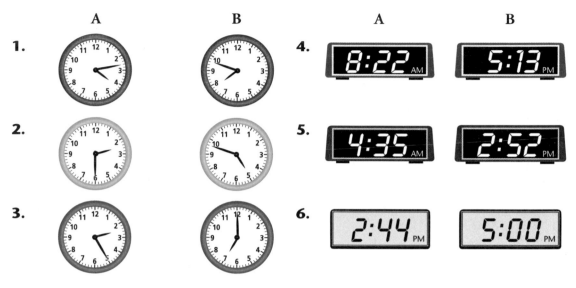

Exercise B Subtract to find the amount of time that has elapsed.

1. From 3:46 A.M. to 7:58 A.M.

2. From 3:45 A.M. to 7:26 A.M.

3. From 5:18 A.M. to 7:25 A.M.

4. From 6:21 P.M. to 11:54 P.M.

5. From 3:59 P.M. to 4:16 P.M.

6. From 3:37 P.M. to 10:21 P.M.

7. From 1:45 P.M. to 11:26 P.M.

8. From 12:15 P.M. to 2:30 P.M.

9. From 5:36 P.M. to 12:52 A.M.

10. From 6:27 P.M. to 3:49 A.M.

11. From 4:17 P.M. to 7:30 P.M.

12. From 6:30 P.M. to 10:42 P.M.

13. From 4:56 A.M. to 1:23 P.M.

14. From 5:45 A.M. to 9:51 A.M.

Technology Connection

Clocks have been used to tell time for thousands of years. The earliest devices for telling time were sundials. Do Internet or library research to find out how clocks have changed through the ages. Find out about sundials, sandtimers, water clocks, pendulum clocks, mechanical clocks, and today's electronic and atomic clocks. How would your daily life be different if there were no accurate clocks or watches?

Exercise C Solve these word problems. Use the clock above each problem to help you.

1. Jeff waits for a bus that is scheduled to arrive at 11:45 A.M. How long will Jeff wait?

2. Carlo's favorite TV program, *Albuquerque,* comes on at 9:00 P.M. How long must Carlo wait for his show?

3. Ginny went to sleep at 10:42 last night. When she awoke this morning, she looked at the clock by her bed. How long did she sleep?

4. Barry arrives at the dentist's office at 12:15 P.M. for his appointment. He looks at his watch when his name is called. How long has Barry been waiting?

5. Maria leaves the house at 9:23 A.M. and drives to Dewey Beach. She arrives at the beach and looks at her dashboard clock. How long has Maria been driving?

6. The umpire stops the game because of rain at 7:23 P.M. When play is resumed, Georgia looks at her watch. How long has the game been delayed?

In some situations, you know the time now and you know how many hours and minutes until a future event begins. You may want to know what time it will be at the time of the event. To do a problem like this, you would add the hours and minutes to the current time.

EXAMPLES Tell what time it will be when the given amount of time elapses from the time shown on the clock.

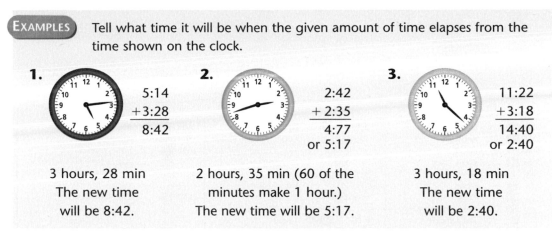

1.

$$\begin{array}{r} 5:14 \\ +3:28 \\ \hline 8:42 \end{array}$$

3 hours, 28 min
The new time
will be 8:42.

2.

$$\begin{array}{r} 2:42 \\ +2:35 \\ \hline 4:77 \\ \text{or } 5:17 \end{array}$$

2 hours, 35 min (60 of the minutes make 1 hour.)
The new time will be 5:17.

3.

$$\begin{array}{r} 11:22 \\ +3:18 \\ \hline 14:40 \\ \text{or } 2:40 \end{array}$$

3 hours, 18 min
The new time
will be 2:40.

Exercise D Find the time after the given amount of time has elapsed.

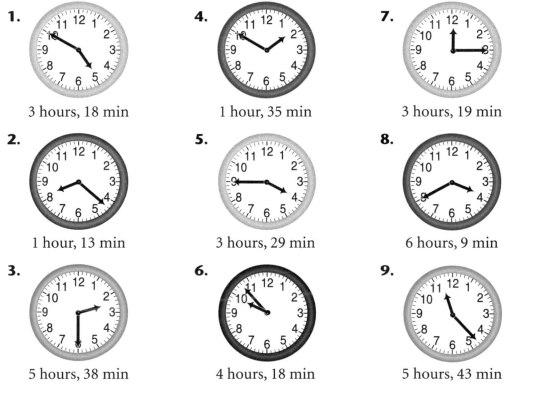

1. 3 hours, 18 min

4. 1 hour, 35 min

7. 3 hours, 19 min

2. 1 hour, 13 min

5. 3 hours, 29 min

8. 6 hours, 9 min

3. 5 hours, 38 min

6. 4 hours, 18 min

9. 5 hours, 43 min

Try This

Don has 3 hr to clean his room and the garage. It will take 45 min to clean his room and 2 hr, 10 min to clean the garage. It is now 1:37 P.M. At what time will he finish cleaning his room? What time will he finish cleaning the garage?

To use a TV schedule, it is helpful if you are able to calculate time.

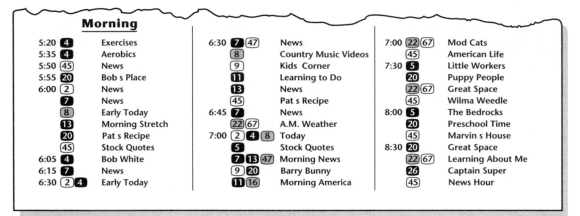

Morning		
5:20 ④ Exercises	6:30 ❼ ㊼ News	7:00 ㉒ ㊲ Mod Cats
5:35 ④ Aerobics	⑧ Country Music Videos	㊺ American Life
5:50 ㊺ News	⑨ Kids Corner	7:30 ❺ Little Workers
5:55 ⑳ Bob s Place	⑪ Learning to Do	⑳ Puppy People
6:00 ② News	⑬ News	㉒ ㊲ Great Space
❼ News	㊺ Pat s Recipe	㊺ Wilma Weedle
⑧ Early Today	6:45 ❼ News	8:00 ❺ The Bedrocks
⑬ Morning Stretch	㉒ ㊲ A.M. Weather	⑳ Preschool Time
⑳ Pat s Recipe	7:00 ② ④ ⑧ Today	㊺ Marvin s House
㊺ Stock Quotes	❺ Stock Quotes	8:30 ⑳ Great Space
6:05 ④ Bob White	❼ ⑬ ㊼ Morning News	㉒ ㊲ Learning About Me
6:15 ❼ News	⑨ ⑳ Barry Bunny	㉖ Captain Super
6:30 ② ④ Early Today	⑪ ⑯ Morning America	㊺ News Hour

PROBLEM SOLVING

Exercise A Answer the questions about this TV program schedule.

1. At what time does *American Life* come on?

2. On what channel can you watch *Country Music Videos*?

3. How long is *Exercises*?

4. How long does the 6:45 news last?

5. What time does *Barry Bunny* come on? What stations carry this program?

6. How long is *Bob White* on?

7. When does *Stock Quotes* come on?

8. How long does *Bob's Place* last?

9. Sharina turns on her TV at 6:43. How much of *Learning to Do* has she missed?

10. At what times does channel 7 news come on?

11. Willie wakes up at 8:17. How many more minutes is *Marvin's House* on?

12. Jim turns on the TV at 6:42. How long does he wait for *Captain Super* to come on?

<table>
<tr><td>

Metered parking space

A space where you must put money in a parking meter

</td></tr>
</table>

When you park your car, you may use a **metered parking space**. You will look at your watch, decide how long you need to run your errands, and then decide what time you must return to avoid getting a parking ticket. Once you know how much time you will be away from your car, you can put the required amount of money into the meter.

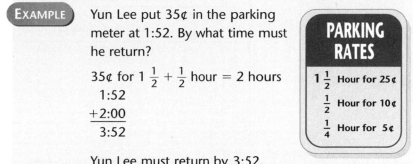

EXAMPLE Yun Lee put 35¢ in the parking meter at 1:52. By what time must he return?

35¢ for $1\frac{1}{2} + \frac{1}{2}$ hour = 2 hours

$$\begin{array}{r} 1:52 \\ +2:00 \\ \hline 3:52 \end{array}$$

Yun Lee must return by 3:52.

PARKING RATES

$1\frac{1}{2}$ Hour for 25¢

$\frac{1}{2}$ Hour for 10¢

$\frac{1}{4}$ Hour for 5¢

PROBLEM SOLVING

Exercise A Answer these questions about parking meters. Use the parking rates above. Use the most quarters that you can when solving each problem.

1. Lynn puts 40¢ in the meter at 2:32. By what time must she return?

2. At 3:52 George puts 15¢ in the meter. By what time must he return?

3. Don puts 45¢ in the meter at 11:42. By what time must he return?

4. Ellie puts 15¢ in the meter at 1:17. When must she return to her car?

5. Sam puts 30¢ in the meter at 12:23. By what time must he return?

6. Anne parks at 10:48. She puts 50¢ in the meter. By what time must Anne return to avoid being ticketed?

7. Olivia needs 20 minutes to complete her errands. How much money should she put in the meter?

Bus schedules indicate the leaving and arriving times for commercial buses. A better understanding of how these schedules work requires an understanding of elapsed time. Elapsed time is the amount of time it takes to complete a trip.

BUFFALO • ELMIRA • WILLIAMSPORT • SUNBURY					
HARRISBURG - BALTIMORE - WASHINGTON					
DOWN		**7144**		**UP**	
EW 195				WE 196	
11:15	- - - -	Lv	BUFFALO, NY . . . .**GL** . .	Ar	- - - -	8:35
11:35	- - - -	Lv	Buffalo Int'l Airport	Ar	- - - -	8:15
12:35	- - - -	Lv	Batavia	Ar	- - - -	7:20
1:15	- - - -	Lv	Mt. Morris	Ar	- - - -	6:40
1:35	- - - -	Lv	Dansville	Ar	- - - -	6:20
2:05	- - - -	Lv	Hornell	Ar	- - - -	5:50
2:45	- - - -	Lv	Bath	Ar	- - - -	5:10
3:15	- - - -	Ar	Corning	Lv	- - - -	4:40
3:30	- - - -	Lv	Corning	Ar	- - - -	4:25
3:55	- - - -	Ar	ELMIRA, NY . . . .**GL** . .	Lv	- - - -	4:00
	2:25	Lv	Binghamton, NY . . . . . .**CPB** . .	Ar	5:05	
	3:55	Ar	Elmira, NY	Lv	3:30	
	4:30	Lv	▲**ELMIRA, NY** . . . .**CPB** . .	Ar	3:30	
- - - -	f		Millerton, PA		f	- - - -
- - - -	hs		Tioga		hs	- - - -
- - - -	5:25		**Mansfield, PA**		2:30	- - - -
- - - -	f		Covington		f	- - - -
- - - -	5:35		Blossburg		2:15	- - - -
	6:40	Ar	▲**Williamsport, PA** . . **CPB** . .	Lv	1:20	
9:00		Lv	Williamsport, PA. . . . . . **TWI** . .	Ar		1:20
9:35		Ar	Lock Haven, PA	Lv		12:35
10:25		Ar	State College, PA	Lv		11:35
- - - -	6:55	Lv	▲**Williamsport, PA**		12:55	- - - -
- - - -	f		Allenwood		f	- - - -
- - - -	7:35		▲**Lewisburg**		12:15	- - - -
- - - -	7:55	Ar	▲**SUNBURY, PA** . . . . . .**CPB** . .	Lv	11:55	- - - -
- - - -	8:00	Lv	SUNBURY, PA . . . .**GL** . .	Ar	11:50	- - - -
- - - -	9:20	Ar	Harrisburg, PA	Lv	10:30	- - - -
- - - -	10:15	Ar	York, PA	Lv	9:10	- - - -
- - - -	11:25	Ar	Baltimore, MD	Lv	8:00	- - - -
- - - -	12:20	Ar	WASHINGTON, DC . . .**GL** . . .	Lv	6:50	- - - -

Bus schedules are really two schedules in one. The first is on the left, reading down. Bus 195 leaves Elmira at 4:30 and arrives in Williamsport at 6:40.

The second schedule is on the right, reading up. Bus 196 leaves Williamsport at 1:20 and arrives in Elmira at 3:30.

Here are some symbols that are used on this bus schedule:

Lv = leaves
Ar = arrives
f = flag stop
hs = highway stop

EXAMPLE   How long does the bus ride take from Mansfield, PA, to Lewisburg, PA? Mansfield is above Lewisburg, so use the left schedule reading down.

$$7:35$$
$$-5:25$$
$$2:10$$

The bus ride takes 2 hours and 10 minutes.

PROBLEM SOLVING

Exercise A Answer these questions. Use the bus schedule to help you.

1. It is now 12:45. How long will it be before the bus for Elmira leaves Dansville, NY?

2. It is now 5:23. How long will it be before the bus for Buffalo leaves Washington, DC?

3. John is riding the bus from Covington, PA, to Batavia, NY. How long will the bus ride last?

4. Frank lives in Lewisburg. Frank needs 20 minutes to walk to the bus station. What time must he leave his house if he is to catch the bus to York?

5. How long is the bus ride from:
 a. Bath to Blossburg?
 b. York to Elmira?
 c. Corning to Batavia?
 d. Hornell to Williamsport?
 e. Elmira to Mt. Morris?
 f. Baltimore to Mansfield?

Writing About Mathematics

Would parking meters be the best choice for an airport parking lot? Why or why not?

Many airports have different parking lots. The lot you park in determines how much you pay.

AIRPORT PARKING RATES

Short-Term Lot

Up to 1/2 hr	$1.50
31 min to 1 hr and 5 min	$2.00
1 hr and 6 min to 1 1/2 hr	$2.50
1 1/2 hr to 2 hr	$3.00
2 hr to 3 hr	$4.00
3 hr to 4 hr	$5.00
4 hr to 5 hr	$6.00
5 hr to 24 hr	$10.00

General Lot

Up to 1 hr	$1.00
1 hr to 3 hr	$2.00
3 hr to 8 hr	$3.50
8 hr to 24 hr	$7.50

Valet Lot

1 day	$15.00
2 days	$20.00
3 days	$25.00
Each additional day	$5.00

Remember that elapsed time is the difference between the starting time and the ending time.

EXAMPLE

Gwen parks her car at 3:16 P.M. She is meeting some friends at the airport. She leaves the lot at 5:38 P.M. How much does Gwen pay for parking?

$$\begin{array}{r} 5:38 \\ -3:16 \\ \hline 2:22 \end{array} = 2 \text{ hours, 22 minutes}$$

The price Gwen pays for parking:
. . . if she is in the short-term lot . . . $4.00
. . . if she is in the general lot $2.00
. . . if she is in the valet lot $15.00

Exercise A Answer these questions about parking at the airport. Use the parking rates on page 184 to help you.

1. Greg parks in the general lot from 12:48 P.M. to 1:19 P.M. How much does he pay?

2. Diane is making a short business trip. She parks her car at 7:23 A.M. She plans to return at 4:50 P.M. Which lot should she use to pay the least amount of parking fees?

3. How much will Diane pay?

4. Cindy and Jackson are going to Seattle for 6 days. How much will they pay for parking in the valet lot while they are gone?

5. How much would you pay for parking:
a. from 8:52 P.M. to 10:03 P.M. in the short-term lot?
b. from 12:34 P.M. to 1:17 P.M. in the general lot?
c. from 9:23 A.M. to 12:31 P.M. in the general lot?

Calculator Practice

Calculator Exercise Convert the following units of time. Use your calculator and the time chart.

To convert larger units to smaller units, you multiply.

1. 5 years = _____ days

2. 13 days = _____ hours

3. 6 hours = _____ minutes

4. 23 hours = _____ minutes

5. 42 days = _____ hours

6. 17 minutes = _____ seconds

Time Chart		
1 year	=	365 days
1 day	=	24 hours
1 hour	=	60 minutes
1 minute	=	60 seconds

A Busy Schedule

Samantha is 17 years old. She is a high school senior, and she just got a part-time job at the local library. She's happy about the job, but it's a challenge to find time for her school activities and homework. This is Samantha's schedule for the week.

Day	School	Work	Homework
Monday	8:30 A.M.– 3:00 P.M.	4:00 P.M.– 6:00 P.M.	7:00 P.M.– 9:00 P.M.
Tuesday	8:30 A.M.– 3:00 P.M.	4:00 P.M.– 7:00 P.M.	8:00 P.M.– 10:00 P.M.
Wednesday	8:30 A.M.– 3:00 P.M.	4:00 P.M.– 6:00 P.M.	7:00 P.M.– 9:00 P.M.
Thursday	8:30 A.M.– 3:00 P.M.	5:00 P.M.– 8:00 P.M.	8:30 P.M.– 10:00 P.M.
Friday	8:30 A.M.– 3:00 P.M.	5:00 P.M.– 7:00 P.M.	7:30 P.M.– 9:00 P.M.

Exercises Use Samantha's schedule to answer these questions.

1. How much time does Samantha spend at work on Mondays?

2. It takes 15 minutes for Samantha to get to work from home. What time should she leave her house on Wednesday to get to work on time?

3. It takes 10 minutes to get home from school and 15 minutes to get to work from home. On Friday, how much time does Samantha have at home in between school and work to chat online with her friends?

4. Samantha plays the piano. On which nights does she have time to play after she finishes her homework, but before 10:00 P.M.?

5. On which days does Samantha have the most free time in between school and work?

Chapter 11 REVIEW

Write the letter of the best answer to each question.

1. What is the elapsed time from the start time on Clock A to the end time on Clock B?

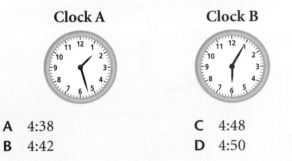

Clock A	Clock B

A   4:38   C   4:48

B   4:42   D   4:50

2. Jonathan's alarm clock rings at 7:17 A.M. He hits the snooze button so he can sleep 15 minutes longer. At what time will his alarm clock ring again?

A   7:29 A.M.   C   7:31 A.M.

B   7:30 A.M.   D   7:32 A.M.

3. Mr. Johnston missed the 6:57 A.M. train to work. It is now 7:01 A.M. The next train leaves the station at 7:14 A.M. How long will Mr. Johnston have to wait for that train?

A   13 minutes   C   17 minutes

B   15 minutes   D   19 minutes

4. It takes Marisol 23 minutes to walk to school. Her first class starts at 8:30 A.M. By what time should she leave her house to get to school on time?

A   8:05 A.M.   C   8:07 A.M.

B   8:06 A.M.   D   8:08 A.M.

5. Simon leaves his house at 6:47 P.M. It takes 41 minutes to drive to the football stadium. What time is it when Simon arrives at the stadium?

A   7:18 P.M.   C   7:38 P.M.

B   7:28 P.M.   D   7:48 P.M.

Answer these questions.

6. Sheldon left school at the time shown on the clock. He arrived home at 3:26 P.M. How long did it take Sheldon to walk home?

7. How much time has elapsed from Clock A to Clock B?

8. The baseball game begins at 12:15 P.M. It is now 12:08 P.M. How long will it be until the game starts?

9. How much time elapses from 11:23 A.M. to 2:45 P.M.?

10. What will the time be when it is 3 hours and 25 minutes later than the time shown on this clock?

11. The sign on the parking meter reads "Half-hour for 10¢." You put 30¢ in the meter at 11:42 A.M. By what time must you return?

12. How much time elapses from 9:16 A.M. to 8:40 P.M.?

13. Dean sets his VCR to record a TV show at 7:00 P.M. It is now 4:30 P.M. How much time will pass before the VCR starts recording?

14. A new movie, *Dinosaur Patrol,* is showing at 8:00 P.M. It is 2 hours and 13 minutes long. What time will the movie end?

15. At what time will the news on Channel 45 end?

16. Abbey likes to do the exercises on Channel 4 each day. How long is Channel 4's exercise program?

17. How long is Channel 45's news program?

5:20	**4**	Exercises
5:35	**4**	Aerobics
5:50	**45**	News
5:55	**20**	Bob's Place
6:00	**2**	News
	5	Panorama
	7	News
	8	Early Today
	13	Morning Stretch
	45	Stock Quotes

18. Murray's Parking Lot charges $1.25 for the first hour and 50¢ for each half-hour after that. How much will you pay at Murray's from 7:52 A.M. to 12:15 P.M.?

19. How long is the bus ride from Sunbury, PA, to Washington, DC?

20. How long is the bus ride from Corning, NY, to Batavia, NY?

BUFFALO • ELMIRA • WILLIAMSPORT • SUNBURY

HARRISBURG - BALTIMORE - WASHINGTON

7144

DOWN EW 195				UP WE 196	
11:15	----	Lv	BUFFALO, NY .... **GL** .. Ar	----	8:35
11:35	----	Lv	Buffalo Int'l Airport .... Ar	----	8:15
12:35	----	Lv	Batavia .... Ar	----	7:20
1:15	----	Lv	Mt. Morris .... Ar	----	6:40
1:35	----	Lv	Dansville .... Ar	----	6:20
2:05	----	Lv	Hornell .... Ar	----	5:50
2:45	----	Lv	Bath .... Ar	----	5:10
3:15	----	Ar	Corning Lv	----	4:40
3:30	----	Lv	Corning .... Ar	----	4:25
3:55	----	Ar	ELMIRA, NY .... **GL** .. Lv	----	4:00
	2:25	Lv	Binghamton, NY ...... **CPB** .. Ar	5:05	
	3:55	Ar	Elmira, NY Lv	3:30	
	4:30	Lv	▲ELMIRA, NY .... **CPB** .. Ar	3:30	
----	f		Millerton, PA	f	----
----	hs		Tioga	hs	----
----	5:25		**Mansfield, PA**	2:30	----
----	f		Covington	f	----
----	5:35		Blossburg	2:15	----
	6:40	Ar	▲**Williamsport, PA** . . **CPB** .. Lv	1:20	
9:00		Lv	Williamsport, PA ...... **TWI** .. Ar		1:20
9:35		Ar	Lock Haven, PA Lv		12:35
10:25		Ar	State College, PA Lv		11:35
----	6:55	Lv	▲**Williamsport, PA**	12:55	----
----	f		Allenwood	f	----
----	7:35		▲**Lewisburg**	12:15	----
	7:55	Ar	▲ **SUNBURY, PA** ...... **CPB** .. Lv	11:55	
----	8:00	Lv	SUNBURY, PA .... **GL** .. Ar	11:50	----
----	9:20	Ar	Harrisburg, PA Lv	10:30	----
----	10:15	Ar	York, PA Lv	9:10	----
----	11:25	Ar	Baltimore, MD Lv	8:00	----
----	12:20	Ar	WASHINGTON, DC .... **GL** ... Lv	6:50	----

Test-Taking Tip

Decide which questions you will do first and last. Do not spend too much time on any question.

12 Baseball Statistics

Baseball is often called America's favorite game. It has also been described as an ocean of statistics. Pitchers talk about their ERAs, hitters work on their batting averages, and teams boast their standings in a league. Player statistics can be found on baseball cards and in newspapers. The numbers you find there have a mathematical meaning that helps you tell how well the players are doing. Baseball statistics are a fun way to become familiar with the branch of mathematics called data and statistics.

In Chapter 12, you will use data to find baseball statistics.

Goals for Learning

◆ To rename fractions as decimals and percents

◆ To determine slugging percentages and baserunning averages

◆ To find a player's fielding percentage

◆ To compute the ERA of a pitcher

◆ To find and use the won-lost percentage to determine league standings

Batting average

A ratio of hits to at bats

Statistic

Fact collected and arranged so as to show certain information

Sacrifice out

Out made to advance base runners

A baseball player's **batting average** is a **statistic** that measures how well the player hits. The higher the batting average, the better the player hits. A batting average is written as a decimal rounded to three places. A player's batting average is found by dividing the number of hits by the number of official at bats. Walks and **sacrifice outs** do not count as official at bats.

EXAMPLE   If a player has 26 hits for 72 at bats, then what is the player's batting average?

$$\text{Batting Average} = \frac{\text{Number of Hits}}{\text{Number of Official at Bats}} = \frac{26}{72}$$

```
        0.3611 ≈ .361
   72 ) 26.0000
      − 21 6
         4 40
       − 4 32
            80
          − 72
            80
          − 72
             8
```

Exercise A Find the batting average for each player.

1. Ymato Ma
45 at bats
18 hits

2. Gail Wills
32 at bats
12 hits

3. Mike Speer
90 at bats
26 hits

4. Sol Lausch
51 at bats
15 hits

5. Gil French
43 at bats
25 hits

6. Walt Jones
73 at bats
37 hits

7. Gwen Smith
28 at bats
9 hits

8. Ben Cardin
63 at bats
35 hits

9. Vic Salski
29 at bats
15 hits

10. Jake Shane
51 at bats
20 hits

11. Tom Foster
28 at bats
10 hits

12. Robin Jay
22 at bats
6 hits

Slugging percentage

Ratio of total bases to official at bats

Two baseball players may have the same batting average, but the first player may hit the ball farther, resulting in getting to more bases—either a double, triple, or home run. The player who hits the ball a shorter distance may only make it to first base—a single. A baseball statistic that fans use to measure how well a player bats is the **slugging percentage**, given as a decimal rounded to three places.

EXAMPLE

What is this player's slugging percentage? Remember, walks and sacrifice outs do not count when finding a player's official at bats.

$$\text{Slugging Percentage} = \frac{\text{Total Bases}}{\text{Official at Bats}}$$

Home runs count as four bases, triples count as three bases, as so on.

home run = 4 bases
triple = 3 bases
double = 2 bases
single = 1 base
an out = 1 at bat

2 home runs	→	8 →	2
3 triples	→	9 →	3
10 doubles	→	20 →	10
14 singles	→	+ 14 →	14
8 walks		51 Bases	+ 33 Outs
33 outs			62 At Bats
9 sacrifice outs			

```
        0.8225 ≈ .823
  62 ) 51.0000
      − 49 6
         1 40
       − 1 24
          160
        − 124
           360
         − 310
            50
```

Exercise A Find each player's slugging percentage. Remember that walks and sacrifice outs do not count as official at bats.

1. Bill Light
1 home run
4 triples
6 doubles
16 singles
5 walks
21 outs
7 sacrifices

2. Skip Carr
4 home runs
12 triples
6 doubles
11 singles
8 walks
12 outs
15 sacrifices

3. George Gill
0 home runs
1 triple
4 doubles
15 singles
3 walks
21 outs
3 sacrifices

4. Riva Lewis
5 home runs
1 triple
11 doubles
21 singles
4 walks
20 outs
9 sacrifices

5. Iona Williams
2 home runs
6 triples
5 doubles
13 singles
18 walks
32 outs
6 sacrifices

6. Joe Leake
3 home runs
0 triples
2 doubles
8 singles
10 walks
18 outs
8 sacrifices

Hitters work hard to improve their slugging percentages.

Percent

Number per hundred

Writing About Mathematics

Explain why you divide to four decimal places in Step 2. Think about how baseball statistics are written.

Multiplying a number by 100 moves the decimal point two places to the right.

A fraction may be written as a **percent** by following these steps:

Step 1 Divide the denominator into the numerator.

Step 2 Divide to four decimal places.

Step 3 Round to three decimal places.

Step 4 Multiply the rounded quotient by 100.

One way to perform the last step is to move the decimal point two places to the right.

EXAMPLES Rewrite $\frac{6}{13}$ as a decimal. Then convert the decimal to a percent.

$$0.4615 \approx 0.46.2 = 46.2\%$$

$$
\begin{array}{r}
13 \overline{)6.0000} \\
-5\,2 \\
\hline
80 \\
-78 \\
\hline
20 \\
-13 \\
\hline
70 \\
-65 \\
\hline
5
\end{array}
$$

Rewrite $\frac{7}{9}$ as a decimal. Then convert the decimal to a percent.

$$0.777 \approx 0.77.8 = 77.8\%$$

$$
\begin{array}{r}
9 \overline{)7.000} \\
-6\,3 \\
\hline
70 \\
-63 \\
\hline
70 \\
-63 \\
\hline
7
\end{array}
$$

Exercise A Rewrite these fractions as percents. If the division does not divide evenly, then round to three decimal places.

1. $\frac{4}{7}$

2. $\frac{7}{12}$

3. $\frac{3}{8}$

4. $\frac{8}{9}$

5. $\frac{4}{11}$

6. $\frac{3}{4}$

7. $\frac{5}{6}$

8. $\frac{2}{3}$

9. $\frac{4}{5}$

10. $\frac{5}{7}$

11. $\frac{6}{13}$

12. $\frac{1}{8}$

13. $\frac{7}{15}$

14. $\frac{5}{9}$

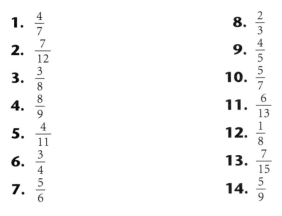

PROBLEM SOLVING

Exercise B Solve each problem.

1. William attended 10 out of 15 home games. What percent of the home games did he attend?

2. Audrey served in the refreshment stand for 8 out of the 15 home games. What percent of the home games did she work?

3. Kennedy Middle School's baseball team won 13 of the 16 games they played. What percent of their games did they win?

4. Joshua played in 7 of the 11 away baseball games. What percent of the away games did he play?

Baserunning average

Ratio of stolen bases to attempted steals

Putout

A play in which the batter or runner is retired

After getting on base, a player may try to steal the next base. This adds to the excitement of the game and advances the base runner to scoring position. How successful a base runner is at stealing bases is measured by the **baserunning average**. The baserunning average is found by dividing the number of bases stolen by the number of attempts. It is given as a percent. The percent is found by multiplying the decimal by 100.

EXAMPLES

Bella Kemp has 16 steals and 30 **putouts** while attempting to steal. What is Bella's baserunning average?

$$\text{Baserunning Average} = \frac{\text{Bases Stolen}}{\text{Attempted Steals}}$$

$$\text{Baserunning Average} = \frac{16}{46} \quad (16 + 30 = 46)$$

$$
\begin{array}{r}
0.3478 \approx 0.34.8 = 34.8\% \leftarrow \text{Baserunning} \\
46 \overline{)16.0000} \qquad\qquad \text{Average} \\
-13\,8 \\
\hline
2\,20 \\
-1\,84 \\
\hline
360 \\
-322 \\
\hline
380 \\
-368 \\
\hline
12
\end{array}
$$

Bernie Mason has 27 steals and 35 putouts while attempting to steal. What is Bernie's baserunning average?

$$\text{Baserunning Average} = \frac{27}{62}$$

$$
\begin{array}{r}
0.4354 \approx 0.43.5 = 43.5\% \leftarrow \text{Baserunning} \\
62 \overline{)27.0000} \qquad\qquad \text{Average} \\
-24\,8 \\
\hline
2\,20 \\
-1\,86 \\
\hline
340 \\
-310 \\
\hline
300 \\
-248 \\
\hline
52
\end{array}
$$

Exercise A Find the baserunning average for each record.

1. 16 steals
   8 putouts

2. 24 steals
   30 putouts

3. 45 steals
   18 putouts

4. 19 steals
   7 putouts

5. 41 steals
   28 putouts

6. 16 steals
   6 putouts

7. 21 steals
   12 putouts

8. 14 steals
   18 putouts

9. 36 steals
   14 putouts

10. 38 steals
    16 putouts

PROBLEM SOLVING

Exercise B Solve each problem.

1. Jen has 10 steals and 20 putouts while attempting to steal. What is Jen's baserunning average?

2. Boris has 15 steals and 21 putouts attempting to steal. What is his baserunning average?

Stealing a base often means the player slides to avoid being called out.

Fielding percentage

Ratio of assists and putouts to total chances

Assist

A defensive play by a fielder that helps to make a putout

Error

Misplay in fielding a ball that allows a player to advance

The ability of a fielder is measured with the **fielding percentage**. It is found by dividing the total number of chances that the fielder has to make a play into the number of **assists** plus the number of putouts. A player's fielding percentage is given as a decimal rounded to three places. Use this formula to find the total chances: assists + putouts + **errors**.

EXAMPLE During one game, Mario Martinez makes 15 assists and 8 putouts while committing 1 error. What is Mario's fielding percentage?

$$\text{Fielding Percentage} = \frac{\text{Assists} + \text{Putouts}}{\text{Number of Chances}}$$

$$\text{Fielding Percentage} = \frac{15 + 8}{15 + 8 + 1} = \frac{23}{24}$$

```
        0.9583 ≈ .958  Fielding Percentage
 24 ) 23.0000
    − 21 6
       1 40
     − 1 20
         200
       − 192
          80
        − 72
           8
```

Exercise A Express each player's fielding percentage as a decimal rounded to three places.

1. J. J. John   8 assists
               7 putouts
               2 errors

2. Chris Sehr   8 assists
               13 putouts
               1 error

3. Elva Ellis   8 assists
               15 putouts
               0 errors

4. John Gans   16 assists
               23 putouts
               3 errors

5. Beth Wells   5 assists
               2 putouts
               1 error

6. Jiang Wu   11 assists
               0 putouts
               3 errors

Earned run average

A statistic that describes how many runs a pitcher allows

A pitcher's most important statistic is probably the **earned run average** (ERA). The ERA is a measure of how many runs a pitcher allows in a game. It is found by multiplying the number of runs that the pitcher has allowed by 9 and then dividing by the number of innings that the pitcher has pitched. The ERA is expressed as a decimal number rounded to two places.

$$\text{Earned Run Average} = \frac{\text{Earned Runs} \times 9}{\text{Innings Pitched}}$$

Multiply by 9 since there are 9 innings in a game.

EXAMPLE Cara Yamamoto allows 5 runs in $27\frac{1}{3}$ innings. What is her earned run average?

$$\text{Earned Run Average} = \frac{5 \times 9}{27\frac{1}{3}}$$

Step 1 Change $27\frac{1}{3}$ to an improper fraction.

$$27\frac{1}{3} = \frac{82}{3}$$

Step 2 Rewrite the problem.

$$\frac{45}{27\frac{1}{3}} = \frac{45}{\frac{82}{3}} = \frac{45}{1} \div \frac{82}{3} = \frac{45}{1} \times \frac{3}{82}$$

Step 3 Solve.

$$\frac{45}{1} \times \frac{3}{82} = \frac{135}{82} \approx 1.646 \approx 1.65 \text{ Earned Run Average}$$

Exercise A Find each pitcher's earned run average in these problems. Express the ERA as a decimal rounded to two places.

1. Lee Gonzalez
16 innings
3 earned runs

2. Gina Statham
24 innings
2 earned runs

3. Larry McCoy
18 innings
2 earned runs

4. Bob Gold
$17\frac{2}{3}$ innings
6 earned runs

Exercise B Solve each problem.

1. Crystal pitched 24 innings and allowed 6 runs. What is her earned run average?

2. Byron allowed 10 runs in 22 innings. What is Byron's earned run average?

3. Thomas pitched $23\frac{1}{3}$ innings and allowed 5 runs. What is his earned run average?

4. Linda allowed 5 runs in 14 innings. What is her earned run average?

5. Pedro pitched $21\frac{1}{3}$ innings and allowed 4 runs. What is his earned run average?

6. Michele allowed 3 runs in 8 innings. What is her earned run average?

Pitchers practice for hours to keep their ERAs as low as possible.

**Won-lost
percentage**

*Ratio of wins to games
played*

One of the most important statistics for a team is its **won-lost
percentage**. The won-lost percentage is written as a decimal
rounded to three places. It is found by dividing the number
of team wins by the number of games that the team has played.

$$\text{Won-Lost Percentage} = \frac{\text{Number of Wins}}{\text{Games Played}}$$

Games played
include both wins
and losses.

EXAMPLE The Metros win 13 games and lose 12 games.
What is their won-lost percentage?

$$\text{Won-Lost Percentage} = \frac{13}{13 + 12} = \frac{13}{25}$$

$$\begin{array}{r} .52 \approx .520 \text{ Won-lost percentage} \\ 25\overline{)13.00} \\ -12\,5 \\ \hline 50 \\ -50 \\ \hline \end{array}$$

**Writing About
Mathematics**

What do you know
if two teams have
the same won-lost
percentages?

Exercise A Use the tables on page 203. Find each team's won-
lost percentage for the Pacific and Atlantic leagues. Then list
the teams in order of their standing. The team with the largest
won-lost percentage in each division is in first place. The other
teams follow in the order of their won-lost percentages.

1.

Pacific League—East Division			
Team	Won	Lost	W-L Pct.
Sabers	37	48	
Sharks	46	39	
Kodiaks	45	39	
Wolves	39	46	
Stallions	41	44	

2.

Atlantic League—East Division			
Team	Won	Lost	W-L Pct.
Mustangs	42	40	
Grizzlies	41	45	
Robins	50	35	
Avengers	39	47	
Flyers	44	42	

Pacific League—Central Division			
Team	Won	Lost	W-L Pct.
Rascals	42	42	
Torpedos	41	42	
Rivets	38	43	
Miners	35	51	
Dingoes	52	32	

Atlantic League—Central Division			
Team	Won	Lost	W-L Pct.
Redbirds	40	45	
Crows	38	48	
Eagles	48	35	
Hawks	48	38	
Seals	37	47	

Pacific League—West Division			
Team	Won	Lost	W-L Pct.
Sea Lions	44	42	
Zebras	43	44	
Buffaloes	52	34	
Rockets	42	43	
Bats	33	52	

Atlantic League—West Division			
Team	Won	Lost	W-L Pct.
Ospreys	42	41	
Wildcats	41	45	
Pumas	46	42	
Caribou	40	46	
Muskies	38	47	

You may use a calculator to help you convert fractions to decimals and then to percents.

EXAMPLE Express $\frac{7}{12}$ as a percent.

Step 1 Divide the numerator by the denominator.
$7 \div 12 = 0.5833333$

Step 2 Round the answer to the nearest thousandth.
$0.5833333 \approx 0.583$

Step 3 Move the decimal point two places to the right. Write the answer as a percent.
$0.58.3 = 58.3\%$

Calculator Exercise Express these fractions as decimals, then as percents. Use a calculator to help you.

1. $\frac{7}{8}$

2. $\frac{5}{6}$

3. $\frac{4}{12}$

4. $\frac{9}{11}$

5. $\frac{9}{10}$

6. $\frac{4}{5}$

7. $\frac{1}{7}$

8. $\frac{2}{7}$

9. $\frac{2}{3}$

10. $\frac{9}{13}$

11. $\frac{3}{17}$

12. $\frac{5}{19}$

13. $\frac{2}{21}$

14. $\frac{1}{6}$

15. $\frac{11}{16}$

16. $\frac{2}{5}$

Try This

For Step 3, use your calculator to multiply the answer in Step 1 by 100, then round your answer. How does your answer to Exercise 13 compare to your answer when you followed the three steps?

A statistic given with the won-lost percentage is the number of games that each team is back from first place. The number of **games back** from first place is found by comparing the wins and losses of each team with those of the first-place team.

$$\text{Games Back} = \frac{\text{Difference of Each Team's Wins} + \text{Difference of Each Team's Losses}}{2}$$

EXAMPLE

Team	Won	Lost	Pct.	GB
Buffaloes	23	14	.622	–
Sea Lions	19	18	.514	■
Zebras	17	19	.472	■

$$\text{Sea Lions—Games Back} = \frac{(23 - 19) + (18 - 14)}{2} = \frac{(4 + 4)}{2} = 4$$

$$\text{Zebras—Games Back} = \frac{(23 - 17) + (19 - 14)}{2} = \frac{6 + 5}{2} = 5\frac{1}{2}$$

Exercise A For each baseball league, compute the teams' won-lost percentage and the number of games back.

Pacific League					Atlantic League				
Team	**Won**	**Lost**	**Pct.**	**GB**	**Team**	**Won**	**Lost**	**Pct.**	**GB**
Sharks	32	20			Robins	36	20		
Rascals	29	21			Flyers	34	23		
Kodiaks	30	22			Grizzlies	34	24		
Sea Lions	28	24			Hawks	29	28		
Torpedoes	27	24			Redbirds	28	30		
Stallions	27	24			Ospreys	27	30		
Rivets	25	28			Wildcats	22	36		
Rockets	24	28			Seals	21	36		
Zebras	18	33			Caribou	18	38		

Recruiter's Choice

Joe Brown visited Ridge High School while on a recruiting tour for his college. He showed interest in two of Ridge's baseball players: LeRoy Townsend and Dominic Schlickman. The following data pertains to the two students.

	Leroy Townsend	Dominic Schlickman
Times at bat	73	59
Hits	48	27
Home runs	3	2
Triples	5	6
Doubles	11	4
Singles	22	10
Outs	7	5
Steals	9	8
Putouts	14	15
Assists	6	4
Errors	2	1
Innings	36	42
Earned runs	6	6

Exercises Use the data for each problem below.

1. Find the batting average for each.

2. Find the slugging percentage for each.

3. Find the baserunning average for each.

4. Find the fielding percentage for each.

5. Find the earned run average for each.

6. Based on the above statistics, if you were Joe Brown, which of the two players would you try to recruit for your college? Why?

Technology Connection

Do a Web search for "baseball" + "improve skills." Some of the selections listed provide free information, such as improving your batting average or summer camp schedules. Send for some information. Share the information with your class when it arrives.

Chapter 12 REVIEW

Write the letter of the best answer to each question.

1. What is $\frac{3}{10}$ renamed as a percent rounded to one decimal place?

A 0.3

B 0.30

C 30%

D 30.0%

2. Jamie had 8 hits for 26 times at bat. What is Jamie's batting average?

A .235

B .308

C 765

D 3.25

3. Djuana steals 15 bases and is put out 21 times while attempting to steal. What is Djuana's baserunning average?

A 41.7%

B 58.3%

C 71.4%

D 140%

4. Pat has 4 assists and 10 putouts. He makes 3 errors. What is Pat's fielding percentage?

A .235

B .400

C .824

D 4.667

5. Tonya pitches 28 innings and allows 5 earned runs. What is her ERA?

A .15

B .18

C 1.61

D 5.60

Rename each fraction as a decimal rounded to three places.

6. $\frac{7}{8}$ **7.** $\frac{5}{13}$

Rename each fraction as a percent. Round to one decimal place.

8. $\frac{3}{7}$ **9.** $\frac{7}{12}$

Give the batting average for each player as a decimal number rounded to three places.

10. Patty Chan/8 hits for 21 at bats

11. Jo Cox/15 hits for 38 at bats

Give the slugging percentage for each player as a decimal number rounded to three places.

12. Henry Wolpert
    1 home run
    2 triples
    4 doubles
    8 singles
    3 walks
  10 outs
    8 sacrifices

13. Juan Cortez
    0 home runs
    1 triple
    3 doubles
  12 singles
    6 walks
    9 outs
    2 sacrifices

Give each baserunning average as a percent rounded to one decimal place.

14. Juanita Sanchez steals 18 bases and is put out 13 times while attempting to steal.

15. Sam Foxtree steals 9 bases and is put out 14 times while attempting to steal.

Give each player's fielding percentage as a decimal number rounded to three places.

16. Joe Shaw has 8 assists and 4 putouts. He makes 2 errors.

17. Morris Corona has 7 assists and 9 putouts. He makes 1 error.

Give each pitcher's ERA as a decimal number rounded to two places.

18. Don Coleman pitches 14 innings and allows 8 earned runs.

19. Marian Finney pitches 24 innings and allows 8 earned runs.

For each team, find the won-lost percentage and the number of games back.

20.

Team	Won	Lost	Pct.	GB
Sea Lions	33	15		
Torpedoes	29	18		
Buffaloes	27	21		

Test-Taking Tip

If you don't know the answer to a question, put a check beside it and go on. When you are finished, go back to any checked questions and try to answer them.

13 Using Percent

As you find ways to spend or try to budget your hard-earned money, you will discover that you need to understand percent. Sales tax, discounts, and credit cards are some of the areas that calculate amounts of money by using a percent. Even if you save your money and never spend it, you will do better if you know more about percent. Certainly, if you wish to be a wise consumer, then you will be glad to know more about the mathematics of percent.

In Chapter 13, you will explore ways that percent helps you to find the best buy and make the best investment.

Goals for Learning

◆ To compute the discount, given the original price

◆ To compute the sales tax and the price plus sales tax

◆ To find the percent of spending

◆ To make a circle graph to display budgets

A state **sales tax** is collected for most sales. Although not all states have a sales tax, most do. The state uses this money for such things as education, police protection, and keeping the highways in good condition. To compute a sales tax is to find a **percentage**.

Sales tax	A state **sales tax** is collected for most sales.

Sales tax

A tax on sales or services, added to the price

Percentage

A given part or amount in every hundred; the part in a percent

Rate

Percent

 EXAMPLE Bill buys a school notebook for $4.35. The sales tax is 4%. What is the price of the notebook with tax?

Step 1 Multiply the price by the **rate** of the tax.

$$\begin{array}{r} \$ \quad 4.35 \quad \text{Original price} \\ \times \quad .04 \quad \text{Rate of tax} \\ \hline \$ .17\,40 \quad \text{Tax} \end{array}$$

$\$ .17\,40 \approx \$0.18$ (State sales tax is rounded up to the next cent.)

Step 2 Add the tax to the original price.

$$\begin{array}{r} \$4.35 \quad \text{Original price} \\ + \ 0.18 \quad \text{Tax} \\ \hline \$4.53 \quad \text{Total price including tax} \end{array}$$

Exercise A Find the sales tax and the total price including tax.

1. CD $12.95 with a 5% sales tax

2. Calculator $9.65 with a 5% sales tax

3. Breath mints $2.20 with a 6% sales tax

4. Shirt $22.99 with a 5% sales tax

5. Shoes $55 with a 4% sales tax

6. Dictionary $13 with a 5% sales tax

7. Granola bar $1.09 with a 5% sales tax

8. Computer cable $8.50 with a 7% sales tax

9. Bookshelf $59.95 with a 5% sales tax

10. Blanket $32.00 with a 6% sales tax

11. Picture frame $16 with a 4% sales tax

12. Car $18,741.87 with a 5% sales tax

Sales are often advertised in the form of **discounts**, such as "10% off." Knowing the exact amount of the discount is important for wise shopping. To calculate a discount is to find a percentage.

Discount

The amount taken off the usual price

Sale price

Reduced price of an item

The higher the percent is, the greater the discount. For example, 10% of $1.00 is a $0.10 (10¢) discount, and 30% of $1.00 is a $0.30 (30¢) discount.

Writing About Mathematics

Write about a time when you bought something for a discounted price and about how much money you saved.

EXAMPLES Jenny wants a bike that originally cost $180. If she gets a 25% discount, how much will the bike cost?

Step 1 Multiply the original price by the rate of discount.

$$
\begin{array}{rl}
\$\ 180.00 & \text{Original price} \\
\times\quad .25 & \text{Rate of discount} \\
\hline
9\ 0000 & \\
+\ 36\ 000 & \\
\hline
\$\ 45.0000 & \text{Discount}
\end{array}
$$

Step 2 Subtract the discount from the original price.

$$
\begin{array}{rl}
\$\ 180.00 & \text{Original price} \\
-\quad 45.00 & \text{Discount} \\
\hline
\$\ 135.00 & \text{Sale price}
\end{array}
$$

With a 25% discount, the bike costs $135.00.

Kristina picks out a coat with a price tag of $98.50. The coat is on sale at 15% off the marked price. How much of a discount does she get? What is the **sale price**?

Step 1 Multiply.

$$
\begin{array}{rl}
\$\ 98.50 & \text{Original price} \\
\times\quad .15 & \text{Rate of discount} \\
\hline
4\ 9250 & \\
+\ 9\ 850 & \\
\hline
\$14.7750 \approx \$14.78 & \text{Discount}
\end{array}
$$

Step 2 Subtract.

$$
\begin{array}{rl}
\$\ 98.50 & \text{Original price} \\
-\quad 14.78 & \text{Discount} \\
\hline
\$\ 83.72 & \text{Sale price}
\end{array}
$$

Exercise A Find the discount and the new sale price for each.

1. Radio $169.00 with a discount rate of 20%

2. Calculator $14.20 with a discount rate of 10%

3. Shirt $27.00 with a discount rate of 15%

4. Shoes $32.50 with a discount rate of 20%

5. Blouse $16.75 with a discount rate of 25%

6. Purse $18 with a discount rate of 10%

7. Flashlight $3.95 with a discount rate of 10%

8. Baseball $6.50 with a discount rate of 25%

9. Television $289 with a discount rate of 30%

10. Rug $175.92 with a discount rate of 10%

11. Chair $109.68 with a discount rate of 15%

12. Shovel $10.99 with a discount rate of 25%

13. Stapler $6.25 with a discount rate of 20%

14. Computer $749 with a discount rate of 15%

15. Scarf $6.75 with a discount rate of 50%

16. Bike $110.25 with a discount rate of 10%

17. Skates $52.98 with a discount rate of 40%

18. CD player $48.95 with a discount rate of 12%

19. Computer game $200 with a discount rate of 20%

20. Keyboard $159 with a discount rate of 25%

21. Lawn mower $289 with a discount rate of 15%

22. Hammer $18.60 with a discount rate of 10%

Budget

A plan for managing money

Income

Money earned

One step in **budget** planning is to find what percent of **income**, or earnings, is usually spent on certain items. You can find the percent, or rate, by dividing.

Remember to put the decimal point in the correct place in the dividend.

EXAMPLE Sandee earns $326 per week and spends $50 per week on food. What percent of her salary does she spend on food per week?

Rate × Base = Percentage

■% of $326 = $50

■% = $50 ÷ $326

$$\begin{array}{r} 0.153 \\ 326 \overline{)50.000} \\ -32\ 6 \\ \hline 17\ 40 \\ -16\ 30 \\ \hline 1\ 100 \\ -\ 978 \\ \hline 122 \end{array}$$

◄— Insert enough zeros to allow three decimal places.

Writing About Mathematics

Talk to someone in your family about ways he or she saves money on food each week. Write a paragraph describing that person's ideas.

To express a decimal as a percent, move the decimal point two places to the right.

0.153 = 15.3%

Sandee spends 15.3% of her salary on food.

People often try to stretch their food budget by buying food items that are on sale.

PROBLEM SOLVING

Exercise A Find the rate of earnings spent. Round your answers to the nearest tenth of a percent.

1. Each week, Lee spends $50 of his income on apartment rent. If he earns $170 per week, what percent does he spend on rent?

2. Yoko earns $65 per week and spends $18 on bus fare. What percent does she spend on bus fare?

3. Laurie needs $14 each week for lunch. If she earns $36 per week, what percent is spent for lunch?

4. Marnie earns $170 during the week and spends $40 for food. What percent is spent for food?

5. Nicholas earns $83 during the week and spends $45 for food. What percent is spent for food?

6. Cara earns $67 during the week and spends $15 on bus fare. What percent is spent on bus fare?

7. José earns $52 during the week and spends $25 on clothes. What percent is spent on clothes?

8. Ben earns $48 during the week. He spends $5 on bus fare and $10 on lunches. What percent is spent on bus fare? What percent is spent on lunches?

9. Rita earns $125 during the week. She spends $10 for bus fare and $16 on lunches. What percent is spent on bus fare? What percent is spent on lunches?

10. Malcolm earns $262 during the week. He spends $16 during the week on food and $50 for a car payment. What percent is spent on food? What percent is spent on the car payment?

11. Jesse earns $350 during the week. He spends $15 on clothes and $75 for rent. What percent is spent on clothes? What percent is spent on the rent?

12. Luis earns $220 during the week. He spends $25 on books and $35 on his gas bill. What percent is spent on books? What percent is spent on the gas bill?

13. Erica earns $275. She spends $55 on her phone bill and $51 on a birthday gift for a friend. What percent is spent on her phone bill? What percent is spent on the birthday gift?

Base

An amount that a percent is taken of

When working with percents, remember to write the percent as a decimal number. For example, 72% is equal to 0.72

Writing About Mathematics

Write about a time when you saved money each week to buy something special.

If you know the rate of earnings saved and the percentage of earnings saved, then you can find the total earnings by dividing.

EXAMPLES   Donnell is saving 20% of his earnings for college. If he saves $45 per week, then how much does he earn per week?

Rate $\times$ **Base** = Percentage
20% $\times$ Base = $45
               Base = $45 $\div$ 0.20   Because 20% is 0.20

$$
\begin{array}{r}
\$\ \ 225. \\
.20)\overline{\$45.00.} \\
-\,40\ \ \ \ \ \\
\hline
5\,0 \\
-\,4\,0 \\
\hline
1\,00 \\
-\,1\,00 \\
\hline
\end{array}
$$

Base = $225. Donnell earns $225 per week.

Lionel saves 15% of his weekly wages. If he saves $23.40 per week, then what are his weekly wages?

Rate $\times$ Base = Percentage
15% $\times$ Base = $23.40
               Base = $23.40 $\div$ 0.15

$$
\begin{array}{r}
\$\ \ 156. \\
.15)\overline{\$23.40.} \\
-\,15\,0\ \ \\
\hline
8\,4 \\
-\,7\,5 \\
\hline
90 \\
\end{array}
$$

Base = $156. Lionel earns $156 per week.

Exercise A Find the earnings.

1. Abbott is saving 30% of his weekly salary for a car. If he saves $24.60 per week, how much does he earn per week?

2. Manuel deposits 25% of his weekly earnings in a savings account. If he deposits $19.50 weekly, then how much does he earn?

3. Rachel saves $32.90 per week from her part-time job. If she saves 35% of her earnings, then how much does she earn?

4. Bo wants to save 25% of his weekly income for college. How much will he have to make to save $11.75 per week?

Try This

Jennifer has a part-time job. She earns $150.00 per week and is saving some of her earnings each week for different things. She is saving 48% for college, 25% for a car, and 12% for concert tickets. How much money is she saving each week for these items? How much money does she have left over?

Exercise B Find the weekly earnings.

1. 20% saved
   Saved $80
   Earned ____

2. 25% saved
   Saved $22.50
   Earned ____

3. 20% saved
   Saved $33
   Earned ____

4. 30% saved
   Saved $97.50
   Earned ____

5. 35% saved
   Saved $63.00
   Earned ____

6. 22% saved
   Saved $12.10
   Earned ____

7. 15% saved
   Saved $12.15
   Earned ____

8. 40% saved
   Saved $84
   Earned ____

9. 10% saved
   Saved $22.50
   Earned ____

10. 12% saved
    Saved $18
    Earned ____

Budgets are often shown with a **circle graph**. Each section of the graph represents a different kind of expense. You can clearly see what rate of total earnings is spent for each purpose.

EXAMPLE Make a circle graph to show Jiang's budget.

Jiang's Budget

Rent	30%
Car	10%
Savings	25%
Other	35%

Follow these steps:

Step 1 Draw a circle. Mark the center.

Step 2 There are 360° in a circle. Find the number of **degrees** needed for each item by multiplying the percent by 360°.

$0.30 \times 360° = 108°$ Rent
$0.10 \times 360° = 36°$ Car
$0.25 \times 360° = 90°$ Savings
$0.35 \times 360° = 126°$ Other

Step 3 Draw a **radius** and use a **protractor** to measure and help draw each segment.

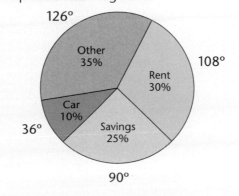

Circle graph

Way to show comparisons by using segments of a circle

Degree

1/360th of a circle

Radius

A line from the center to the edge of a circle

Protractor

An instrument used for drawing and measuring angles

When you mark the center of the circle, use your protractor to check that the mark is exactly in the center.

Try This

Many family budgets are more complicated than those in Exercise A. Make a circle graph for this family budget:

Housing: 30%
Food: 20%
Transportation: 15%
Entertainment: 10%
Clothing: 5%
Medical Bills: 5%
Savings: 15%

Exercise A Make a circle graph for each budget. Round degrees to the nearest whole number.

1. Rent 25%
Food 15%
Car 15%
Other 45%

2. Rent 30%
Food 25%
Car 10%
Other 35%

3. Rent 20%
Clothing 15%
Savings 5%
Other 60%

4. Entertainment 14%
Housing 26%
Savings 10%
Other 50%

5. Transportation 15%
Savings 20%
Food 35%
Housing 20%
Clothing 10%

6. Entertainment 5%
Housing 20%
Food 30%
Clothing 15%
Other 30%

7. Rent 25%
Food 22%
Clothing 18%
Other 35%

8. Savings 15%
Food 17%
Clothing 13%
Other 55%

Technology Connection

Have you ever created a circle graph? If you have, you know how difficult it can be to make each section of the graph exactly the right size. With the latest technology, creating circle graphs is a snap. Many computer programs can take the information you enter and create a graph with just a click of the mouse. You can try these programs at your school or local library. Think about how this technology is helpful to someone planning a family budget or to someone creating a business presentation.

You can use a calculator to help you find discounts.

EXAMPLE Find the discount of 30% on $83.77.

Step 1 Multiply the price by the discount rate.

$$83.77 \;\boxed{\times}\; 0.30 \;\boxed{=}\; 25.131$$

Step 2 Round your answer to the nearest cent.
$25.131 = $25.13

> When you round a number to the nearest cent, you round to the number in the hundredths place.

Calculator Exercise Use your calculator to help you find the discounts. Round your answers to the nearest cent.

1. $25 at 25%
2. $13.50 at 22%
3. $125.52 at 32%
4. $18.95 at 10%
5. $120 at 35%
6. $1.95 at 20%
7. $32.89 at 15%
8. $103.75 at 60%
9. $1,069.45 at 16%
10. $753.79 at 23%
11. $176.40 at 49%
12. $16.02 at 18%
13. $62,673.58 at 52%
14. $93 at 33%
15. $444.44 at 44%
16. $62 at 56%

Shopping for Bargains

Tena likes to shop for new clothes. She visits one of her favorite stores because they are having a clearance sale. Tena has saved $80 for this shopping trip. She finds several items to buy, and she calculates the total bill carefully before going to the register. When she gets the total bill, it is more than she expected to pay. She studies the bill carefully.

```
               RECEIPT

Pants . . . . . . . $21.99   30% off  $18.71

T-shirt . . . . . . $12.99   20% off  $10.39

Sweater . . . . . $24.99   30% off  $17.49

Skirt . . . . . . . . $18.95   25% off  $15.16


                    Subtotal  $61.75
                    6% Tax   $  3.71

                    TOTAL  $65.46
```

Exercises Use the receipt to answer the questions.

1. There is a mistake in the discount given for one of the items Tena buys. Which item has the wrong discounted price? What is the correct discounted price?

2. What is the subtotal, before taxes, on the receipt?

3. What is the corrected subtotal on the receipt before taxes?

4. There is a 6% sales tax on clothing. How much should Tena pay in sales tax after the subtotal is corrected?

5. What is the corrected total amount?

Chapter 13 R E V I E W

Write the letter of the best answer to each question.

1. Judi saves $22.00. She spends 77% of that on a new shirt. How much does she spend?
   A $16.00
   B $16.54
   C $16.94
   D $16.99

2. Alfonzo buys a drill for $28.80, which is 20% off the original price. What is the original price?
   A $36.00
   B $36.50
   C $37.00
   D $37.50

3. LaShonda puts 20% of her earnings into a savings account each week. She earns $72.00 a week. How much does she save?
   A $14.30
   B $14.40
   C $14.50
   D $14.60

4. A DVD player costs $252.00. There is a 35% discount. What is the sale price?
   A $163.20
   B $163.50
   C $163.80
   D $163.90

5. A cell phone costs $79.99. There is a 17% discount. How much is the discount?
   A $13.60
   B $13.65
   C $66.39
   D $66.49

Find the discount and the new sale price for each.

6. A shirt priced at $23 with a 20% discount

7. Jeans priced at $26.95 with a 10% discount

8. Running shoes priced at $78.57 with a 35% discount

Find the sales tax and the total price including tax.

9. Radio $19.75 with a 5% sales tax

10. Computer $1,039.16 with a 6% sales tax

11. Television $621.97 with a 6% sales tax

Find the rate of earnings spent. Round your answers to the nearest whole number.

12. Karen spends $29.75 of her savings for a coat. Find the percent spent if her savings is $85.

13. Patrice earns $36 one week tutoring. She spends $3.96 for school supplies. What percent does Patrice spend on school supplies?

14. John earns $83 per week. He spends $10 at the movies. What percent does John spend at the movies?

Find the earnings.

15. Kirk saves 15% of his part-time earnings for clothes. If he saves $8.25 for clothes, then how much does he earn?

16. Luke saves 30% of his weekly part-time earnings for college. If he saves $13.50 weekly, then how much does he earn per week?

17. Steve saves $18 a week for a car, which is 40% of his weekly part-time earnings. How much does Steve earn per week?

Make a circle graph for each budget. Use a protractor to help you.

18. Housing 25%
Transportation 10%
Other 65%

19. Housing 30%
Food 20%
Entertainment 20%
Other 30%

20. Housing 40%
Food 20%
Transportation 10%
Savings 30%

Test-Taking Tip

Before taking a test, find out what tools, such as a calculator or protractor, you need to bring with you.

14 Working With Interest

Banks, finance companies, and sometimes even friends charge interest for the money that you borrow from them. A loan may be in the form of a bank loan, such as a home mortgage. Or, interest may be in the form of charges on a credit card. Whatever the reason, you are sure to encounter interest charges throughout your life. Understanding interest and how it is calculated is another way in which you can use mathematics to help you solve problems in your everyday life.

In Chapter 14, you will apply the skills necessary to compute interest and to help you make informed money decisions.

Goals for Learning

◆ To compute simple and compound interest

◆ To use a table to compute payments

◆ To use the addition and subtraction methods to compute loan payments

Interest

Amount paid for the use of money

Principal

Amount of a loan or a deposit

Time

Duration of a loan or deposit

Loan

Money given to a borrower that is to be returned with interest

Interest rate

Percent paid or charged for the use of money

Simple interest

Interest computed on principal only

Calculate **interest** by multiplying the **principal** times the rate of interest times the **time**. The principal is the amount of the **loan** or the amount in your savings account. The rate is a percent paid for each time period. The time is how long you have the loan or the time the money is in the account.

 EXAMPLE Felipe's car costs $3,180.07. His uncle agrees to loan Felipe the money at a simple **interest rate** of 6% per year for $2\frac{1}{4}$ years. How much **simple interest** will Felipe have to pay?

Compute the simple interest on $3,180.07 at 6% per year for $2\frac{1}{4}$ years. Convert the rate and time to decimals: 6% = 0.06; $2\frac{1}{4}$ = 2.25

Interest = Principal × Rate × Time in Years
Interest = $3,180.07 × 0.06 × 2.25

Step 1

$ 3,180.07	Principal
× .06	Interest rate
$190.8042	
$190.80	Rounded interest for 1 year

Step 2

$ 190.80	Interest
× 2.25	Time in years
$ 429.30	Total interest

Converting Months to Years					
Months	**Fractional Part of Year**	**Rounded Decimals**	**Months**	**Fractional Part of Year**	**Decimals**
1	$\frac{1}{12}$	0.08	7	$\frac{7}{12}$	0.58
2	$\frac{2}{12}$	0.17	8	$\frac{8}{12}$	0.67
3	$\frac{3}{12}$	0.25	9	$\frac{9}{12}$	0.75
4	$\frac{4}{12}$	0.33	10	$\frac{10}{12}$	0.83
5	$\frac{5}{12}$	0.42	11	$\frac{11}{12}$	0.92
6	$\frac{6}{12}$	0.50			

Exercise A Find the simple interest.

1. $60 × 4% × 2 years

2. $120 × 6% × 1 year

3. $250 × 6% × 4 years

4. $96 × 3% × 5 years

5. $320 × 7% × 4 years

6. $136 × 3% × 3 years

PROBLEM SOLVING

Exercise B Find the simple interest. Annual interest rates are given.

1. Huilde has a principal of $165 with a rate of interest of 6% for 4 years. How much is the interest?

2. Elise borrows $235 from her sister with a rate of interest of 7% for 3 years. How much will she pay in interest?

3. Eduardo borrows $1,095 from his mother for 6 months at 9% interest. What is the amount Eduardo pays in interest?

4. Preeti needs $49.92 more to buy a new CD player. Her brother agrees to loan her the money if Preeti will pay back her brother at the rate of 5% over 4 months. How much will Preeti need to pay in interest if she accepts her brother's offer?

5. Sigfredo borrows $2,065 from an uncle to buy a motorcycle. He agrees to pay back his uncle 6% for 2 years. How much interest does Sigfredo pay to his uncle?

6. John has a loan from the garden shop for $38. He agrees to pay it back in 6 months at 6% interest. How much is the interest?

7. Ung borrows $92 from a friend to buy a new drill. If Ung agrees to pay his loan in 8 months at 9% interest, then how much interest does Ung pay?

8. Latrice borrows $102.26 from her grandmother for 2 years at 7% interest. How much interest does Latrice pay?

9. Tamara gets a loan from her bank for $1,000 at 7% for 10 years. How much is the interest?

10. Maggie agrees to give Glen a loan for $23.40. However, Glen must pay the money back in 6 months at 5% interest. How much will Glen pay Maggie in interest?

$\frac{1}{4} = 0.25$

$\frac{1}{2} = 0.5$

$\frac{3}{4} = 0.75$

The rate of interest may contain a fraction. To compute the interest, you can change the fraction to its decimal equivalent. Then multiply.

EXAMPLE Compute the simple interest on a principal of $350 at $7\frac{1}{2}$% per year for 3 years.

Interest = Principal × Rate × Time

$7\frac{1}{2}$% = 0.075

$350	Principal
× .075	Rate of interest
1 750	
24 500	
$26.250	Interest for 1 year
$ 26.25	Interest for 1 year
× 3	Time in years
$ 78.75	Interest for 3 years

Exercise C Find the simple interest. Annual interest rates are given.

1. $400 at $8\frac{1}{2}$% for 2 years

2. $175 at $6\frac{1}{4}$% for 2 years

3. $200 at $6\frac{3}{4}$% for 3 years

4. $75 at $6\frac{1}{2}$% for 6 months

5. $62 at $7\frac{3}{4}$% for 9 years

6. $380 at $6\frac{3}{4}$% for 5 years

7. $1,800 at $9\frac{3}{4}$% for 1 year

8. $350 at $7\frac{1}{4}$% for 3 years

9. $395 at $7\frac{3}{4}$% for 2 years

10. $80 at $8\frac{1}{2}$% for 6 months

11. $267 at $9\frac{3}{4}$% for 3 years

12. $132 at $5\frac{1}{4}$% for 5 years

13. $17 at $9\frac{1}{4}$% for 2 years

14. $500 at $6\frac{1}{4}$% for 4 years

Compound interest

Interest computed on principal plus interest

Quarterly

Happening at regular intervals four times a year

Balance

The amount due

To compound interest quarterly, use a quarterly interest rate, or the annual rate divided by 4.

Round compound interest to the nearest penny. $5.202 rounds to $5.20.

You earn **compound interest** when the bank pays interest on the principal and on the interest already earned on money in a savings account.

EXAMPLE Janna deposits $250 in her savings account and receives 2% interest compounded **quarterly**. What is her **balance** at the end of 1 year?

Interest = Principal × Rate × Time

First Quarter

a) $250.00 Principal
    × .005 (2% divided by 4)
    $ 1.25 Interest

b) $250.00 Principal
    + 1.25 Interest
    $251.25 New principal

Second Quarter

c) $ 251.25 Principal
    ×   .005 Rate
    $1.25625 Interest

d) $ 251.25 Principal
    +   1.26 Interest
    $ 252.51 New principal

Third Quarter

e) $ 252.51 Principal
    ×   .005 Rate
    $1.26255 Interest

f) $ 252.51 Principal
    +   1.26 Interest
    $ 253.77 New principal

Fourth Quarter

g) $ 253.77 Principal
    ×   .005 Rate
    $1.26885 Interest

h) $253.77 Principal
    + 1.27 Interest
    $255.04 New principal

The balance at the end of 1 year is $255.04.

Exercise A Find the interest compounded quarterly and the new balance at the end of 1 year.

1. $200 at 8%
2. $500 at 6%
3. $250 at 10%
4. $300 at 10%
5. $450 at 8%
6. $1,000 at 9%
7. $850 at 12%
8. $960 at 12%
9. $2,000 at 7%
10. $1,500 at 9%

11. $1,600 at 8%
12. $145 at 10%
13. $350 at 5%
14. $750 at 3%
15. $800 at 6%
16. $150 at 2%
17. $575 at 4%
18. $625 at 10%
19. $720 at 8%
20. $4,000 at 5%

Your money begins earning compound interest as soon as you make a deposit at the bank.

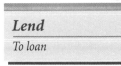
Lend

To loan

For loan interest, *always* round payments up.

Writing About Mathematics

Explain why the final payment can be an amount that is different from other payments.

The Subtraction Method Some lenders of money subtract the interest due from the total amount that they **lend**. The borrower does not receive the full amount but does pay back the full amount.

EXAMPLE   Hideo wants to borrow $2,000 at 10% annual interest for 30 months, making 30 monthly payments. How much is each payment?

Step 1
$ 2,000	Loan
× .10	Interest rate
$200.00	Interest for 1 year

$2,000 is the amount Hideo will pay back.

Step 2
$ 200	Interest for 1 year
× 2.5	Time in years
$ 500	Total interest

Step 3
$2,000	Loan
− 500	Interest
$1,500	Loan minus interest

$1,500 is the amount Hideo will receive.

Step 4
Months

$2,000 ÷ 30 = $66.666
Always round the payment up.
$2,000 ÷ 30 = $66.67

$66.67 is the monthly payment for 29 months.

Step 5
Notice that $66.67 × 30 = $2,000.10.
The last payment, then, is $66.67 − $0.10, or $66.57.

Exercise A Find the monthly payment. Write the amount of the last payment if it differs from the first payment. Use the subtraction method.

1. $600 at 10% for 12 months

2. $700 at 12% for 12 months

3. $950 at 12% for 18 months

4. $550 at 10% for 12 months

5. $1,000 at 14% for 6 months

6. $1,000 at 10% for 18 months

7. $1,500 at 10% for 12 months

8. $1,100 at 12% for 18 months

The Addition Method Some lenders add the interest to the amount of the loan. The borrower pays back the full amount of the loan plus interest.

> **EXAMPLE** Lanita wants to borrow $2,000 at 10% annual interest for 30 months, making 30 monthly payments. How much is each payment?

Step 1

$ 2,000	Loan
× .10	Interest rate
$200.00	Interest for 1 year

$2,000 is the amount Lanita will receive.

Step 2

$200	Interest for 1 year
×2.5	Number of years
$500	Total interest

Step 3

$2,000	Loan
+ 500	Interest
$2,500	Loan plus interest

$2,500 is the amount Lanita will pay back.

Step 4

$2,500 ÷ 30 = $83.333
Always round the payment up.
$2,500 ÷ 30 = $83.34

$83.34 is the monthly payment for 29 months.

Step 5

Notice that $83.34 × 30 = $2,500.20.
The last payment, then, is $83.34 − $0.20, or $83.14.

Exercise B Find the monthly payment. Write the amount of the last payment if it differs from the first payment. Use the addition method.

1. $600 at 10% for 12 months
2. $800 at 12% for 18 months
3. $1,200 at 8% for 6 months
4. $950 at 9% for 12 months
5. $75 at 10% for 12 months
6. $200 at 20% for 12 months
7. $500 at 12% for 6 months
8. $150 at 8% for 9 months
9. $1,000 at 7% for 9 months
10. $1,500 at 14% for 9 months
11. $2,500 at 15% for 12 months
12. $230 at 8% for 24 months

Exercise C Find the monthly payment. Write the amount of the last payment if it differs from the first payment. Use the subtraction method.

1. $500 at 12% for 12 months
2. $750 at 10% for 12 months
3. $650 at 12% for 12 months
4. $850 at 9% for 12 months
5. $780 at 10% for 9 months
6. $900 at 10% for 12 months
7. $900 at 9% for 18 months
8. $800 at 14% for 18 months
9. $500 at 8% for 12 months
10. $1,200 at 6% for 10 months
11. $1,000 at 10% for 18 months
12. $1,100 at 10% for 12 months
13. $1,300 at 9% for 10 months
14. $1,250 at 15% for 9 months

Try This

Use the subtraction method for Exercise D, problem 14. How much less do you pay using the subtraction method?

Exercise D Find the monthly payment. Write the amount of the last payment if it differs from the first payment. Use the addition method.

1. $2,000 at 8% for 18 months
2. $1,900 at 10% for 18 months
3. $1,850 at 14% for 12 months
4. $2,000 at 12% for 6 months
5. $1,700 at 16% for 9 months
6. $1,700 at 10% for 12 months
7. $1,600 at 12% for 12 months
8. $400 at 12% for 12 months
9. $350 at 9% for 12 months
10. $450 at 14% for 18 months
11. $960 at 10% for 12 months
12. $825 at 10% for 6 months
13. $1,350 at 14% for 6 months
14. $1,735 at 16% for 9 months

Buying with **credit** is like borrowing money. Credit allows you to buy an item now and pay for it later. When you pay later, you pay a percent of interest for the use of the money. This interest is charged to your account each month. The first month is usually interest free.

Credit

The right to buy now and to pay later

Finance charge

Money paid for the use of money

Monthly payments can change if you charge more to your credit account. Most accounts allow you to make extra payments at any time with no penalty. This allows you to pay off the account earlier than planned.

EXAMPLE Mariah purchases a lawn mower on sale for $132 on the condition that she makes monthly payments of $20 per month with a **finance charge** of $1\frac{3}{4}\%$ on any unpaid balance. She will make her first payment on the first day of January. What will Mariah's March balance be?

Step 1
$132	Balance
− 20	January payment
$112	New balance for February

Step 2
$ 112	Previous balance
× .0175	Finance rate
$ 1.96	Finance charge

Step 3
$112.00	Previous balance
+ 1.96	Finance charge
$113.96	Before payment

Step 4
$113.96	Before payment
− 20.00	Payment
$ 93.96	New balance for March

Exercise A Complete the information for this chart for the lawn mower.

Month	Previous Balance	Finance Charge	Before Payment	Monthly Payment	New Balance
Jan.	$132.00	$—	$132.00	$20.00	$112.00
Feb.	$112.00	$1.96	$113.96	$20.00	$93.96
March	$93.96	$1.64	$95.60	$20.00	$75.60
April	$75.60				
May					
June					
July					

When you use a credit card to make a purchase, you will receive a monthly statement. It shows the balance due and any finance charges that you owe.

Exercise B Complete the information for these charts.

1. Rolf purchases his school clothes for a total of $111. He agrees to make $15 monthly payments with first month interest free. His finance charge is $1\frac{1}{2}\%$ on any unpaid balance.

Month	Previous Balance	Finance Charge	Before Payment	Monthly Payment	New Balance
Aug.	$111.00	$ —	$111.00	$15	$96.00
Sept.	$96.00	$1.44	$97.44	$15	$82.44
Oct.	$82.44				
Nov.					
Dec.					
Jan.					
Feb.					
March					

2. Nicole purchases a birthday gift for $143. She agrees to make payments of $20 per month with a finance charge of 2% on any unpaid balance. Her first month will be interest free.

Month	Previous Balance	Finance Charge	Before Payment	Monthly Payment	New Balance
Feb.	$143.00	$ —	$143.00	$20	$123.00
March	$123.00	$2.46	$125.46	$20	$105.46
April	$105.46				
May					
June					
July					
Aug.					
Sept.					

Calculator Exercise Budgeting often requires you to find a percentage of earnings. Use a calculator to help you find the percentages for the budget below. Round your answers to the nearest cent.

Eduardo's Budget With $175 per Week		Amount
1. Rent	25%	
2. Car	20%	
3. Savings	10%	
4. Food	15%	
5. Clothes	5%	
6. Miscellaneous	25%	

Megan's Budget With $200 per Week		Amount
7. Entertainment	5%	
8. Food	20%	
9. Car	25%	
10. Rent	19%	
11. Savings	15%	
12. Miscellaneous	16%	

Technology Connection

You can use a spreadsheet program on a computer to help you find the amount of money set aside for each budgeted item in Megan's budget shown above. Enter each budgeted item in column A of a blank spreadsheet, starting with cell A1. Enter the percentage of earnings for each item expressed as a decimal in column B, starting with cell B1. To find the amount of money budgeted for entertainment, enter the formula B1*0.05 in cell C1. To find the amount of money budgeted for food, enter the formula B2*200 in cell C2. To quickly find the amounts for the remaining items, highlight cells C1–C6, click on the Edit menu, and choose Fill Down. The amounts for the remaining items will be filled in automatically.

How Much Interest?

Jerome wants to borrow $5,000.00 for a car. His bank charges 14% annual interest. Jerome is trying to decide how long it will take him to repay the loan. Simple interest will be used.

Exercises Answer these questions about Jerome's loan.

How much interest will Jerome pay if he takes out the loan for each of the following lengths of time?

1. 1 year

2. 18 months

3. 2 years

4. 30 months

5. 3 years

6. For which length of time would the monthly payments be the least?

7. Why should Jerome try to pay the loan back in 1 year?

Chapter 14 REVIEW

Write the letter of the best answer to each question.

1. Which of the following is the simple interest on a loan of $200 at 8% interest for 3 years?
   A $16.00
   B $32.00
   C $48.00
   D $4,800.00

2. What is the total amount owed at the end of 1 year if $200 is compounded quarterly at an annual interest rate of 8%?
   A $16.00
   B $16.48
   C $216.00
   D $216.48

3. A purchase of $150 will have monthly payments of $20 and a finance charge of 2% on the unpaid balance. The first month will be interest free. What is the balance after the second month's payment?
   A $260.00
   B $110.00
   C $112.60
   D $132.60

4. A loan of $250 at 10% interest is taken out for 10 months. If the subtraction method is used, what is the last payment?
   A $20.83
   B $25.00
   C $27.02
   D $27.50

5. A loan of $300 at 10% interest is taken out for 15 months. If the addition method is used, what is the last payment?
   A $20.00
   B $22.00
   C $22.50
   D $25.00

Compute the simple interest.

6. $125 at 10% for 3 years

7. $110 at 7% for 6 months

8. 290 at $6\frac{1}{2}$% for 5 years

9. $206 at $7\frac{1}{4}$% for 2 years

Compute the compound interest quarterly.

10. $300 at 8% for 1 year

11. $275 at 10% for 1 year

12. $1,200 at 5% for 1 year

13. $600 at 4% for 1 year

Complete the information in the chart on buying with credit.

14. A purchase of $175 with monthly payments of $50 and a finance charge of $1\frac{1}{2}$% on the unpaid balance. The first month will be interest free.

Month	Previous Balance	Finance Charge	Before Payment	Monthly Payment	New Balance
Jan.	$175.00	$ —	$175.00	$50.00	$125.00
Feb.	$125.00	$1.88		$50.00	
March				$50.00	
April					$0.00

Find the payments.

15. Use the addition method to compute the first and last payments on a loan of $175 at 10% for 12 months.

16. Use the subtraction method to compute the first and last payments on a loan of $200 at 15% for 10 months.

17. Use the addition method to compute the first and last payments on a loan of $100 at 8% for 6 months.

Niko decides to budget the earnings from his part-time job. Complete the chart to show the amount of money that Niko set aside for each item.

	Niko's Budget—$200 per Month		Amount
18.	School lunches	20%	
19.	Video game rentals	10%	
20.	Movie tickets	15%	
21.	Tickets for sports events	10%	
22.	Comic books	5%	
23.	Computer games	30%	
24.	Miscellaneous	10%	

Test-Taking Tip

If you have time, compute problems a second time, then check your original answer.

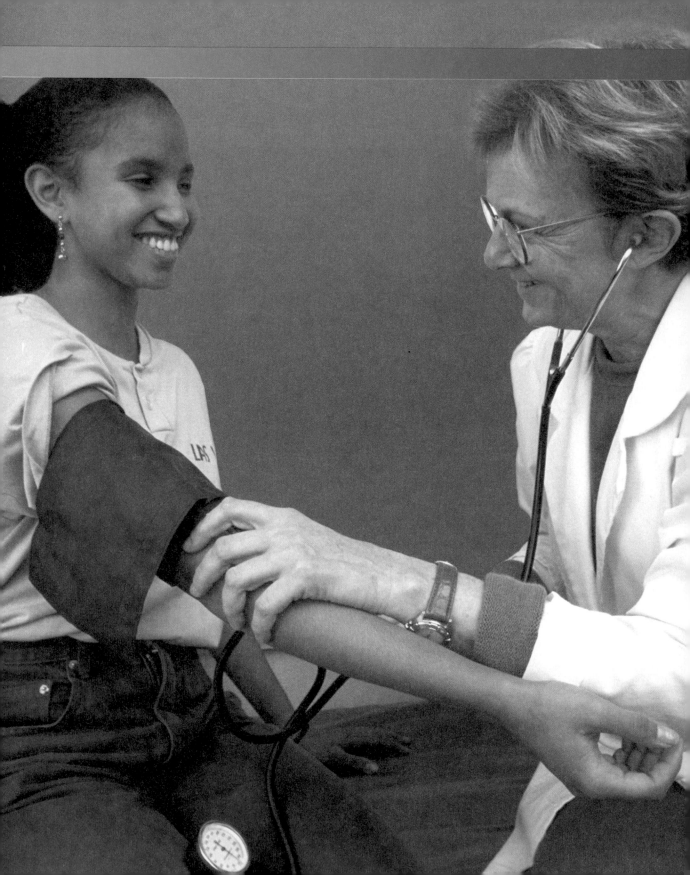

15 Insurance

People buy insurance as a way to protect themselves financially. Home insurance protects a person's home and belongings. Life insurance provides money for the survivors when death occurs. Automobile insurance lets a car owner know that in the event of an accident, damages are covered. Insurance is available for many catastrophes, including floods, earthquakes, and other disasters. As people invest their income in cars and homes, it is wise for them also to invest in insurance, which protects those investments.

In Chapter 15, you will explore the ways to compute the cost of insurance before you make an investment.

Goals for Learning

◆ To use a chart to determine cost of health insurance

◆ To identify the types of life insurance

◆ To use replacement cost and location multiplier to find the cost of homeowners insurance

◆ To use a rate chart to determine premiums

◆ To compute automobile insurance costs with the aid of a table

Insurance

*Coverage by a contract
in which one party
guarantees another
against loss*

Coverage

Insurance for a loss

Premium

*Amount paid for
insurance*

Premium chart

*List of amounts to be
paid for insurance*

Families buy health **insurance** so that they have less worry about how they will pay their doctors' and hospital bills if they have an accident or become ill. Most health care companies offer a variety of health insurance plans. Better **coverage** costs more money. The amount of money that you pay for the health insurance is called the **premium**. You can determine the premium by reading an insurance **premium chart**.

> **EXAMPLE**   Tom is 46 years old. His wife, Susan, is 44 years old. They and their two children are enrolled in Plan B of the health care program. How much is their monthly premium? Use the chart on page 247 to help you.
>
> $127.57
> $104.54
> +$137.56
> $369.67   Monthly premium

Exercise A Use the chart on page 247 to find the monthly premium for each coverage described below.

1. Single adult 43 years old, Plan A

2. Single adult 51 years old, Plan C

3. Husband 28 years old, wife 27 years old, Plan B

4. Husband 41 years old, wife 38 years old, three children, Plan B

5. Husband 54 years old, wife 52 years old, Plan A

6. Husband 32 years old, wife 29 years old, Plan C

7. Single adult 56 years old, Plan B

8. Husband 63 years old, wife 65 years old, Plan A

9. Husband 27 years old, wife 27 years old, one child, Plan B

10. Husband 36 years old, wife 33 years old, two children, Plan A

Health Care Insurance

Pays 100% benefit from the first day of covered accidents or illnesses.

Age at Enrollment	Monthly Premium per Adult
3 mo.–18 yr.	$69.99
19–29	$80.13
30–34	$87.35
35–39	$94.67
40–44	$106.39
45–49	$129.83
50–54	$168.71
55–59	$219.32
60–64	$240.62
65+	$240.62

Additional Costs:
Children up to age 19
(or 25 if full-time student)

1 child	$69.99
2 children	$139.98
3 or more	$209.97

PLAN B

Pays 80% benefit from the first day of covered accidents or illnesses.

Age at Enrollment	Monthly Premium per Adult
3 mo.–18 yr.	$68.78
19–29	$78.74
30–34	$85.83
35–39	$93.03
40–44	$104.54
45–49	$127.57
50–54	$165.78
55–59	$215.50
60–64	$236.44
65+	$236.44

Additional Costs:
Children up to age 19
(or 25 if full-time student)

1 child	$68.78
2 children	$137.56
3 or more	$206.34

PLAN C

Pays 60% benefit from the first day of covered accidents or illnesses.

Age at Enrollment	Monthly Premium per Adult
3 mo.–18 yr.	$64.01
19–29	$73.29
30–34	$79.88
35–39	$86.58
40–44	$97.30
45–49	$118.74
50–54	$154.30
55–59	$200.58
60–64	$220.06
65+	$220.06

Additional Costs:
Children up to age 19
(or 25 if full-time student)

1 child	$64.01
2 children	$128.02
3 or more	$192.03

Major Medical Insurance Many health care plans place limits on covered expenses. Because of these limits, many companies provide their employees with **major medical insurance** coverage. Payroll deductions for part of the total premium can be made weekly, **semimonthly**, or monthly from employees' paychecks.

Rest Easy Major Medical Program Semimonthly Payroll Deductions	
Employee	$12.22
Employee and spouse	$14.98
Employee and family	$23.67

EXAMPLE Morgan, her husband, and their two children are enrolled in the Rest Easy Major Medical Program. What is their annual premium?

$$
\begin{array}{r}
\$\ 23.67 \\
\times\ \ \ \ \ 24 \\
\hline
94\ 68 \\
+\ 473\ 4 \\
\hline
\$\ 568.08\ \ \text{Annual premium}
\end{array}
$$

Exercise B Use the chart above to find each premium.

1. married employee
with three children
_____ a week

2. single employee
_____ a year

3. single employee
_____ a month

4. married employee
without children
_____ a year

5. married employee
with one child
_____ a month

6. married employee
with five children
_____ a month

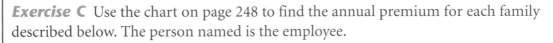

Exercise **C** Use the chart on page 248 to find the annual premium for each family described below. The person named is the employee.

1. Joe Kassa is married and has a two-year-old son. How much is Joe's annual premium?

2. Mary Guthrie has three children. How much is Mary's annual premium for herself and her children?

3. Gail Harrington is single. How much is her annual premium?

4. Louis Kohn provides coverage for himself and his wife. How much is Louis's annual premium?

5. Henry Jones is married with six children living at home. How much is Henry's annual premium if he purchases insurance for himself and his family?

Try This

An employee needs to have some X rays taken. The total cost for the X rays is $743.22, and the employee's health insurance will pay 80% of the cost. How much will the health insurance pay? How much will the employee have to pay?

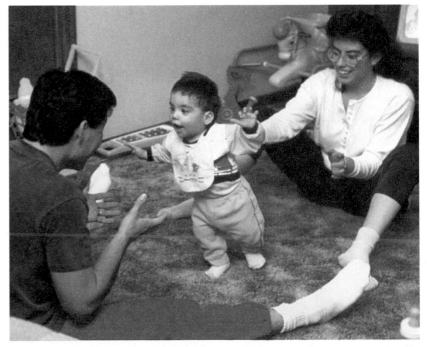

It is important to have a good health insurance plan when raising a family.

Unit count

A way to determine a house's size for insurance purposes

Fixture

Toilet, sink, bathtub, or shower

Most families insure their homes against possible loss by buying insurance. If the house should be damaged by fire or severe weather, then the insurance company pays for the damages up to the amount of the insurance coverage. Most homeowners insure their homes for the full value of the house plus its contents. The first step in determining how much a house is worth is to do a **unit count** for the house.

Count 1 for Each Unit Below:	Count $\frac{1}{2}$ for Each Unit Below:
Kitchen	Half Bathroom (1 or 2 fixtures)
Dining Room	One-Car Garage
Living Room	Dinette
Bedroom	Breakfast Nook
Bathroom (3 or more **fixtures**)	Unfinished Basement
Den or Study	Unfinished Attic
Family Room	Enclosed Porch
Utility Room	Fireplace
Finished Attic	
Finished Basement	
Two-Car Garage	
Central Air-Conditioning	

Technology Connection

It can be very difficult for insurance agents to keep track of all of their clients. As in many other professions, insurance agents use technology to help them do a better job. Talk to an insurance agent. Your parents or someone else in your family may have an insurance agent. Ask the agent how technology makes his or her job easier. Ask the agent to show you how he or she uses computers to write insurance policies and file claims. How do different forms of wireless technology help insurance agents when they are out of the office?

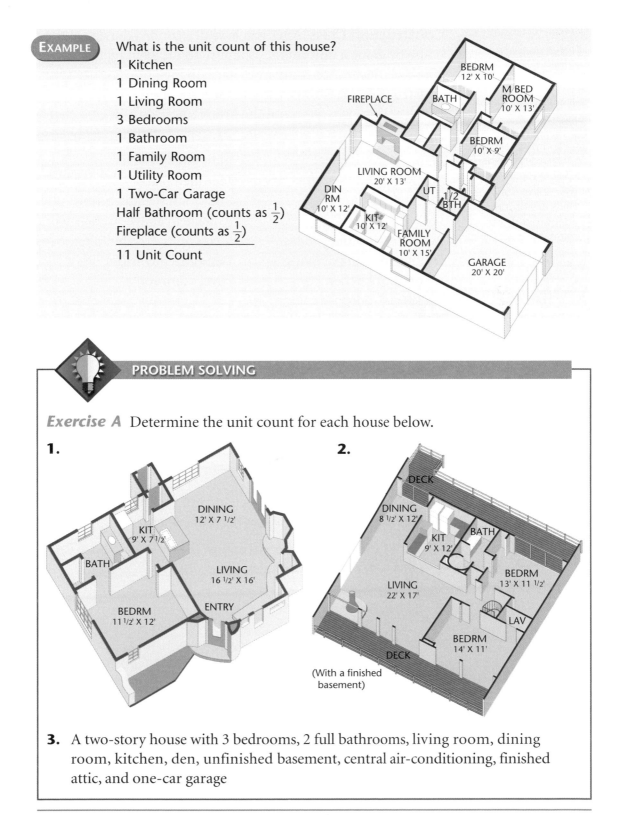

EXAMPLE What is the unit count of this house?

1 Kitchen
1 Dining Room
1 Living Room
3 Bedrooms
1 Bathroom
1 Family Room
1 Utility Room
1 Two-Car Garage
Half Bathroom (counts as $\frac{1}{2}$)
Fireplace (counts as $\frac{1}{2}$)
_____
11 Unit Count

BEDRM 12' X 10'
M BED ROOM 10' X 13'
FIREPLACE
BATH
BEDRM 10' X 9'
LIVING ROOM 20' X 13'
DIN RM 10' X 12'
UT
1/2 BTH
KIT 10' X 12'
FAMILY ROOM 10' X 15'
GARAGE 20' X 20'

PROBLEM SOLVING

Exercise A Determine the unit count for each house below.

1.

DINING 12' X 7 1/2'
KIT 9' X 7 1/2'
BATH
LIVING 16 1/2' X 16'
BEDRM 11 1/2' X 12'
ENTRY

2.

DECK
DINING 8 1/2' X 12'
KIT 9' X 12'
BATH
LIVING 22' X 17'
BEDRM 13' X 11 1/2'
LAV
BEDRM 14' X 11'
DECK
(With a finished basement)

3. A two-story house with 3 bedrooms, 2 full bathrooms, living room, dining room, kitchen, den, unfinished basement, central air-conditioning, finished attic, and one-car garage

Construction Class After you have determined the size of the house by doing a unit count, you must decide what type of house you have. Insurance companies have divided houses into four **construction classes**. When you know the unit count and the construction class, you find the house's base cost from a chart.

Class I
Plain design
Stock-type house
Tract-type house
Low cost
Just meets building codes
Dining area part of living
    room or kitchen
No special-purpose rooms

Class III
Individual design
Modified plans
Built for a specific buyer
Average to above-average work
Meets or exceeds building codes
Den or family room
Foyer common

Class II
Simple design
Standard plans
Some ornamentation
Average quality
Meets or exceeds building codes
Dining room
Den or family room

Class IV
One-of-a-kind design
Architect's plans
Above-average work
Exceeds building codes
Unique floor plan
Large rooms and foyer
Many special rooms

Exercise B Use the chart on page 253 to find the base cost of each house. Write your answers on your paper.

	Unit Count	Construction Class	Base Cost
1.	$10\frac{1}{2}$	III	_____
2.	12	II	_____
3.	7	I	_____
4.	13	IV	_____
5.	$14\frac{1}{2}$	IV	_____
6.	$6\frac{1}{2}$	II	_____
7.	11	III	_____

Unit Count	Construction Class			
	I	II	III	IV
6	$40,900	$66,300	$113,400	$180,100
$6\frac{1}{2}$	$42,900	$69,000	$116,000	$184,000
7	$44,100	$70,600	$119,300	$185,700
$7\frac{1}{2}$	$46,200	$73,200	$122,500	$186,900
8	$47,800	$75,100	$124,900	$190,700
$8\frac{1}{2}$	$49,900	$77,700	$128,100	$197,400
9	$51,400	$79,700	$130,500	$200,300
$9\frac{1}{2}$	$53,400	$82,300	$133,700	$204,200
10	$55,500	$85,000	$136,200	$207,000
$10\frac{1}{2}$	$57,700	$87,600	$139,500	$210,800
11	$60,100	$89,500	$141,800	$213,700
$11\frac{1}{2}$	$60,800	$91,600	$144,500	$216,900
12	–	$94,500	$147,400	$220,400
$12\frac{1}{2}$	–	$97,100	$150,700	$224,300
13	–	$99,600	$153,000	$233,700
$13\frac{1}{2}$	–	$102,300	$156,400	$237,700
14	–	$105,000	$158,800	$238,600
$14\frac{1}{2}$	–	$107,600	$162,100	$239,700

Replacement cost

The cost to replace insured property

Location multiplier

A chart that helps determine a house's replacement cost, based on its ZIP code location

Make sure you put the decimal point in the correct place in the product after you multiply.

Replacement Cost Once you know the base cost of a home, you can find the house's **replacement cost** by using a **location multiplier**. A location multiplier is used because the same house can be built for different prices in different areas. The cost of labor and materials varies from location to location. Insurance companies have researched these differences in building costs and organized their findings by ZIP codes.

EXAMPLE A house of construction class III has a unit count of 11. The ZIP code is 46512. What is its replacement cost?

From the chart: Unit count is 11.
Class III
Base cost = $141,800
ZIP code is 46512
Location multiplier = 1.04

$$\begin{array}{r} \$ \quad 141{,}8\,00 \\ \times \qquad 1.04 \\ \hline 5\,672\,00 \\ +141\,800\,00 \\ \hline \$\,147{,}472.00 \end{array}$$

The replacement cost is $147,472.

Location by First 3 Digits of ZIP Code					
State and ZIP Code	Location Multiplier	State and ZIP Code	Location Multiplier	State and ZIP Code	Location Multiplier
Kentucky		Ohio		Indiana	
400–402	1.02	430–433	1.06	460–462	1.06
403–405	1.02	434, 436	1.16	463–464	1.09
406–410	1.01	435	1.12	465–466	1.04
411–422	0.99	437–439	1.04	467–468	1.01
423–424	1.01	440–443	1.10	469, 478–479	0.96
425–427	0.97	444–450	1.08	470–475	1.05
		451–455, 458	1.07	476–477	1.03
		456–457	1.14		

Exercise C Use the ZIP code chart on page 254 and the construction class chart on page 253 to help you find the replacement cost of each home. Write your answers on your paper.

	Unit Count	Class	ZIP Code	Replacement Cost
1.	12	II	42416	_____
2.	$13\frac{1}{2}$	III	46307	_____
3.	10	I	44321	_____
4.	$7\frac{1}{2}$	I	43516	_____
5.	$12\frac{1}{2}$	IV	45624	_____
6.	12	II	46602	_____
7.	$12\frac{1}{2}$	III	47933	_____
8.	9	II	42620	_____
9.	$13\frac{1}{2}$	IV	43414	_____
10.	6	I	41607	_____
11.	$8\frac{1}{2}$	IV	46401	_____
12.	$11\frac{1}{2}$	III	47221	_____

Calculator Practice

Insurance premiums are often given as an annual rate. You may have to budget your earnings to make your annual payment.

Calculator Exercise Use a calculator to help you divide the annual payments by 52 paychecks. Round the payments to the nearest cent.

1.	$385	**7.**	$201.34
2.	$272	**8.**	$89.90
3.	$776.80	**9.**	$149.50
4.	$105	**10.**	$200
5.	$125	**11.**	$136.75
6.	$603	**12.**	$492.50

When multiplying
money, round the
product to the
nearest cent.

After you find the replacement cost of your home, you can
then determine how much insurance to buy. Many people
insure their homes for replacement cost plus the value of the
items in the home. Insurance is also available for people who
live in apartments. The amount of money paid for insurance
is called the premium. The amount of insurance protection
is called the **face value** of the policy. The premium is found
by multiplying the rate per $100 by the number of 100s in the
face value of the policy. The rate per $100 varies according to
the type of policy.

EXAMPLE   Face value: $82,600
Rate per $100 $0.74
There are 826 hundreds in $82,600.

$$\begin{array}{r} 826 \\ \times\ \$\ .74 \\ \hline \$611.24 \end{array}$$

The yearly premium is $611.24.

*House fires are tragic. You can protect your house and belongings with
fire insurance.*

Exercise A Find the yearly premium for each fire insurance policy. Write your answers on your paper.

Face Value	Rate per $100	Yearly Premium
1. $52,300	$0.96	_____
2. $20,700	$0.73	_____
3. $38,000	$0.84	_____
4. $71,450	$0.88	_____
5. $46,700	$0.92	_____
6. $56,700	$0.80	_____
7. $48,800	$0.92	_____
8. $67,500	$0.93	_____
9. $46,730	$0.87	_____
10. $79,400	$0.96	_____
11. $71,120	$0.78	_____
12. $86,200	$0.99	_____
13. $120,300	$0.88	_____
14. $55,890	$0.80	_____
15. $47,000	$1.04	_____
16. $200,000	$0.82	_____
17. $77,340	$0.70	_____
18. $99,940	$0.95	_____
19. $80,000	$0.91	_____
20. $104,000	$0.89	_____

Liability

Insurance that protects
the owner against
claims resulting from
an accident

Auto liability insurance protects the owner of a car against
claims arising from his or her car being involved in an accident.
Liability insurance can cover both bodily injury and property
damage. The premium that you pay for this protection, or
coverage, is determined by the amount of protection and the
region in which you live.

Coverage for a 50/100/25 Policy

Maximum
of $50,000
for claim per
injured person ⟶ **50/100/25** ⟵ damage

Maximum
of $25,000
for property

Maximum of $100,000 for
claim per accident

	Bodily Injury				Property Damage		
Region	**10/20**	**20/40**	**25/50**	**50/100**	**5,000**	**10,000**	**25,000**
1	$101	$139	$152	$182	$68	$71	$73
2	$59	$81	$89	$106	$52	$55	$56
3	$50	$69	$75	$90	$56	$59	$60
4	$40	$55	$60	$72	$48	$50	$52
5	$53	$73	$80	$95	$47	$49	$51

Liability Insurance Rates

Charts can sometimes be confusing. Read the chart on page 258 carefully to make sure you get the correct information.

Try This

Joseph buys his first car. He lives in Region 2, and he wants the 50/100/5 coverage. He gets a 20% discount for being a good student. How much is the premium he pays?

EXAMPLE Mr. Tanaka lives in Region 2. His coverage is 25/50/25. Using the chart, his premium is $89 plus $56, or $145.

Exercise A Use the chart on page 258 to determine the amount of the basic premium for each liability insurance policy. Write your answers on your paper.

	Coverage	Region	Premium
1.	20/40/5	4	_____
2.	20/40/25	1	_____
3.	20/40/10	3	_____
4.	25/50/10	2	_____
5.	10/20/10	5	_____
6.	20/40/25	3	_____
7.	50/100/25	3	_____
8.	20/40/5	2	_____
9.	50/100/10	1	_____
10.	10/20/10	3	_____
11.	10/20/25	4	_____
12.	25/50/25	2	_____
13.	10/20/5	4	_____
14.	20/40/5	3	_____
15.	50/100/25	1	_____
16.	20/40/25	5	_____
17.	50/100/5	2	_____
18.	10/20/10	4	_____

Rate factor

---

*An amount by which
the basic premium is
multiplied*

Once the auto insurance agent has determined the basic premium for auto liability insurance coverage, the agent consults a **rate factor** table. Women pay less than men for the same insurance coverage. People pay less for insurance if they drive the car for pleasure or farm use than if they drive the car to work each day. Owners pay more if they use their car for business.

Age of Driver	Gender	Pleasure Use	Drives Less Than 10 mi to Work	Drives 10 mi or More to Work	Car Used for Work	Farm Use
17	M	1.80	1.90	2.20	2.30	1.55
	F	1.55	1.65	1.95	2.05	1.30
18	M	1.70	1.80	2.10	2.20	1.45
	F	1.40	1.50	1.80	1.90	1.15
19	M	1.60	1.70	2.00	2.10	1.35
	F	1.25	1.35	1.65	1.75	1.00
20	M	1.50	1.60	1.90	2.00	1.25
	F	1.10	1.20	1.50	1.60	0.85

Rate Factor Table

If you have a car accident, liability insurance pays for car repairs. It also lowers your medical costs if you are injured.

EXAMPLE Sara and Lito both have a basic insurance premium of $153. Each is 19 years old and drives 8 miles to work. Sara's premium is $206.55 ($153 × 1.35). Lito's premium is $260.10 ($153 × 1.70).

PROBLEM SOLVING

Exercise B Find each person's insurance premium by multiplying the basic premium by the appropriate factor from the table on page 260.

1. Heidi is 17 years old. She drives 6 miles to work. Her basic premium is $135.

2. Michael's basic premium is $128. He uses the car only on the farm. He is 17 years old.

3. Gene is 18 years old. His basic premium is $208. He uses the car only for pleasure.

4. Basamih is 20 years old. Her basic premium is $147. She drives 16 miles to work.

5. Rudy drives 8 miles to work. He is 19 years old. His basic premium is $183.

6. Ricardo is 20 years old. He uses the car in his work. His basic premium is $236.

7. Angela is 18 years old. She drives 10 miles to work. Her basic premium is $188.

8. Ronny drives 9 miles to work. He is 20 years old. His basic premium is $306.

9. Ming is 17 years old. He uses his car for pleasure. His basic premium is $294.

10. Sheila is 19 years old. She drives 14 miles to work. Her basic premium is $289.

Try This

Stone and Sandra are twins. They are 17 years old, and they both use their cars for pleasure. Their basic premiums are $281.00. Sandra gets an 11% discount for good grades, and Stone gets a 15% discount for having a good driving record. How much is Sandra's premium? How much is Stone's premium?

People buy life insurance to protect the dependents of the insured person. If the insured person dies, the person's **beneficiary** is paid the face value of the life insurance policy. A person can buy different kinds of life insurance. The four basic kinds of life insurance are:

1. **Term Insurance.** Premiums are paid only for a certain time. The policyholder is insured only during the stated time. Benefits are paid only if the policyholder dies during the term of insurance.

2. **Ordinary Life Insurance.** Premiums are paid until the policyholder dies. When the policyholder dies, the beneficiary is paid the face value of the policy.

3. **Limited-Payment Life Insurance.** The policyholder is insured until death. Premiums are paid for a limited period of time (20 or 30 years, usually). This is also called 20-payment or 30-payment life insurance.

4. **Endowment Insurance.** The policyholder pays premiums for a limited period of time (20 or 30 years, usually). At the end of this period of time, the policyholder is paid the face value of the policy. If the policyholder dies during the payment period, then the beneficiary is paid the face value of the policy.

Beneficiary

A person who receives the face value of an insurance policy

Term insurance

Insurance where payments and insurance last for a fixed amount of time

Ordinary life insurance

Insurance where payments are made as long as the insured is alive

Limited-payment life insurance

Insurance that covers the policyholder until death

Endowment insurance

Insurance where premium is paid and face value is paid to the insured

The premiums are the lowest for term insurance. Ordinary life insurance costs more. Limited-payment insurance is more expensive. The most expensive insurance is endowment insurance.

Many families think about their life insurance needs after a baby is born. They want to make sure their child's needs will be met.

Annual premiums are based not only on the kind of insurance people buy. The face value of the policy raises or lowers the cost. People's age, health, or the work they do may change the premiums. Single people often pay higher annual premiums for car insurance than married people do. However, married people with children usually pay higher health insurance annual premiums than single people do.

Tables are one tool to help insurance companies decide how much premiums will be. The premium tables on the next page show costs based on a policyholder's age. They show that the type of insurance changes how much a person pays.

Here are some premium tables for the four types of life insurance:

Annual Premium per $1,000 of Term Insurance						
Age			5-Year Term Policy		10-Year Term Policy	
Male	Female		$5,000– $9,999	$10,000– $19,999	$5,000– $9,999	$10,000– $19,999
20	23		$6.44	$5.69	$6.51	$5.76
25	28		$6.59	$5.84	$6.72	$5.97
30	33		$6.88	$6.13	$7.19	$6.44
35	38		$7.56	$6.81	$8.27	$7.52
40	43		$9.11	$8.36	$10.24	$9.49
45	48		$11.60	$10.85	$13.43	$12.68
50	53		$15.66	$14.91	$18.47	$17.72
55	58		$21.95	$21.20	$26.28	$25.53
60	63		$31.80	$31.05	$38.40	$37.65

Annual Life Insurance Premium Rates per $1,000							
Age		Ordinary Life		20-Payment Life		20-Year Endowment	
Male	Female	$5,000– $9,999	$10,000– $19,999	$5,000– $9,999	$10,000– $19,999	$5,000– $9,999	$10,000– $19,999
20	23	$15.07	$14.32	$22.90	$22.15	$46.70	$45.95
25	28	$17.08	$16.33	$25.43	$24.68	$46.93	$46.18
30	33	$19.63	$18.88	$28.42	$27.67	$47.36	$46.61
35	38	$22.94	$22.19	$32.02	$31.27	$48.19	$47.44
40	43	$27.25	$26.50	$36.40	$35.65	$49.66	$48.91
45	48	$32.85	$32.10	$41.72	$40.97	$52.01	$51.26
50	53	$40.23	$39.48	$48.33	$47.58	$55.76	$55.01
55	58	$49.93	$49.18	$56.64	$55.89	$61.64	$60.89
60	63	$62.47	$61.72	$67.70	$66.85	$70.59	$69.84

EXAMPLE   What is the annual premium for a 38-year-old
woman if she buys $15,000 of 20-payment life
insurance?

From the chart: Rate per $1,000 = $31.27
Number of 1,000s in $15,000 = 15

$ 31.27
×   15
$469.05   Annual premium

You can see from the premium tables that gender affects the cost
of insurance. Also, the older you are when you buy insurance,
the more you pay.

To determine the annual premium, find the type of insurance
in the charts, find the correct age and gender, and read the rate
per $1,000 of face value. You multiply this rate by the number
of 1,000s in the face value of the policy.

Exercise A Find the annual premium for each life insurance
policy below. Use the tables on page 264 to help you.

1. 45-year-old man, $10,000
   5-year term policy

2. 48-year-old woman, $14,000
   20-payment life policy

3. 40-year-old man, $6,000
   ordinary life policy

4. 58-year-old woman, $14,000
   10-year term policy

5. 33-year-old woman, $15,000
   20-year endowment policy

6. 20-year-old man, $17,000
   20-year endowment policy

7. 40-year-old man, $19,000
   20-payment life policy

8. 50-year-old man, $16,000
   10-year term policy

9. 50-year-old man, $13,000
   ordinary life policy

10. 28-year-old woman, $17,000
    20-year endowment policy

11. 38-year-old woman, $9,000
    ordinary life policy

12. 30-year-old man, $8,900
    10-year term policy

Health Insurance Premiums

Jorge just got a new job. He needs to choose a health insurance plan for his family from three different plans offered by the company. Plan A has a premium of $127.00 a month. The monthly Plan B premium is $136.00. Plan C has a premium of $146.00 a month. Each plan covers procedures at different rates.

	Percent of Benefit Paid From the First Day of Covered Accidents or Illnesses					
	Plan A		**Plan B**		**Plan C**	
Service	**In Network**	**Out of Network**	**In Network**	**Out of Network**	**In Network**	**Out of Network**
Physical exam	100%	0%	80%	60%	50%	50%
Eye exam	0%	0%	50%	0%	50%	50%
Maternity	100%	0%	80%	60%	80%	80%
Dental exam	100%	0%	80%	60%	80%	60%
Prescriptions	100%	0%	80%	0%	80%	0%

Exercises Use the information above to answer the questions.

1. Jorge's son needs a physical exam for school. Including vaccinations, the exam costs $381. How much of that bill will each health insurance plan pay?

2. For regular dental exams every 6 months, Jorge's family spends $453 a year. How much of that bill will each health insurance plan pay?

3. Jorge's wife takes prescription medication every day that costs $82.15 per month. Which insurance plan provides the best prescription coverage?

4. Jorge's daughter wears glasses. Her annual eye exam costs $75. Plan C plan covers 50% of that cost. How much does Plan C plan cover?

5. Which insurance plan do you think is best for Jorge and his family?

Chapter 15 R E V I E W

Write the letter of the best answer to each question.

1. What is the yearly premium for a fire insurance policy with a face value of $276,000 and a rate of $1.18?

  A $325,680

  B $335,680

  C $335,720

  D $345,720

2. Lauren has a base auto insurance premium of $187, and 1.01 is the factor used to determine her premium. How much is Lauren's premium?

  A $187.00

  B $187.50

  C $188.24

  D $188.87

3. The base cost of a house is $402,000, and the location multiplier is 1.03. What is the house's replacement cost?

  A $412,060

  B $413,060

  C $414,060

  D $415,060

4. Stanley's health insurance premium is $1,296 per year. How much is deducted from his paycheck for health insurance semimonthly?

  A $44

  B $54

  C $64

  D $74

5. Teun pays $72.18 per month for her own health insurance. She pays another $61.74 per month for her family. How much is Teun's health insurance premium for 1 year?

  A $1,600.02

  B $1,607.04

  C $1,608.06

  D $1,610.14

Use this chart to find the annual premium for each family described below. The person named is the employee.

Rest Easy Major Medical Program Semimonthly Payroll Deductions	
Employee	$12.22
Employee and spouse	$14.98
Employee and family	$23.67

6. Ung and his wife and two children

7. Linda and her husband

8. Max Baker

Find the replacement cost for each house.

9. base cost = $48,600; location multiplier = 1.08

10. base cost = $67,400; location multiplier = 0.97

Find the yearly premium for each fire insurance policy.

11. The policy's face value is $52,400. The rate per $100 is $0.96.

12. The policy's face value is $67,000. The rate per $100 is $0.80.

Use this rate chart to find the basic premium for each policy.

Liability Insurance Rates							
	Bodily Injury				Property Damage		
Region	**10/20**	**20/40**	**25/50**	**50/100**	**5,000**	**10,000**	**25,000**
1	$101	$139	$152	$182	$68	$71	$73
2	$59	$81	$89	$106	$52	$55	$56
3	$50	$69	$75	$90	$56	$59	$60
4	$40	$55	$60	$72	$48	$50	$52

13. 20/40/10 coverage; Region 3

14. 25/50/25 coverage; Region 2

Find each person's insurance premium by multiplying the basic premium by the appropriate factor from this chart.

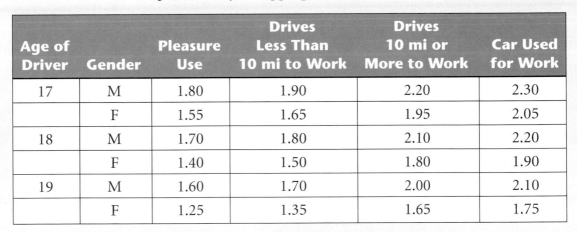

Age of Driver	Gender	Pleasure Use	Drives Less Than 10 mi to Work	Drives 10 mi or More to Work	Car Used for Work
17	M	1.80	1.90	2.20	2.30
	F	1.55	1.65	1.95	2.05
18	M	1.70	1.80	2.10	2.20
	F	1.40	1.50	1.80	1.90
19	M	1.60	1.70	2.00	2.10
	F	1.25	1.35	1.65	1.75

15. Tooky is 18 years old. She drives 12 miles to work. Her basic premium is $165.

16. Mike is 19 years old. He uses his car for pleasure. His basic premium is $147.

17. Denise is 17 years old. She drives 6 miles to work. Her basic premium is $184.

Tell if the life insurance described is *term life, ordinary life, limited-payment life,* or *endowment life* insurance.

18. The policyholder pays premiums for a limited period of time. At the end of this period of time, the policyholder is paid the face value of the policy.

19. The policyholder pays premiums for a limited period of time. The policyholder is insured only during this period.

20. The policyholder pays premiums until death. At death the beneficiary is paid the face value of the policy.

Test-Taking Tip

When studying for a test, review the topics in the chapter. Then make up a practice test for yourself.

16 Lawn Care

Have you ever thought about all the ways you use measurement to make your life run more smoothly? Besides finding your height and weight or adjusting recipes, you can use measurement to help you calculate measurements needed to keep your property attractive. Planting hedges and flower beds, fertilizing lawns and fencing yards, all require measurement and mathematics. Even pouring cement for sidewalks and patios is made easier if you know how to use mathematics to help you.

In Chapter 16, you will find ways to use formulas to help you compute area, perimeter, and volume.

Goals for Learning

◆ To find perimeter and area
◆ To calculate cost for hedging and fencing
◆ To measure to the nearest sixteenth of an inch
◆ To measure to the nearest tenth of a centimeter
◆ To use a ruler to interpret scale drawings
◆ To find volume of rectangular prisms
◆ To calculate cost, using volume and cubic yards

Perimeter

The distance around all the sides of a polygon

One way to enclose your yard is to plant a hedge around its **perimeter**. To find the cost of putting a hedge around the yard, you first add the length of the sides of the area to be enclosed. You then multiply the cost of the hedge per yard by this answer.

Notice from the diagram that a small length of one side will not have a hedge planted on it.

EXAMPLE A hedge costs $4.25 per yard. How much will it cost to plant a hedge around this property?

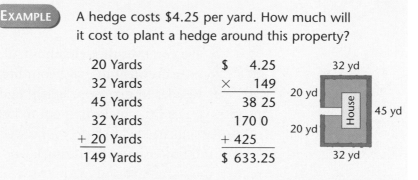

20 Yards	$ 4.25	
32 Yards	× 149	
45 Yards	38 25	
32 Yards	170 0	
+ 20 Yards	+ 425	
149 Yards	$ 633.25	

Length of hedge is 149 yd; cost of hedge is $633.25.

Exercise A Find the cost of planting a hedge along the dark lines for each property. Hedging costs $4.25 per yard. Round to the nearest cent.

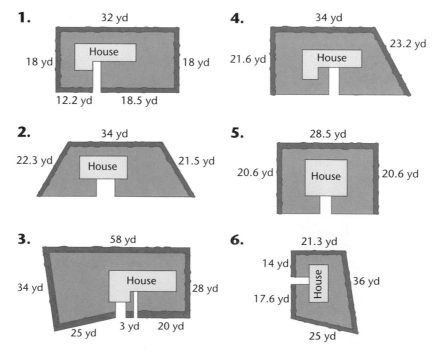

1. 32 yd / House / 18 yd / 18 yd / 12.2 yd / 18.5 yd

4. 34 yd / 23.2 yd / 21.6 yd / House

2. 34 yd / 22.3 yd / House / 21.5 yd

5. 28.5 yd / 20.6 yd / House / 20.6 yd

3. 58 yd / House / 34 yd / 28 yd / 25 yd / 3 yd / 20 yd

6. 21.3 yd / 14 yd / House / 36 yd / 17.6 yd / 25 yd

Writing About Mathematics

Explain how you know there are 36 fence posts in this example.

Another way to enclose your yard is with fencing.

EXAMPLE Find the cost of fencing in this yard. Chain-link fencing costs $7.50 per yard, and fence posts cost $4.25 each. Gates cost $30.25 each.

30 yd

26.4 yd | House | 26.4 yd

Post

11 yd

18.3 yd — Gate

Step 1 Find the length of fence needed.

18.3	Yards
26.4	Yards
30	Yards
26.4	Yards
+ 11	Yards
112.1	Yards

Step 2 Find the cost of fencing.

```
    1 1 2.1
×    $ 7.5 0
    56 0 5 0
+   784 7
  $ 840.7 5 0
```

Step 3 Find the cost of fence posts.

```
$    4.25 Cost per post
×      36 Total posts
     25 50
+   127 5
$ 153.00
```

Step 4 Find the total cost.

```
  $  840.75 Fencing
  $  153.00 Fence posts
+ $   30.25 Gate
  $1,024.00
```

The total cost is $1,024.00

Exercise B Find the total cost of fencing in each yard. Use the prices from the example above.

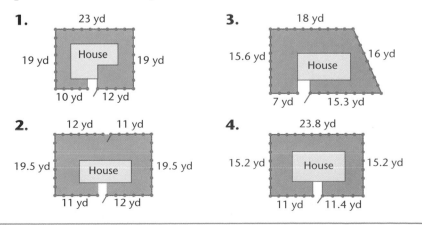

1. 23 yd

19 yd | House | 19 yd

10 yd / 12 yd

2. 12 yd   11 yd

19.5 yd | House | 19.5 yd

11 yd / 12 yd

3. 18 yd

15.6 yd | House | 16 yd

7 yd / 15.3 yd

4. 23.8 yd

15.2 yd | House | 15.2 yd

11 yd / 11.4 yd

| **Line segment** |
| A part of a line |

If you can measure with a ruler, then you will be better able to make plans for your work in the yard. An inch ruler is divided into inches, and each inch can be divided into 16 parts.

EXAMPLE How long is each **line segment** to the nearest sixteenth of an inch?

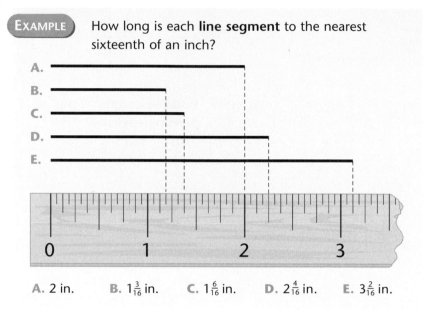

A. 2 in.   B. $1\frac{3}{16}$ in.   C. $1\frac{6}{16}$ in.   D. $2\frac{4}{16}$ in.   E. $3\frac{2}{16}$ in.

Exercise A Use an inch ruler to find the length of each line segment to the nearest sixteenth inch.

You can also measure using a centimeter ruler. Each centimeter can be divided into 10 units.

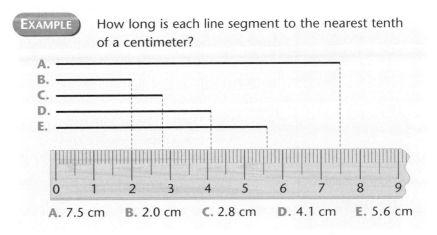

EXAMPLE   How long is each line segment to the nearest tenth of a centimeter?

A. 7.5 cm   B. 2.0 cm   C. 2.8 cm   D. 4.1 cm   E. 5.6 cm

Exercise B Use a centimeter ruler to find the length of each line segment to the nearest tenth of a centimeter.

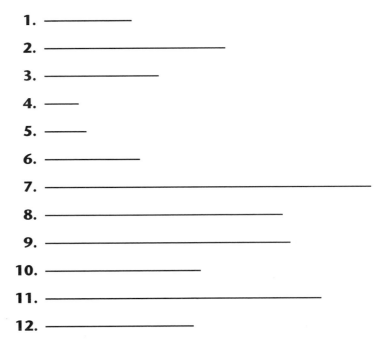

1. ────────

2. ──────────────

3. ──────────

4. ──

5. ──

6. ──────────

7. ────────────────────────

8. ────────────────

9. ──────────────────

10. ────────────

11. ──────────────────────

12. ────────────

Scale drawing

A picture that shows relative sizes of real objects

Scale

Ratio of the map size to the true size of an object or area

Writing About Mathematics

Explain why the scale $\frac{8}{16}$ in. = 16 ft is the same as $\frac{1}{16}$ in. = 2 ft.

When Denise plans her spring yard work, she makes this **scale drawing**. The **scale** at the bottom of the drawing means that $\frac{1}{16}$ inch equals 2 feet in the actual yard. Now Denise can make her plans without being outside in the yard.

EXAMPLE What is the actual length of the lot?
Use a tape measure and measure 92 sixteenths.

$$\frac{1}{2 \text{ feet}} = \frac{92}{\blacksquare} \longleftarrow \text{Number of sixteenths}$$

$$2 \times 92 = \blacksquare$$

$$184 = \blacksquare$$

The lot is 184 feet long.

Exercise A Find these dimensions of the actual lot.

The length of the:
1. house _____
2. garage _____
3. driveway _____
4. sidewalk _____
5. patio _____
6. garden _____

The width of the:
7. lot _____
8. garden _____
9. driveway _____
10. patio _____
11. house _____
12. sidewalk _____

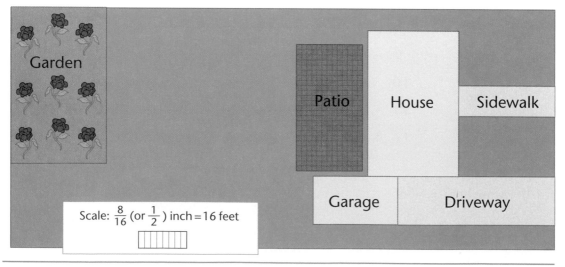

Scale: $\frac{8}{16}$ (or $\frac{1}{2}$) inch = 16 feet

Scales can be shown using metric lengths.

 EXAMPLE What is the actual length of the house?

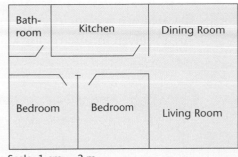

Bath-room	Kitchen		Dining Room
Bedroom	Bedroom		Living Room

Scale: 1 cm = 2 m

Use a ruler to measure 6 cm.

$$\frac{1}{2} = \frac{6}{\blacksquare}$$

$$2 \times 6 = \blacksquare$$

$$12 = \blacksquare$$

The house is 12 meters long.

Exercise B Find these dimensions of the actual lot.

The length of the:

1. house _____

2. lot _____

3. driveway _____

4. sidewalk _____

5. patio _____

The width of the:

6. garage _____

7. tool shed _____

8. driveway _____

9. patio _____

10. house _____

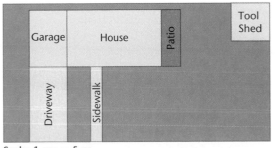

Scale: 1 cm = 5 m

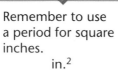

Lesson 4   Area

Remember to use a period for square inches.

in.²

If a shape is irregular, you can divide it into two or more rectangles and find the area of each.

Some yard work requires knowing the area of the yard. To find the area of a rectangle, you can multiply the length by the width. Area is given in square units, like square inches (in.²) or square meters (m²).

EXAMPLE   Find the area of these rectangles:

A.
$$
\begin{array}{r}
17 \\
\times\ 9 \\
\hline
153
\end{array}\ \text{in.}^2
$$

9 in.

17 in.

B.
$$
\begin{array}{r}
16 \\
\times\ 8 \\
\hline
128
\end{array}\ \text{m}^2
$$

$$
\begin{array}{r}
12 \\
\times\ 7 \\
\hline
84
\end{array}\ \text{m}^2
$$

$$
\begin{array}{r}
128 \\
+\ 84 \\
\hline
212
\end{array}\ \begin{array}{l}\text{m}^2 \\ \text{m}^2 \\ \text{m}^2\end{array}
$$

16 m   12 m

9 m

8 m

Writing About Mathematics

Explain how you know that the width of the second rectangle in Example B is 7 m.

Exercise A Find the area of each shape.

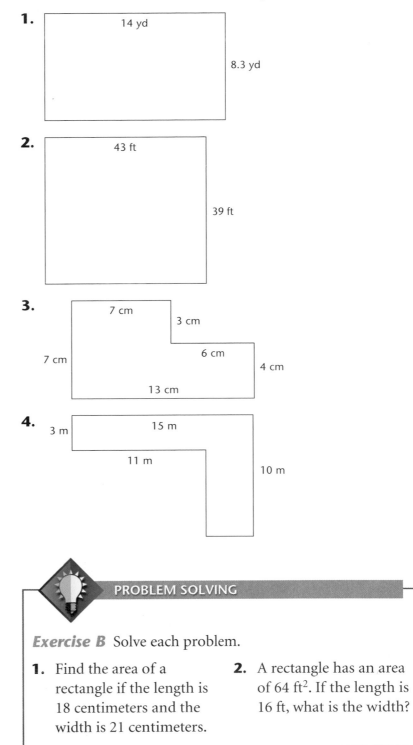

1.

14 yd

8.3 yd

2.

43 ft

39 ft

3.

7 cm

3 cm

7 cm

6 cm

4 cm

13 cm

4.

3 m

15 m

11 m

10 m

PROBLEM SOLVING

Exercise B Solve each problem.

1. Find the area of a rectangle if the length is 18 centimeters and the width is 21 centimeters.

2. A rectangle has an area of 64 ft². If the length is 16 ft, what is the width?

Many people apply fertilizer to their lawn to make the grass healthier. If you apply too much, then it may kill the grass. For best results, you should use 5 pounds of fertilizer per 200 square feet of lawn. To find the number of square feet of lawn, follow these steps:

Step 1 Find the total area of the lot.

Step 2 Find the area of any places that are not to be fertilized.

Step 3 Subtract to find the area of the lawn.

Step 4 Divide by 200 to find the number of 5-pound bags of fertilizer needed. If necessary, round up to the next whole number.

EXAMPLE   Find the amount of fertilizer needed for this lawn.

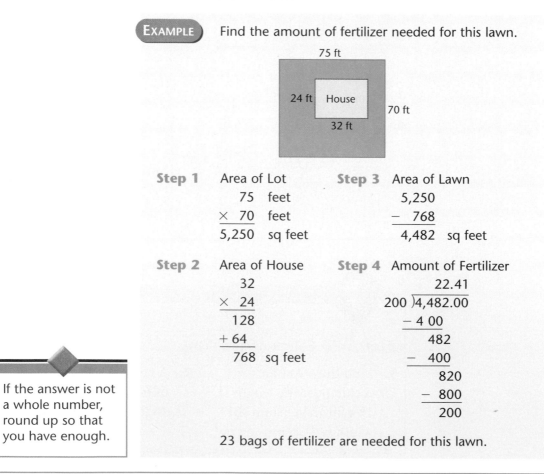

Step 1	Area of Lot	Step 3	Area of Lawn
	75 feet		5,250
	× 70 feet		− 768
	5,250 sq feet		4,482 sq feet

Step 2	Area of House	Step 4	Amount of Fertilizer
	32		22.41
	× 24		200)4,482.00
	128		− 4 00
	+ 64		482
	768 sq feet		− 400
			820
			− 800
			200

If the answer is not a whole number, round up so that you have enough.

23 bags of fertilizer are needed for this lawn.

You should spread fertilizer evenly on your lawn for best results.

Exercise A Find the amount of fertilizer that you need to fertilize the shaded area of each lot.

1.

90 ft

28 ft

14 ft | House

40 ft

3.

70 ft

75 ft

35 ft

House | 20 ft

2.

150 ft

90 ft

28 ft | House

40 ft

4.

135 ft

120 ft

House | 45 ft

60 ft

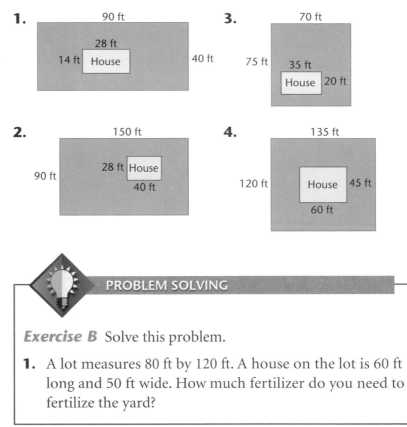

PROBLEM SOLVING

Exercise B Solve this problem.

1. A lot measures 80 ft by 120 ft. A house on the lot is 60 ft long and 50 ft wide. How much fertilizer do you need to fertilize the yard?

Volume

The amount of space occupied in three dimensions

Cubic

Measurement related to volume

Rectangular prism

A solid figure with bases or ends that are parallel and sides that are rectangles

For some jobs and tasks, you need to know the **volume** of a container. Volume is given in **cubic** units, like cubic feet (ft^3) or cubic meters (m^3). You can find the volume of a **rectangular prism** by multiplying the length by the width by the height, or depth.

EXAMPLE

Length = 4 yd
Width = 2 yd
Height = 3 yd
Volume = $l \times w \times h$
= $4 \times 2 \times 3$
= 24 yd^3

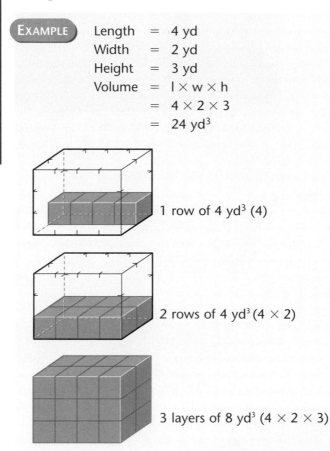

1 row of 4 yd^3 (4)

2 rows of 4 yd^3 (4 × 2)

3 layers of 8 yd^3 (4 × 2 × 3)

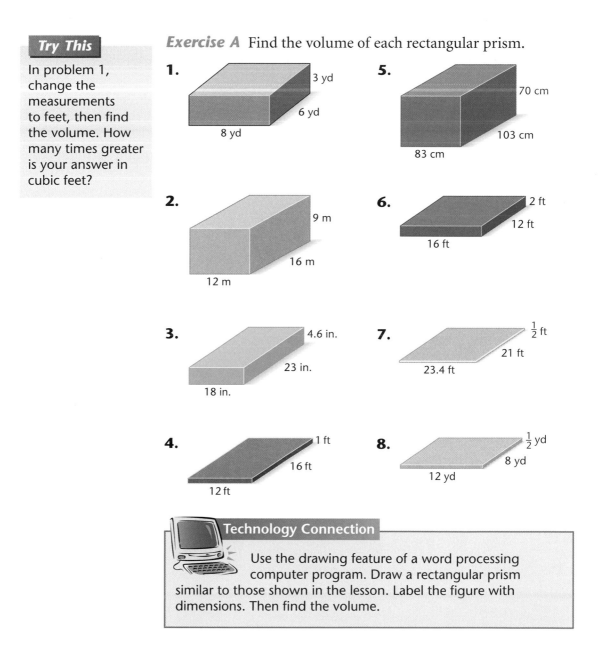

Try This

In problem 1, change the measurements to feet, then find the volume. How many times greater is your answer in cubic feet?

Exercise A Find the volume of each rectangular prism.

1.

3 yd

6 yd

8 yd

2.

9 m

16 m

12 m

3.

4.6 in.

23 in.

18 in.

4.

1 ft

16 ft

12 ft

5.

70 cm

103 cm

83 cm

6.

2 ft

12 ft

16 ft

7.

½ ft

21 ft

23.4 ft

8.

½ yd

8 yd

12 yd

Technology Connection

Use the drawing feature of a word processing computer program. Draw a rectangular prism similar to those shown in the lesson. Label the figure with dimensions. Then find the volume.

You might pour concrete in some yard projects, such as installing a patio or replacing a driveway or sidewalk. Concrete is ordered by the cubic yard. You can find the number of cubic yards of concrete that you will need by finding the volume of the space that the concrete will fill.

EXAMPLE How much concrete will you need to replace a sidewalk that is 20 yards long and 3 yards wide? The sidewalk is to be 3 inches thick. Round up to the next higher whole number. Express 3 inches as part of a yard.

$$\frac{\text{inches}}{\text{yard}} \quad \frac{3}{36} = \frac{1}{12}$$

$$V = l \times w \times h$$
$$V = 20 \times 3 \times \frac{1}{12}$$
$$V = 5$$

You need 5 cubic yards of concrete.

Exercise A Find the amount of concrete needed for each project. Assume that 3 inches is to be the thickness.

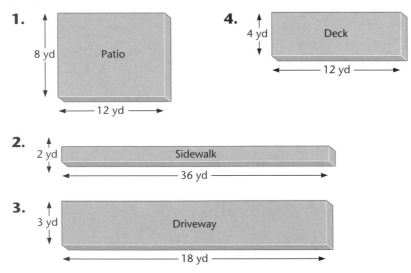

1. 8 yd — Patio — 12 yd

4. 4 yd — Deck — 12 yd

2. 2 yd — Sidewalk — 36 yd

3. 3 yd — Driveway — 18 yd

Exercise B Find the cost of the concrete needed for these projects if concrete costs $80 per cubic yard. Do not round your answers.

	Project	Dimensions	Amount of Concrete	Amount of Concrete
1.	Driveway	$3 \times 48 \times \frac{1}{12}$	_____	_____
2.	Patio	$4 \times 6 \times \frac{1}{12}$	_____	_____
3.	Sidewalk	$1 \times 12 \times 0.1$	_____	_____
4.	Wall	$14 \times 21 \times 0.2$	_____	_____
5.	Deck	$6 \times 5 \times \frac{1}{12}$	_____	_____

Calculator Practice

You can use a calculator to help you solve proportion problems.

EXAMPLE $\frac{15}{\blacksquare} = \frac{3}{45}$

Step 1 Find the cross products.

Step 2 $15 \boxed{\times} 45 \boxed{=} 675$. While 675 is still on the display, press $\boxed{\div} 3$.

$675 \div 3 = 225$

$$\frac{15}{\blacksquare} \underset{\nearrow}{\overset{\searrow}{\times}} \frac{3}{45}$$

$\blacksquare \times 3 = 15 \times 45$

$\blacksquare = \dfrac{15 \times 45}{3}$

$\blacksquare = 225$

Calculator Exercise Use a calculator to help you solve these proportions.

1. $\dfrac{5}{16} = \dfrac{\blacksquare}{256}$

2. $\dfrac{7}{28} = \dfrac{\blacksquare}{308}$

3. $\dfrac{\blacksquare}{16} = \dfrac{7}{56}$

4. $\dfrac{\blacksquare}{576} = \dfrac{7}{18}$

Maximizing Winnings

You've just won a contest! The prize is as many dimes as you can fit in a box. The only catch is that you must build the box. The length plus the width plus the height of the box must add up to 30 inches.

EXAMPLE   Let the length = 2 inches, the width = 4 inches, and the height = 24 inches.

length + width + height = 2 + 4 + 24 = 30

volume = 2 × 4 × 24 = 192 in.^{3}

Exercises Answer the following questions.

1. Why would you want to find a box with the greatest volume?

2. Try using 5 inches, 5 inches, and 20 inches. Does the sum equal 30 inches? What is the volume?

3. Try using 6 inches, 8 inches, and 16 inches. Does the sum equal 30 inches? What is the volume?

4. Try using 7 inches, 10 inches, and 13 inches. Does the sum equal 30 inches? What is the volume?

5. Look at the answers for the example and questions 2–4. What do you notice about the volumes? What do you notice about the three dimensions you are using?

6. What dimensions do you think will give the greatest volume in this contest? What is the greatest volume?

Chapter 16 REVIEW

Write the letter of the best answer to each question.

1. What is the perimeter of the shape?

A   26 ft
B   40 ft
C   60 ft
D   216 ft

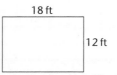

18 ft

12 ft

2. What is the cost of planting a hedge along the dark line of the property? Hedging costs $5.10 per yard.

A $98.00
B $397.80
C $561.00
D $4,998.00

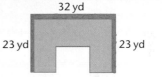

32 yd

23 yd   23 yd

3. A scale used in a drawing is $\frac{4}{16}$ inch = 2 feet. If a line in the scale drawing measures $\frac{12}{16}$ inch, what is the actual length?

A   6 ft
B   10 ft
C   16 ft
D   32 ft

4. Find the area of the shape.

A   70 m²
B   96 m²
C   166 m²
D   180 m²

8 m
2 m
7 m
10 m   12 m
15 m

5. What is the number of bags of fertilizer you will need to fertilize the area of the lawn? You need one 5-lb bag of fertilizer per 200 square feet.

A   19 bags
B   71 bags
C   72 bags
D   90 bags

150 ft
75 ft
120 ft   House   50 ft

Find the perimeter of each shape.

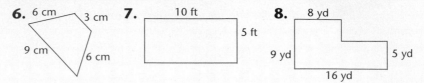

6. 6 cm   3 cm   9 cm   6 cm

7. 10 ft   5 ft

8. 8 yd   9 yd   5 yd   16 yd

Find the cost of planting a hedge along the dark lines for each property. Hedging costs $4.38 per yard.

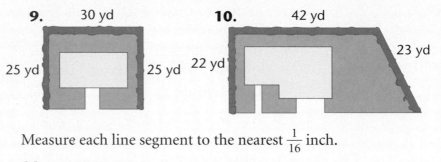

9. 30 yd   25 yd   25 yd

10. 42 yd   23 yd   22 yd

Measure each line segment to the nearest $\frac{1}{16}$ inch.

11. _____

12. _____

Use a ruler and this scale drawing of a yard to help you answer the following questions.

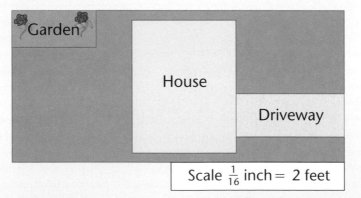

Garden

House

Driveway

Scale $\frac{1}{16}$ inch = 2 feet

13. What is the width of the garden?

14. What is the length of the driveway?

15. What is the width of the house?

16. What is the length of the garden?

Find the area of each shape.

17.
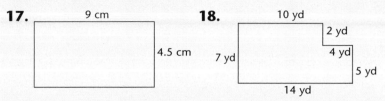
9 cm

4.5 cm

18.
10 yd

2 yd

7 yd

4 yd

5 yd

14 yd

Find the number of bags of fertilizer needed to fertilize the shaded area of each lot. You need one 5-pound bag of fertilizer per 200 square feet.

19.
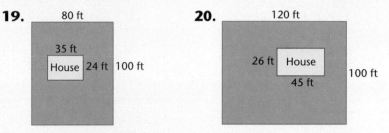
80 ft

35 ft

House | 24 ft | 100 ft

20.
120 ft

26 ft | House

45 ft

100 ft

Find the volume of each rectangular prism.

21.
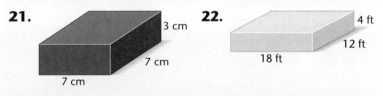
3 cm

7 cm

7 cm

22.
4 ft

12 ft

18 ft

Find the cost of the concrete that you will need for these projects if concrete costs $80 per cubic yard.

23. Sidewalk: 1 yd × 10 yd × 0.1 yd

24. Driveway: 4 yd × 20 yd × 0.16 yd

25. Patio: 5 yd × 8 yd × 0.1 yd

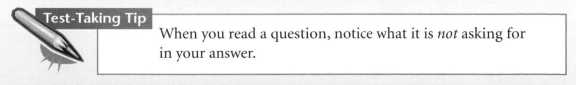

Test-Taking Tip

When you read a question, notice what it is *not* asking for in your answer.

17 Using Energy

Computers have changed the way many businesses operate. Businesses can use computers to help calculate costs, issue bills for customers, even allow customers to pay by phone. However, there is still at least one job in many cities that computers do not do. Take a guess what that job is. It is the job of a meter reader. These employees still drive and visit apartments, houses, and other buildings to read water, gas, or electric meters. The numbers the meter reader records tell the company how much of something a customer has used. Contact your local water, gas, or electric company to find how to read the meters in your home.

In Chapter 17, you will learn more about reading meters and calculating the costs of energy products such as gas.

Goals for Learning

- ◆ To read a meter dial
- ◆ To convert from hours of use to kilowatt-hours
- ◆ To find the amount of savings with different wattage bulbs
- ◆ To convert gas readings to hundreds of cubic feet
- ◆ To convert from Celsius to Fahrenheit, and from Fahrenheit to Celsius

Kilowatt

A unit of electrical power equal to 1,000 watts

Watt

A unit of electrical power

The amount of electricity a household uses is measured in **kilowatts.** However, light bulbs and electrical appliances are labeled to show their power requirements in **watts.** You need to be able to convert watts to kilowatts to understand your electric bill. *Kilo-* means "one thousand." A kilowatt is 1,000 watts. The abbreviation for kilowatt is kW.

EXAMPLE   How many kilowatts do 4,000 watts equal? To convert watts to kilowatts, divide the watts by 1,000.

$$\begin{array}{r} 4 \\ 1{,}000 \overline{)\,4{,}000} \\ \underline{4{,}000} \\ 0 \end{array}$$

4,000 watts = 4 kilowatts or 4 kW

There is an easier way to convert watts to kilowatts. Just move the decimal point three places to the left.

EXAMPLES   2,890 watts = 2.890 kilowatts or 2.890 kW

36 watts = 0.036 kilowatts or 0.036 kW

Moving a decimal point three places to the left can be confusing if there are not enough digits. Put a zero in each place where there is no digit.

Electricity travels to your home from large power plants.

Exercise A Convert these watts to kilowatts.

1. 2,000 watts	**11.** 39 watts
2. 1,500 watts	**12.** 58 watts
3. 3,500 watts	**13.** 80 watts
4. 4,000 watts	**14.** 29 watts
5. 2,300 watts	**15.** 64 watts
6. 1,600 watts	**16.** 913 watts
7. 3,800 watts	**17.** 51 watts
8. 92,000 watts	**18.** 12.3 watts
9. 5,305 watts	**19.** 2.63 watts
10. 60,000 watts	**20.** 75 watts

Electric companies bill their customers for the kilowatt-hours of electricity they use. You can estimate the watt-hours of electricity used. The abbreviation for watt-hours is whr.

EXAMPLES A 100-watt bulb that burns for 2 hours uses 200 watt-hours of electricity (100 watts × 2 hours = 200 watt-hours).

Two 100-watt bulbs that burn for 1 hour use 200 watt-hours of electricity (200 watts × 1 hour = 200 watt-hours).

On the other hand, three 100-watt bulbs that burn for 8 hours use 2,400 watt-hours of electricity (300 watts × 8 hours = 2,400 watt-hours).

Number of Watts × Number of Hours = Watt-Hours

To convert watt-hours to kilowatt-hours, divide the watt-hours by 1,000.

Exercise B Complete the information for this chart. Convert the total watt-hours to kilowatt-hours. The abbreviation for kilowatt-hours is kWh. Write your answers on your paper.

	Number of Lights	Watts	Hours Burned	Watt-Hours
1.	3	100	6	
2.	2	75	3	
3.	1	150	4	
4.	4	200	3	
5.		Total watt-hours		
6.		Total kilowatt-hours		

Reading Electric Meters You can read your electric **meter** to determine the number of kilowatt-hours used. Read the dials from right to left. Read the number the pointer has just passed. Take the lower number.

EXAMPLE

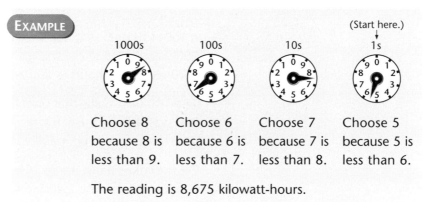

The reading is 8,675 kilowatt-hours.

Even though the pointer appears to be exactly on a number, read the next lower number—unless the pointer to its right has passed zero.

EXAMPLE

3   8   2   0

| On 4, but the pointer to the right has not passed 0. | Choose the lower of the two numbers. | On 2; the pointer to the right has passed 0. | Choose 0 because 0 is less than 1. |

The reading is 3,820 kilowatt-hours.

Some meters are digital. Look at these digital meters and read the numbers from left to right.

EXAMPLES

6,528 kWh   5,394 kWh   4,816 kWh

Exercise C Read the following electric meters.

1.

2.

3. 9 9 8 3   4. 0 5 3 4

The Electric Bill The electric company bills its customers for the number of kilowatt-hours used during a billing period, which is usually 1 month. The cost per kilowatt-hour varies from one city or area to another.

EXAMPLE Olivia's family uses 1,328 kilowatt-hours for the month of April. Find the cost if the electric company charges 7¢ per kilowatt-hour.

$$
\begin{array}{rl}
1,328 & \text{Kilowatt-hours (kWh)} \\
\times \quad .07 & \text{Price per kWh} \\
\hline
\$\,92.96 & \text{Cost for April}
\end{array}
$$

The electric company may add additional charges, such as fuel costs and customer service charges. The customer service charge covers the expense of reading the meter and keeping account records.

EXAMPLE Compute the electric bill for 1,760 kWh at 6¢ with a customer service charge of $2.89.

$$
\begin{array}{rl}
1,760 & \text{kWh} \\
\times \quad .06 & \text{Cost per kWh} \\
\hline
\$105.60 &
\end{array}
$$

$$
\begin{array}{rl}
\$105.60 & \\
+ \quad 2.89 & \text{Customer service charge} \\
\hline
\$108.49 & \text{Total bill}
\end{array}
$$

PROBLEM SOLVING

Exercise D Solve these problems.

1. Dino's family uses 1,098 kWh in May. Find the cost if the electric company charges 6.5¢ per kWh.

2. Compute the electric bill for 2,284 kWh at 7.3¢ with a customer service charge of $4.95.

3. Karina's total electric bill for July was $64.64 for using 1,050 kWh. Find how much her electric company charges per kWh if Karina's bill includes a $5 monthly service charge.

Exercise E Compute each bill with a $2.89 customer service charge. Write your answers on your paper.

	kWh Used	Rate per kWh	Total
1.	2,150	6¢	_____
2.	1,765	5¢	_____
3.	5,020	7¢	_____
4.	2,315	7¢	_____
5.	983	6¢	_____
6.	1,700	8¢	_____
7.	671	5¢	_____
8.	2,175	6¢	_____

Calculator Practice

You can use your calculator to determine the number of kilowatt-hours used.

Calculator Exercise Subtract the smaller reading from the larger reading.

1. 2,368 to 2,815

2. 5,872 to 6,023

3. 8,211 to 9,903

4. 4,020 to 5,107

5. 3,083 to 5,116

6. 4,135 to 6,102

7. 7,319 to 8,082

8. 6,129 to 7,815

9. 3,002 to 4,726

10. 8,362 to 9,108

11. 4,554 to 6,218

12. 2,315 to 4,063

13. 2,912 to 3,244

14. 6,691 to 8,354

15. 2,963 to 4,185

16. 8,615 to 9,031

17. 5,620 to 7,516

18. 8,001 to 9,532

19. 1,316 to 2,235

20. 2,273 to 3,442

21. 6,083 to 8,510

22. 5,174 to 7,002

Many electric companies encourage customers to avoid running appliances during **peak hours**. They do this by offering time-of-use (TOU) rates to consumers. The consumer pays a little more for a monthly charge but pays less for a kilowatt-hour during nonpeak hours. These charts help explain TOU rates.

Peak hours

The time when usage is greatest

Writing About Mathematics

Explain why the peak hours for electricity use are different in the summer than they are for the other seasons.

When getting information from a chart, double-check to make sure you are getting the data you need.

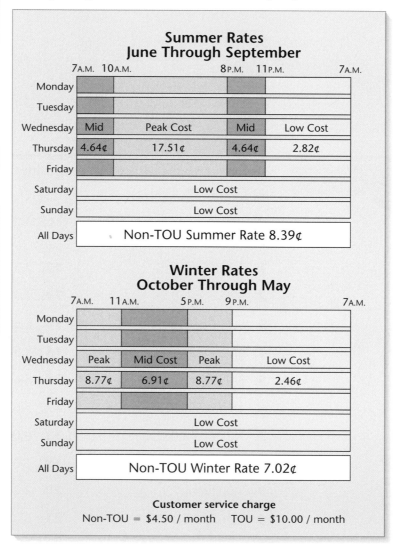

Summer Rates
June Through September

	7 A.M.	10 A.M.		8 P.M.	11 P.M.	7 A.M.
Monday						
Tuesday						
Wednesday	Mid	Peak Cost		Mid	Low Cost	
Thursday	4.64¢	17.51¢		4.64¢	2.82¢	
Friday						
Saturday		Low Cost				
Sunday		Low Cost				
All Days		Non-TOU Summer Rate 8.39¢				

Winter Rates
October Through May

	7 A.M.	11 A.M.	5 P.M.	9 P.M.	7 A.M.
Monday					
Tuesday					
Wednesday	Peak	Mid Cost	Peak	Low Cost	
Thursday	8.77¢	6.91¢	8.77¢	2.46¢	
Friday					
Saturday		Low Cost			
Sunday		Low Cost			
All Days		Non-TOU Winter Rate 7.02¢			

Customer service charge
Non-TOU = $4.50 / month   TOU = $10.00 / month

Try This

Steven hangs holiday lights outside his house in December. The watts used are equal to four 100-watt bulbs. If he leaves the lights on 24 hours a day, what is the total cost for 1 weekday for the TOU rates? What is the total cost for 1 day for the non-TOU rates?

EXAMPLE How much does it cost to burn a 60-watt bulb for 8 hours if you have TOU rates? How much will it cost if you have non-TOU rates?

$$
\begin{array}{r}
60 \quad \text{watts} \\
\times \quad 8 \quad \text{hours} \\
\hline
480 \quad \text{watt-hours} = .48 \text{ kWh}
\end{array}
$$

	Low	Mid	Peak	Non-TOU
TOU Summer	2.82¢	4.64¢	17.51¢	8.39¢
	× .48	× .48	× .48	× .48
	1.3536¢	2.2272¢	8.4048¢	4.0272¢
TOU Winter	2.46¢	6.91¢	8.77¢	7.02¢
	× .48	× .48	× .48	× .48
	1.1808¢	3.3168¢	4.2096¢	3.3696¢

Exercise A Find the cost of burning a light bulb for TOU rates during low, mid, and peak hours and for non-TOU rates. Write your answers on your paper.

TOU	Low	Mid	Peak	Non-TOU
1. A 75-watt bulb for 6 hours during March				
2. A 60-watt bulb for 15 hours during August				
3. A 40-watt bulb for 8 hours during April				
4. A 100-watt bulb for 6 hours during July				
5. A 60-watt bulb for 4 hours during June				

Remember, the abbreviation for watt-hours is whr.

Cutting Back You can save money by replacing a light bulb with a lower-watt bulb in areas where bright lights are not needed.

EXAMPLE   The light in the hall closet burns 12 hours each month. Electricity costs 8.39¢ per kWh. How much will be saved each month if the 100-watt bulb is replaced by a 60-watt bulb?

Cost of 100-watt bulb

100 watts	8.39¢ /kWh
× 12 hours	× 1.2 kWh
1,200 whr = 1.2 kWh	10.068¢

Cost of 60-watt bulb

60 watts	8.39¢ /kWh
× 12 hours	× .72 kWh
720 whr = .72 kWh	6.0408¢

Savings   10.0680¢   About 4¢ per month
          − 6.0408¢   will be saved.
            4.0272¢

The savings could also be found by subtracting 60 watts from 100 watts to find the savings in watts. Multiplying by hours and cost per kilowatt-hour would provide the savings.

Exercise B Find the savings per month. Write your answers on your paper.

	Old Bulb	New Bulb	Hours Used	Cost per kWh	Savings
1.	100 watts	60 watts	32 hours	8.77¢	_____
2.	75 watts	60 watts	25 hours	17.51¢	_____
3.	100 watts	75 watts	16 hours	4.64¢	_____
4.	75 watts	40 watts	36 hours	7.02¢	_____
5.	100 watts	40 watts	35 hours	8.39¢	_____
6.	75 watts	60 watts	80 hours	2.82¢	_____
7.	100 watts	20 watts	70 hours	4.64¢	_____

The gas meter, like the electric meter, is read from right to left. A meter may have three or four dials, but all gas and electric meters are read the same way.

502 thousand cubic feet

> **If you don't remember how to read a meter, refer back to the example on page 294.**

Try This

Is your home heated with natural gas? If it is, find and read your gas meter. How many thousands of cubic feet does it show? How many hundreds?

Gas is measured in thousands of cubic feet. Gas customers, however, are billed for the hundreds of cubic feet they use. You can convert the reading to hundreds of cubic feet by multiplying the meter reading by 10.

EXAMPLE   502 thousand cubic feet = 5,020 hundred cubic feet because 502 × 10 = 5,020.

Exercise A Convert each gas reading to hundreds of cubic feet.

1. 236 thousand cu ft

2. 400 thousand cu ft

3. 356 thousand cu ft

4. 210 thousand cu ft

5. 109 thousand cu ft

6. 3,001 thousand cu ft

7. 291 thousand cu ft

8. 801 thousand cu ft

9. 407 thousand cu ft

10. 725 thousand cu ft

11. 4,063 thousand cu ft

12. 2,912 thousand cu ft

13. 762 thousand cu ft

14. 1,000 thousand cu ft

15. 2,000 thousand cu ft

16. 3,022 thousand cu ft

17. 543 thousand cu ft

18. 304 thousand cu ft

19. 1,200 thousand cu ft

20. 206 thousand cu ft

21. 885 thousand cu ft

22. 2,934 thousand cu ft

Exercise B Read each gas meter. Convert the reading to hundreds of cubic feet.

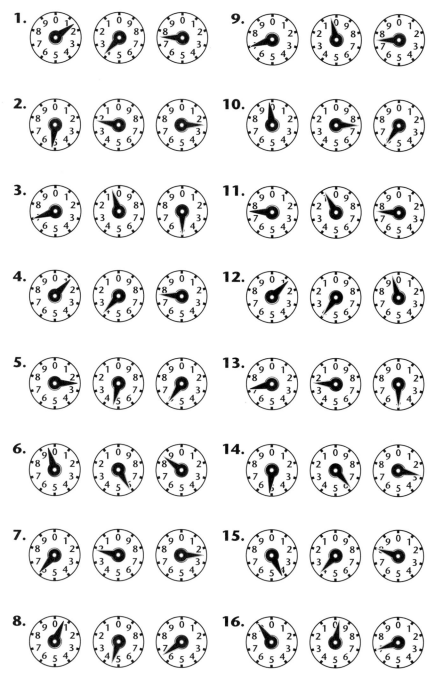

Celsius

A thermometer on which 0 degrees is the freezing point

Fahrenheit

A thermometer on which 32 degrees is the freezing point

When solving a problem without parentheses, always multiply before you add.

The amount of energy you use to heat or cool your home depends on weather conditions. Furnaces and water heaters work extra hard during freezing winter temperatures. Air conditioners and fans are used more during hot summer days.

Converting Celsius Readings to Fahrenheit Temperatures may be reported in **Celsius** readings.

30°C is the same as 86°F. To convert Celsius to **Fahrenheit**, use this formula:

$$F = \frac{9}{5} \times C + 32$$

Fahrenheit temperature   Celsius temperature

EXAMPLES   Convert 35° Celsius to Fahrenheit.

$F = \frac{9}{5} \times C + 32$

$F = \frac{9}{5} \times 35 + 32$

$F = 63 + 32$

$F = 95°$

Convert 34° Celsius to Fahrenheit.

$F = \frac{9}{5} \times C + 32$

$F = \frac{9}{5} \times 34 + 32$

$F = 61\frac{1}{5} + 32$

$F = 93\frac{1}{5}°$

Converting Fahrenheit Readings to Celsius To convert a Fahrenheit reading to Celsius, use this formula:

$$C = \frac{5}{9} \times (F - 32)$$

Celsius temperature   Fahrenheit temperature

EXAMPLES Convert 86° Fahrenheit to Celsius.

$$C = \frac{5}{9} \times (F - 32)$$

$$C = \frac{5}{9} \times (86 - 32)$$

$$C = \frac{5}{9} \times 54$$

$$C = 30°$$

Convert 90° Fahrenheit to Celsius.

$$C = \frac{5}{9} \times (90 - 32)$$

$$C = \frac{5}{9} \times 58$$

$$C = 32\frac{2}{9}°$$

Many thermometers show both Fahrenheit and Celsius temperatures.

Exercise A Convert the following Celsius temperatures to Fahrenheit.

1. 25°C

2. 30°C

3. 60°C

4. 15°C

5. 55°C

6. 36°C

7. 42°C

8. 45°C

9. 20°C

10. 53°C

11. 18°C

12. 23°C

Exercise B Convert the following Fahrenheit temperatures to Celsius.

1. 68°F

2. 50°F

3. 122°F

4. 104°F

5. 32°F

6. 80°F

7. 62°F

8. 35°F

9. 44°F

10. 98°F

11. 72°F

12. 85°F

Technology Connection

What kinds of energy can be used to heat a home? Use the Internet and electronic encyclopedias to learn about different sources for home heat. Some homes use natural gas, some use heating oil, some use electricity, and some use solar energy. Which heat source costs the least? Which is best for the environment? Think about why people are using technology to find alternative forms of energy.

Reading an Electric Bill

Frank Stevens and his family moved into their new home in October. Each month since that time, their electricity use has risen, so their costs have risen, too. Frank wants to make sure that his family does everything possible to reduce their electricity use and costs. Each month, Frank and his wife read the electric bill very carefully. Below is a copy of their latest bill.

Meter Information	Read Date	Load Type	Reading Type	Meter Reading Previous	Present	Diff	Mult X	Usage
	01/08	General Service	Tot kWh	23292 kWh	24359 kWh	1067	1	1067

Service from 12/05/2002 to 01/08/2003 - 34 Days

Current Period				
	Customer service charge			$ 7.58
	Energy charge	400 kWh X	$ .08275	33.10
	Energy charge discount	667 kWh X	$ .06208	41.41
	Franchise cost	$82.92 X	.70840%	0.59
	State tax			3.52
	Total current charges			**$ 86.20**
Other Charges				
	Total amount due			**$ 86.20**

Your Usage Profile

13 month Usage (Total kWh)

	Monthly Billed	Total Demand	Avg Daily kWh	Avg Daily Temp
Current Month		0.0	31.3	32
Last Month		0.0	24.5	51
Last Year		0.0	0.0	0

```
1500
1000
 800
 600
 400
 200
    J F M A M J J A S O N D J
    02  MONTHS BILLED  03
```

Exercises Use the electric bill to answer the questions.

1. What is the difference between the previous meter reading and the present meter reading?

2. How many kilowatt-hours are charged at 8.275¢?

3. Approximately how many kilowatt-hours were used in October? How many were used in December?

4. How many kilowatt-hours are charged at a discounted rate?

5. What suggestions do you have for Frank's family to reduce their energy use and costs?

Chapter 17 R E V I E W

Write the letter of the best answer to each question.

1. A 100-watt light bulb burns in a bedroom for 60 hours per month. Electricity costs 7.25¢ per kWh. How much is the cost of using the light bulb?

   A 43.5¢

   B 43.6¢

   C 43.7¢

   D 43.8¢

2. What is the correct reading for this gas meter?

   A 328 thousand cubic feet

   B 418 thousand cubic feet

   C 428 thousand cubic feet

   D 518 thousand cubic feet

3. How many hundred cubic feet are equal to 571 thousand cubic feet?

   A 5.71 hundred cubic feet

   B 57.1 hundred cubic feet

   C 571 hundred cubic feet

   D 5,710 hundred cubic feet

4. What are the electricity charges for 1,822 kWh used at 9.20¢ per kWh?

   A $167.62

   B $168.63

   C $169.64

   D $170.62

5. What is 23°C converted to Fahrenheit?

   A 73°F

   B $73\frac{1}{10}$°F

   C $73\frac{2}{5}$°F

   D $73\frac{1}{2}$°F

Convert to kilowatts.

6. 2,639 watts

7. 37 watts

Choose the correct answer.

8. 700 watts burning for 5 hours equals:
  A 35 kWh
  B 0.35 kWh
  C 3.5 kWh
  D 3,500 kWh

Read this digital electric meter.

9.

Answer these questions.

10. What are the charges for 2,367 kWh used at 7¢ per kWh?

11. What is the bill for 3,076 kWh used at 8¢ per kWh, with an added fuel cost of $15.16?

12. How many hundred cubic feet are equal to 28 thousand cubic feet?

13. What is 11°C converted to Fahrenheit?

14. What is 65°F converted to Celsius?

Read this gas meter.

15.

16. A 100-watt light bulb in a hallway burns 8 hours per month. Electricity costs 8.39¢ per kWh. About how much is saved each month if the 100-watt bulb is replaced with a 60-watt bulb?

17. Explain why a customer saves money by using a 60-watt bulb instead of a 100-watt bulb in a lamp.

18. Draw four dials of an electric meter. Place the dials on the meters to show the amount of electricity used. Read your dials and record your reading.

19. Suppose you are a meter reader. Write a paragraph to explain your job to a friend.

20. If you are the supervisor at the electric company, would you recommend that the company increase the monthly charge, or change the time-of-use rates? Explain your thinking.

Test-Taking Tip

When answering multiple-choice questions, first identify the answer choices that you know are incorrect.

Whole Numbers

Identifying the Place Value of Whole Numbers

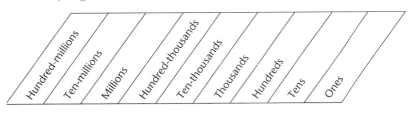

Example Write the name of the place for each underlined digit.

6<u>5</u>,823   thousands

2,9<u>0</u>6   tens

<u>4</u>,790,098   millions

Exercise Write the name of the place for each underlined digit.

1. <u>2</u>3,456

2. 5<u>3</u>6

3. 5,1<u>2</u>6

4. 6<u>2</u>1

5. 150,<u>3</u>41

6. 780,<u>2</u>96

7. 3,10<u>3</u>,615

8. <u>8</u>2,605

9. <u>2</u>6

10. 7,<u>4</u>05

11. <u>4</u>1,811

12. 9<u>6</u>3

13. 3<u>1</u>,005

14. <u>1</u>,815

15. 1,<u>0</u>07

16. <u>8</u>1,001

17. 56<u>7</u>

18. <u>3</u>14,152

19. <u>7</u>2,855

20. <u>6</u>,293,000

Whole Numbers

Rounding Whole Numbers

To the nearest ten	Step 1	To the nearest hundred
582 ↑ tens	Find the place to be rounded.	68,154 ↑ hundreds
582 ↑	**Step 2** If the digit to the right is greater than or equal to 5, add 1 to the place to be rounded.	68,154 ↑
580	**Step 3** Change all digits to the right of the rounded place to zeros.	68,200

Exercise Round these numbers to the nearest:

		Ten	Hundred	Thousand
1.	26,311	_____	_____	_____
2.	40,592	_____	_____	_____
3.	7,098	_____	_____	_____
4.	415	_____	_____	_____
5.	89	_____	_____	_____
6.	49	_____	_____	_____
7.	2,900	_____	_____	_____
8.	3,200	_____	_____	_____
9.	4	_____	_____	_____
10.	129	_____	_____	_____

Whole Numbers

Adding Whole Numbers

Example $26 + 451 + 2 = $ ■

Solution
$$
\begin{array}{r}
26 \ \rbrace \\
451 \ \rbrace \ \text{Addends} \\
+ \ 2 \ \rbrace \\
\hline
479 \leftarrow \text{Sum or total}
\end{array}
$$

Example $7 + 0 = $ ■

Solution
$$
\begin{array}{r}
7 \leftarrow \text{Addend} \\
+ \ 0 \leftarrow \text{Addend} \\
\hline
7 \leftarrow \text{Sum or total}
\end{array}
$$

Exercise Write these addends in vertical form. Then add.

1. $235 + 62$

2. $503 + 263$

3. $211 + 623$

4. $26 + 78 + 9$

5. $395 + 75 + 37$

6. $314 + 625 + 893$

7. $512 + 726 + 89$

8. $1,033 + 78 + 201$

9. $1,515 + 301 + 201$

10. $51 + 8,992 + 7$

11. $72 + 6,203 + 45$

12. $10,638 + 2,957$

13. $6,203 + 89 + 1,458$

14. $1,502 + 84 + 201$

15. $302 + 895 + 102$

16. $4,403 + 789 + 62$

17. $5,067 + 29,835$

18. $26 + 2,419 + 231$

19. $45 + 671$

20. $215 + 823$

21. $305 + 876$

22. $516 + 23 + 8$

23. $3,007 + 926 + 85$

24. $27 + 851 + 623$

25. $351 + 603 + 1,151$

26. $403 + 1,151 + 69$

27. $62 + 89 + 5 + 301$

28. $702 + 98 + 304$

29. $1,346 + 62 + 891$

30. $29,063 + 29 + 305$

31. $62,301 + 89 + 901$

32. $375 + 1,002 + 962$

33. $1,302 + 63 + 115$

34. $463 + 891 + 200$

35. $135 + 60,039 + 12$

36. $48 + 121 + 2,635$

Whole Numbers

Subtracting Whole Numbers

Example   Subtract 26 from 235. The number following *from* is written first.

Solution

$$\begin{array}{r} 235 \\ -\ \ 26 \\ \hline 209 \end{array}$$ Minuend
Subtrahend
Difference

Check

$$\begin{array}{r} 26 \\ +\ 209 \\ \hline 235 \end{array}$$

Exercise   Write these problems in vertical form. Then subtract.

1. $208 - 45$

2. $351 - 290$

3. $265 - 28$

4. $208 - 177$

5. $1,066 - 815$

6. $1,210 - 986$

7. $6,213 - 866$

8. $7,019 - 669$

9. $5,287 - 2,008$

10. $1,010 - 935$

11. $37,115 - 235$

12. $5,351 - 709$

13. $17,315 - 9,115$

14. $20,061 - 4,805$

15. $30,155 - 7,132$

16. $23,103 - 9,163$

17. $50,167 - 12,735$

18. $37,451 - 16,203$

19. $81,131 - 17,788$

20. $16,683 - 6,891$

21. $55,103 - 2,317$

22. $88,471 - 73,115$

23. $400 - 28$

24. $614 - 326$

25. $3,105 - 106$

26. $4,992 - 885$

27. $3,001 - 223$

28. $8,191 - 310$

29. $3,355 - 2,665$

30. $3,274 - 2,275$

31. $8,101 - 4,283$

32. $9,000 - 862$

33. $2,113 - 421$

34. $48,300 - 9,301$

35. $41,041 - 8,597$

36. $14,724 - 7,026$

37. $65,913 - 27,261$

38. $10,991 - 2,815$

39. $41,568 - 29,321$

40. $20,972 - 3,811$

41. $10,014 - 2,560$

42. $57,221 - 10,811$

43. $51,371 - 5,119$

44. $14,014 - 7,958$

Whole Numbers

Multiplying Whole Numbers

Example $23 \times 6 = $ ■

Solution

$$
\begin{array}{r}
23 \\
\times\ 6 \\
\hline
138
\end{array}
$$

23, × 6 } Factors
138   Product

Example $46 \times 35 = $ ■

Solution

46, × 35 } Factors

$$
\begin{array}{r}
46 \\
\times\ \ 35 \\
\hline
230 \\
+\ 1\ 38 \\
\hline
1,610
\end{array}
$$

1,610   Product

Multiplying Whole Numbers With Zeros

Example $267 \times 10 = $ ■

Solution

$$
\begin{array}{r}
267 \\
\times\ \ 10 \\
\hline
2,670
\end{array}
$$
←One zero
←One zero

Example $342 \times 100 = $ ■

Solution

$$
\begin{array}{r}
342 \\
\times\ \ 100 \\
\hline
34,200
\end{array}
$$
←Two zeros
←Two zeros

Exercise Write these problems in vertical form. Then multiply.

1. 23×6

2. 403×5

3. 313×4

4. 26×45

5. 72×35

6. 567×10

7. 109×50

8. 815×400

9. 701×202

10. 511×120

11. $2,215 \times 63$

12. $6,057 \times 40$

13. $5,063 \times 41$

14. $2,267 \times 19$

15. $2,830 \times 110$

16. $5,011 \times 300$

(continued on page 316)

(continued from page 315)

17. 7,706 × 250

18. 1,127 × 277

19. 90,681 × 22

20. 15,012 × 50

21. 21,305 × 100

22. 89,000 × 62

23. 4,805 × 1,001

24. 57,119 × 1,010

25. 77,805 × 601

26. 38 × 9

27. 206 × 8

28. 231 × 11

29. 52 × 60

30. 391 × 20

31. 435 × 39

32. 623 × 67

33. 516 × 200

34. 870 × 270

35. 603 × 250

36. 4,120 × 10

37. 1,403 × 27

38. 8,010 × 50

39. 3,115 × 28

40. 4,100 × 310

41. 8,214 × 200

42. 5,066 × 305

43. 6,405 × 115

44. 40,363 × 100

45. 71,106 × 602

46. 28,015 × 101

47. 10,376 × 203

48. 72,011 × 78

49. 90,301 × 201

50. 53,103 × 111

Whole Numbers

Dividing Whole Numbers With Zeros

Example   576 ÷ 12 = ■

Solution

```
        48
  12) 576
     − 48
       96
     − 96
        0
```

Check

```
       48
   ×   12
       96
   + 48
      576
```

Dividing Whole Numbers With Fractional Remainders

Example   3,191 ÷ 25 = ■

Solution

```
       127 16/25
  25) 3,191
     − 2 5                Write the
        69                remainder
      − 50                over the
       191                divisor.
     − 175
        16
```

Check

```
         127
     ×    25
         635
     + 2 54
       3,175
     +    16     Remainder
       3,191
```

Dividing Whole Numbers With Zeros in the Quotient

Example   2,380 ÷ 14 = ■

Solution

```
        170
  14) 2,380
     − 1 4
        98
      − 98
        00
```

Check

```
       170
   ×    14
       680
   + 1 70
     2,380
```

Example   4,864 ÷ 16 = ■

Solution

```
         304
   16) 4,864
      − 4 8
        064
      − 64
          0
```

Check

```
        304
    ×    16
      1,824
    + 3 04
      4,864
```

Whole Numbers

Exercise Divide.

1. 138 ÷ 6

2. 882 ÷ 9

3. 1,030 ÷ 5

4. 1,806 ÷ 6

5. 1,631 ÷ 7

6. 3,060 ÷ 4

7. 1,404 ÷ 52

8. 4,980 ÷ 60

9. 5,040 ÷ 70

10. 5,700 ÷ 95

11. 6,510 ÷ 105

12. 9,108 ÷ 18

13. 30,954 ÷ 77

14. 15,257 ÷ 73

15. 9,646 ÷ 91

16. 19,520 ÷ 32

17. 30,310 ÷ 70

18. 32,040 ÷ 40

19. 45,150 ÷ 15

20. 56,221 ÷ 11

21. 44,520 ÷ 12

22. 65,160 ÷ 36

23. 51,090 ÷ 13

24. 80,080 ÷ 40

25. 12,524 ÷ 31

26. 371 ÷ 7

27. 3,159 ÷ 9

28. 1,744 ÷ 8

29. 3,018 ÷ 6

30. 2,564 ÷ 4

31. 6,033 ÷ 3

32. 1,539 ÷ 27

33. 4,100 ÷ 82

34. 8,820 ÷ 90

35. 3,375 ÷ 25

36. 3,450 ÷ 15

37. 19,418 ÷ 38

38. 31,626 ÷ 63

39. 19,530 ÷ 62

40. 10,160 ÷ 80

41. 34,310 ÷ 47

42. 52,920 ÷ 60

43. 8,866 ÷ 22

44. 138,253 ÷ 23

45. 738,500 ÷ 35

46. 50,300 ÷ 10

47. 103,200 ÷ 24

48. 82,212 ÷ 51

49. 90,900 ÷ 30

50. 57,414 ÷ 14

Whole Numbers

Exercise Divide. Write any remainders as fractions.

1. $335 \div 6$

2. $50 \div 8$

3. $711 \div 9$

4. $393 \div 6$

5. $7,151 \div 8$

6. $6,205 \div 15$

7. $60,600 \div 15$

8. $181,819 \div 18$

9. $30,091 \div 25$

10. $70,111 \div 80$

11. $41,015 \div 32$

12. $26,031 \div 26$

13. $13,315 \div 25$

14. $60,031 \div 81$

15. $53,010 \div 52$

16. $10,008 \div 50$

17. $27,023 \div 62$

18. $15,132 \div 25$

19. $90,615 \div 23$

20. $46,023 \div 23$

21. $23,310 \div 70$

22. $50,003 \div 85$

23. $22,022 \div 60$

24. $463,201 \div 71$

25. $57,231 \div 500$

26. $573 \div 6$

27. $908 \div 9$

28. $630 \div 9$

29. $721 \div 8$

30. $3,900 \div 9$

31. $8,003 \div 15$

32. $7,440 \div 22$

33. $32,331 \div 16$

34. $7,910 \div 19$

35. $51,631 \div 25$

36. $10,631 \div 81$

37. $35,103 \div 34$

38. $14,401 \div 72$

39. $42,002 \div 60$

40. $73,106 \div 73$

41. $53,010 \div 38$

42. $14,108 \div 80$

43. $62,031 \div 20$

44. $72,150 \div 80$

45. $81,035 \div 90$

46. $34,210 \div 81$

47. $78,311 \div 30$

48. $37,101 \div 51$

49. $72,101 \div 82$

50. $80,031 \div 198$

Whole Numbers

Finding Values of Numbers With Exponents

Example   Find 3^4.

Solution $3^4 = 3 \times 3 \times 3 \times 3$ (4 times)
                    $= 81$

Example   Find 2^3.

Solution $2^3 = 2 \times 2 \times 2$ (3 times)
                    $= 8$

Exercise Find the value of each expression.

1. 3^2	**26.** 4^3	**51.** 5^2
2. 5^3	**27.** 4^2	**52.** 8^2
3. 9^2	**28.** 2^5	**53.** 9^3
4. 19^2	**29.** 7^3	**54.** 4^5
5. 3^5	**30.** 2^4	**55.** 6^2
6. 8^2	**31.** 11^2	**56.** 13^3
7. 9^4	**32.** 16^3	**57.** 12^2
8. 18^2	**33.** 5^4	**58.** 18^2
9. 6^3	**34.** 10^4	**59.** 28^2
10. 2^6	**35.** 15^2	**60.** 17^2
11. 25^2	**36.** 5^5	**61.** 24^2
12. 7^2	**37.** 8^4	**62.** 150^2
13. 2^7	**38.** 50^3	**63.** 300^4
14. 26^2	**39.** 5^3	**64.** 70^3
15. 7^4	**40.** 40^3	**65.** 22^2
16. 30^2	**41.** 77^2	**66.** 500^3
17. 200^3	**42.** 60^3	**67.** 15^3
18. 70^2	**43.** 92^2	**68.** 13^2
19. 100^3	**44.** 30^3	**69.** 42^2
20. 80^3	**45.** 80^2	**70.** 90^3
21. 30^4	**46.** 32^2	**71.** 10^3
22. $1{,}000^2$	**47.** 16^2	**72.** 30^4
23. 46^2	**48.** 10^2	**73.** 63^2
24. 5^6	**49.** 8^3	**74.** 10^5
25. 10^4	**50.** 23^2	**75.** 3^3

Whole Numbers

Using the Order of Operations

Rules **1.** Evaluate expressions with exponents first.

2. Multiply and divide from left to right in order.

3. Add and subtract from left to right in order.

Example $\quad 2 \quad + \quad 3 \times 4 \quad - \quad 8 \div 4 \quad = \quad \blacksquare$

Solution $\quad 2 \quad + \quad \underset{\downarrow}{3 \times 4} \quad - \quad \underset{\downarrow}{8 \div 4} \quad =$

$\quad\quad\quad\quad 2 \quad + \quad 12 \quad - \quad 2 \quad = \quad 12$

Example $\quad 2^3 \quad + \quad 3 \times 4 \div 2 \quad - \quad 48 \div 4^2 \quad = \quad \blacksquare$

Solution $\quad 8 \quad + \quad \underset{\downarrow}{3 \times 4} \div 2 \quad - \quad 48 \div 16 \quad =$

$\quad\quad\quad\quad\quad\quad\quad \underset{\downarrow}{12 \div 2} \quad\quad\quad \underset{\downarrow}{3} \quad =$

$\quad\quad\quad\quad 8 \quad + \quad 6 \quad - \quad 3 \quad = \quad 11$

Exercise Use the rules for the order of operations. Find the answers.

1. $3 + 8 \times 2 \div 4$

2. $5 + 9 \times 4 \div 12 - 2$

3. $8 - 8 \div 4 + 3 \times 2$

4. $13 - 16 \times 3 \div 12 - 1$

5. $9 + 6 \times 3 - 8 \times 2 \div 4$

6. $1 + 16 \times 3 \div 12 - 4$

7. $14 + 32 \div 16 - 4 \times 2$

8. $32 \div 16 + 9 \div 3 \times 2$

9. $5 - 16 \div 4 + 1 + 3$

10. $35 - 25 \times 4 \div 20 + 5$

11. $2^3 + 8 \times 2^2 + 3$

12. $8 - 6^2 \div 12 + 2 \times 5$

13. $15 + 8^2 \div 4 - 6$

14. $26 + 13^2 \div 13 - 20$

15. $9^2 + 32 \div 8 \times 4 - 6$

16. $3 + 2^3 \div 2^2 - 4$

17. $5 + 8 \times 9 \div 6^2 - 4$

18. $25 + 11^2 + 8 \times 2 - 3$

19. $39 \div 13 + 12^2 \div 6 - 5$

20. $52 + 12 \div 2^2 - 82 \div 2 + 3^2$

21. $35 + 2^5 \div 2^4 \times 3^2 - 2^3$

22. $18 \div 3^2 + 6 \times 8 \div 4^2 - 5$

23. $4 \times 3 \times 5 \div 10 + 8 \times 2^3 \div 2^4$

24. $9 - 16 \times 3 \div 12 + 8 \div 2^2 - 2^2$

Whole Numbers

Finding an Average

Example Compute the average for 98, 88, and 80.

Solution Add the numbers. Divide the sum by the number of addends.

$$\left. \begin{array}{r} 98 \\ 88 \\ + \ 80 \end{array} \right\} \ 3 \text{ addends}$$

$$266 \leftarrow \text{Sum or total}$$

$$\begin{array}{r} 88\frac{2}{3} \\ 3 \overline{)\ 266} \\ -\ 24 \\ \hline 26 \\ -\ 24 \\ \hline 2 \end{array}$$

Answer The average is $88\frac{2}{3}$.

Exercise Compute the average for each set of numbers.

1. 25, 63, 48, 52, 49, 38, 42, 67, 38

2. 98, 53, 42, 56, 72, 36, 72

3. 39, 40, 39, 62, 53, 86, 29, 34

4. 95, 83, 39, 42, 88, 77, 75, 42, 67

5. 88, 62, 42, 53, 96, 35, 35

6. 53, 60, 72, 43, 35, 39, 53

7. 52, 65, 83, 96, 35, 100, 92, 53

8. 91, 62, 39, 50, 42, 88, 53, 60, 83, 72

9. 36, 50, 42, 53, 46, 82, 80, 50, 52, 39

10. 81, 90, 92, 90, 83, 43, 46, 72, 53

11. 100, 103, 96, 105, 105, 97, 102, 120

12. 36, 42, 85, 92, 30, 33, 88, 29, 62, 50

13. 109, 156, 95, 108, 90, 83, 45, 80, 90, 98, 93, 96

14. 40, 42, 43, 40, 41, 42, 43, 48, 44, 42, 45, 42

15. 40, 38, 37, 35, 42, 43, 36, 49, 48, 53, 42, 39, 34

16. 21, 20, 23, 28, 25, 23, 20, 25, 24, 29, 28, 24, 22, 20

17. 52, 50, 59, 62, 63, 55, 54, 58, 60, 50, 52, 53, 57, 52, 51

Fractions

Comparing Fractions

Example Compare $\frac{3}{4}$ and $\frac{5}{8}$.

Solution $\begin{array}{cc} 24 & 20 \end{array}$

$$\frac{3}{4} \bowtie \frac{5}{8}$$

Because   Because

$4 \times 5 = 20$ $3 \times 8 = 24$

24 is greater than 20; therefore, $\frac{3}{4}$ is greater than $\frac{5}{8}$.

Changing Fractions to Higher Terms

Example Write $\frac{5}{6}$ as a fraction with 30 as the new denominator.

Solution **Step 1** $\frac{5}{6} = \frac{\blacksquare}{30}$

           Step 2   Divide 30 by 6. $\longrightarrow$ $6\overline{)30}$ ... 5

           Step 3   Multiply $\frac{5}{6}$ by $\frac{5}{5}$. $\longrightarrow$ $\frac{5 \times 5}{6 \times 5} = \frac{25}{30}$

Answer $\frac{5}{6} = \frac{25}{30}$

Exercise Express these fractions in higher terms.

1. $\frac{3}{4} = \frac{\blacksquare}{48}$

2. $\frac{1}{3} = \frac{\blacksquare}{21}$

3. $\frac{2}{3} = \frac{\blacksquare}{15}$

4. $\frac{5}{6} = \frac{\blacksquare}{18}$

5. $\frac{7}{8} = \frac{\blacksquare}{56}$

6. $\frac{3}{5} = \frac{\blacksquare}{20}$

7. $\frac{1}{7} = \frac{\blacksquare}{49}$

8. $\frac{5}{12} = \frac{\blacksquare}{24}$

9. $\frac{3}{7} = \frac{\blacksquare}{21}$

10. $\frac{4}{12} = \frac{\blacksquare}{36}$

11. $\frac{4}{9} = \frac{\blacksquare}{45}$

12. $\frac{3}{3} = \frac{\blacksquare}{18}$

13. $\frac{2}{11} = \frac{\blacksquare}{121}$

14. $\frac{15}{16} = \frac{\blacksquare}{48}$

15. $\frac{3}{10} = \frac{\blacksquare}{30}$

16. $\frac{12}{14} = \frac{\blacksquare}{70}$

17. $\frac{9}{12} = \frac{\blacksquare}{144}$

18. $\frac{5}{15} = \frac{\blacksquare}{45}$

19. $\frac{2}{8} = \frac{\blacksquare}{96}$

20. $\frac{1}{6} = \frac{\blacksquare}{72}$

21. $\frac{17}{24} = \frac{\blacksquare}{120}$

Fractions

Renaming Fractions to Simplest Terms

Example Rename $\frac{14}{16}$ to simplest terms.

Solution Choose a number that can be divided into the denominator and the numerator.

$$\frac{14 \div 2}{16 \div 2} = \frac{7}{8}$$

Answer $\frac{14}{16} = \frac{7}{8}$

Example Rename $\frac{24}{30}$ to simplest terms.

Solution $\frac{24 \div 3}{30 \div 3} = \frac{8}{10}$

The division process may occur more than once if the divisor is not large enough in the first step.

$$\frac{8 \div 2}{10 \div 2} = \frac{4}{5}$$

Answer $\frac{24}{30} = \frac{4}{5}$

Exercise Rename these fractions to simplest terms.

1. $\frac{24}{48}$

2. $\frac{10}{230}$

3. $\frac{45}{99}$

4. $\frac{5}{25}$

5. $\frac{13}{39}$

6. $\frac{56}{58}$

7. $\frac{63}{81}$

8. $\frac{6}{54}$

9. $\frac{16}{112}$

10. $\frac{39}{52}$

11. $\frac{12}{60}$

12. $\frac{16}{64}$

13. $\frac{18}{36}$

14. $\frac{22}{121}$

15. $\frac{53}{106}$

16. $\frac{18}{72}$

17. $\frac{5}{15}$

18. $\frac{55}{242}$

19. $\frac{10}{52}$

20. $\frac{48}{96}$

21. $\frac{28}{56}$

Fractions

Renaming Improper Fractions as Mixed Numbers or Whole Numbers

Example   Rename $\frac{13}{5}$.

Solution   Divide the numerator by the denominator.

$$\begin{array}{r} 2 \\ 5\overline{)13} \\ -10 \\ \hline 3 \end{array} \longleftarrow \text{Remainder}$$

Answer $\frac{13}{5} = 2\frac{3}{5}$ $\longleftarrow$ Write the remainder over the divisor.

Example   Rename $\frac{42}{16}$.

Solution

$$\begin{array}{r} 2 \\ 16\overline{)42} \\ -32 \\ \hline 10 \end{array}$$

$$2\frac{10}{16} = 2\frac{5}{8}$$

Answer $\frac{42}{16} = 2\frac{5}{8}$

Writing Mixed Numbers in Simplest Terms

Example   Write $12\frac{4}{6}$ in simplest terms.

Solution $12\frac{4}{6} = 12 + \frac{4}{6} = 12 + \frac{2}{3} = 12\frac{2}{3}$

Answer $12\frac{4}{6} = 12\frac{2}{3}$

Fractions

Exercise Rename these improper fractions as either mixed numbers or whole numbers.

1. $\dfrac{13}{5}$

2. $\dfrac{18}{3}$

3. $\dfrac{19}{6}$

4. $\dfrac{14}{3}$

5. $\dfrac{23}{4}$

6. $\dfrac{12}{2}$

7. $\dfrac{38}{5}$

8. $\dfrac{66}{11}$

9. $\dfrac{56}{11}$

10. $\dfrac{19}{5}$

11. $\dfrac{52}{32}$

12. $\dfrac{55}{8}$

13. $\dfrac{28}{6}$

14. $\dfrac{32}{4}$

15. $\dfrac{90}{3}$

16. $\dfrac{63}{8}$

17. $\dfrac{50}{6}$

18. $\dfrac{58}{7}$

19. $\dfrac{52}{10}$

20. $\dfrac{37}{3}$

21. $\dfrac{120}{10}$

22. $\dfrac{73}{8}$

23. $\dfrac{13}{2}$

24. $\dfrac{51}{4}$

25. $\dfrac{82}{9}$

26. $\dfrac{23}{5}$

27. $\dfrac{52}{8}$

28. $\dfrac{32}{15}$

Fractions

Renaming Mixed Numbers as Improper Fractions

Example Write $2\frac{3}{4}$ as an improper fraction.

Solution **Step 1** Multiply the whole number by the denominator.

$$2 \times 4 = 8$$

Step 2 Add the numerator to the product from Step 1.

$$3 + 8 = 11$$

Step 3 Write the sum over the original denominator.

$$\frac{11}{4}$$

Answer $2\frac{3}{4} = \frac{11}{4}$

Exercise Rename these mixed numbers as improper fractions.

1. $3\frac{2}{5}$

2. $6\frac{2}{5}$

3. $5\frac{1}{6}$

4. $7\frac{2}{12}$

5. $2\frac{1}{6}$

6. $9\frac{1}{2}$

7. $4\frac{1}{9}$

8. $8\frac{2}{11}$

9. $5\frac{2}{3}$

10. $8\frac{1}{3}$

11. $6\frac{10}{13}$

12. $16\frac{2}{3}$

13. $7\frac{3}{8}$

14. $15\frac{2}{3}$

15. $13\frac{9}{14}$

16. $9\frac{2}{3}$

17. $5\frac{11}{10}$

18. $20\frac{2}{3}$

19. $16\frac{5}{21}$

20. $11\frac{1}{8}$

Fractions

Multiplying Fractions

Example $\frac{5}{6} \times \frac{3}{4} = \blacksquare$

Solution $\frac{5 \times 3}{6 \times 4} = \frac{15}{24}$

$\frac{15}{24} = \frac{5}{8}$

Answer $\frac{5}{8}$

Example $7 \times \frac{4}{5} = \blacksquare$

Solution $\frac{7 \times 4}{1 \times 5} = \frac{28}{5}$

$\frac{28}{5} = 5\frac{3}{5}$

Answer $5\frac{3}{5}$

Exercise Multiply. Write your answers in simplest terms.

1. $\frac{1}{2} \times \frac{2}{3}$

2. $\frac{3}{5} \times \frac{5}{6}$

3. $\frac{7}{8} \times \frac{6}{13}$

4. $\frac{2}{9} \times \frac{3}{5}$

5. $\frac{6}{7} \times \frac{1}{2}$

6. $\frac{3}{11} \times \frac{2}{5}$

7. $\frac{2}{7} \times \frac{2}{9}$

8. $\frac{1}{6} \times \frac{1}{5}$

9. $\frac{5}{11} \times \frac{1}{4}$

10. $\frac{1}{6} \times \frac{2}{9}$

11. $\frac{5}{6} \times \frac{1}{4}$

12. $\frac{3}{11} \times \frac{2}{12}$

13. $\frac{4}{5} \times \frac{2}{9}$

14. $\frac{4}{7} \times \frac{1}{8}$

15. $\frac{3}{16} \times \frac{13}{21}$

16. $\frac{5}{21} \times \frac{7}{10}$

17. $\frac{5}{24} \times \frac{3}{13}$

18. $\frac{6}{28} \times \frac{7}{12}$

19. $\frac{2}{3} \times \frac{5}{6}$

20. $\frac{12}{21} \times \frac{7}{8}$

21. $\frac{13}{32} \times \frac{8}{26}$

22. $\frac{24}{25} \times \frac{5}{16}$

23. $\frac{1}{12} \times \frac{2}{7}$

24. $\frac{2}{17} \times \frac{3}{4}$

25. $\frac{10}{13} \times \frac{39}{100}$

26. $\frac{12}{18} \times \frac{9}{32}$

27. $\frac{2}{15} \times \frac{45}{50}$

28. $\frac{5}{11} \times \frac{55}{75}$

29. $\frac{4}{5} \times \frac{2}{13}$

30. $\frac{2}{11} \times \frac{3}{10}$

31. $\frac{3}{14} \times \frac{28}{30}$

32. $\frac{7}{13} \times \frac{39}{63}$

33. $\frac{24}{36} \times \frac{1}{3}$

Fractions

Multiplying Mixed Numbers

Example $3\frac{2}{3} \times 1\frac{1}{2} = \blacksquare$

Solution $3\frac{2}{3} = \frac{11}{3}$ $\left.\vphantom{\begin{array}{c}a\\b\end{array}}\right\}$ Rename mixed numbers as improper fractions.

$1\frac{1}{2} = \frac{3}{2}$

$\frac{11}{3} \times \frac{3}{2} = \frac{11}{2}$

$\frac{11}{2} = 5\frac{1}{2}$

Answer $5\frac{1}{2}$

Exercise Multiply. Write your answers in simplest terms.

1. $2\frac{1}{2} \times \frac{1}{3}$
2. $\frac{1}{2} \times 1\frac{1}{5}$
3. $\frac{2}{7} \times 1\frac{1}{3}$
4. $\frac{1}{5} \times 1\frac{1}{7}$
5. $3\frac{1}{5} \times \frac{3}{4}$
6. $5\frac{2}{3} \times \frac{1}{5}$
7. $\frac{5}{7} \times 2\frac{3}{8}$
8. $1\frac{1}{2} \times \frac{15}{18}$
9. $4\frac{5}{7} \times \frac{7}{11}$
10. $2\frac{3}{5} \times 1\frac{1}{5}$
11. $2\frac{3}{7} \times 2\frac{1}{2}$

12. $5\frac{1}{7} \times 2\frac{1}{5}$
13. $5\frac{1}{6} \times 1\frac{1}{5}$
14. $1\frac{5}{6} \times 1\frac{1}{3}$
15. $1\frac{2}{7} \times 2\frac{1}{8}$
16. $6\frac{1}{2} \times 2\frac{3}{4}$
17. $2\frac{2}{5} \times 1\frac{3}{4}$
18. $4\frac{1}{2} \times 1\frac{1}{4}$
19. $3\frac{3}{7} \times 2\frac{1}{3}$
20. $5\frac{2}{9} \times 1\frac{1}{8}$
21. $5\frac{1}{4} \times 2\frac{1}{7}$
22. $6\frac{2}{5} \times 1\frac{1}{7}$

23. $13\frac{1}{3} \times 2\frac{1}{4}$
24. $1\frac{5}{9} \times 1\frac{3}{4}$
25. $3\frac{2}{5} \times 2\frac{2}{4}$
26. $5\frac{2}{5} \times 1\frac{1}{9}$
27. $5\frac{1}{3} \times 1\frac{1}{8}$
28. $5\frac{3}{9} \times 1\frac{1}{6}$
29. $1\frac{2}{8} \times 3\frac{1}{2}$
30. $3\frac{1}{2} \times 5\frac{1}{6}$
31. $2\frac{4}{5} \times 2\frac{1}{7}$
32. $4\frac{1}{5} \times 1\frac{5}{7}$
33. $3\frac{7}{8} \times 1\frac{1}{2}$

Fractions

Dividing Fractions

Example $\frac{4}{7} \div \frac{1}{2} = \blacksquare$

Solution $\frac{4}{7} \div \frac{1}{2} = \blacksquare$

$\frac{4}{7} \times \frac{2}{1} = \frac{8}{7}$ ◄————Invert the divisor. Then multiply.

$\frac{8}{7} = 1\frac{1}{7}$

Answer $1\frac{1}{7}$

Exercise Divide. Write your answers in simplest terms.

1. $\frac{2}{5} \div \frac{2}{7}$

2. $\frac{5}{6} \div \frac{1}{3}$

3. $\frac{2}{7} \div \frac{1}{8}$

4. $\frac{4}{5} \div \frac{1}{6}$

5. $\frac{2}{7} \div \frac{5}{6}$

6. $\frac{3}{8} \div \frac{1}{2}$

7. $\frac{4}{5} \div \frac{5}{6}$

8. $\frac{8}{9} \div \frac{4}{5}$

9. $\frac{5}{6} \div \frac{2}{5}$

10. $\frac{5}{11} \div \frac{2}{22}$

11. $\frac{8}{11} \div \frac{5}{11}$

12. $\frac{5}{12} \div \frac{5}{6}$

13. $\frac{3}{8} \div \frac{5}{12}$

14. $\frac{2}{11} \div \frac{3}{22}$

15. $\frac{8}{13} \div \frac{24}{26}$

16. $\frac{3}{9} \div \frac{1}{5}$

17. $\frac{11}{12} \div \frac{24}{30}$

18. $\frac{5}{7} \div \frac{48}{49}$

19. $\frac{1}{2} \div \frac{5}{7}$

20. $\frac{5}{7} \div \frac{5}{14}$

21. $\frac{8}{9} \div \frac{3}{6}$

22. $\frac{3}{4} \div \frac{6}{7}$

23. $\frac{13}{14} \div \frac{3}{7}$

24. $\frac{8}{15} \div \frac{2}{5}$

25. $\frac{1}{2} \div \frac{1}{2}$

26. $\frac{2}{3} \div \frac{1}{7}$

27. $\frac{3}{7} \div \frac{15}{21}$

28. $\frac{5}{10} \div \frac{2}{6}$

29. $\frac{4}{7} \div \frac{5}{14}$

30. $\frac{2}{3} \div \frac{14}{21}$

31. $\frac{18}{20} \div \frac{15}{40}$

32. $\frac{22}{27} \div \frac{11}{18}$

33. $\frac{16}{30} \div \frac{8}{15}$

Fractions

Dividing Mixed Numbers

Example $2\frac{3}{4} \div 3\frac{1}{3} = \blacksquare$

Solution
$\left.\begin{array}{l} 2\frac{3}{4} = \frac{11}{4} \\[6pt] 3\frac{1}{3} = \frac{10}{3} \end{array}\right\}$ Rename mixed numbers as improper fractions.

$\frac{11}{4} \div \frac{10}{3} = \blacksquare$

$\frac{11}{4} \times \frac{3}{10} = \frac{33}{40}$ ←——Invert the divisor and multiply.

Answer $\frac{33}{40}$

Exercise Divide. Write your answers in simplest terms.

1. $1\frac{1}{2} \div \frac{1}{2}$

2. $3\frac{2}{3} \div \frac{1}{9}$

3. $1\frac{1}{5} \div \frac{2}{5}$

4. $2\frac{1}{6} \div \frac{3}{12}$

5. $\frac{3}{12} \div 3\frac{1}{6}$

6. $\frac{13}{15} \div 1\frac{3}{5}$

7. $1\frac{2}{5} \div \frac{14}{15}$

8. $3\frac{1}{2} \div \frac{5}{6}$

9. $1\frac{1}{2} \div 1\frac{2}{5}$

10. $\frac{1}{2} \div 1\frac{1}{2}$

11. $1\frac{1}{12} \div 2\frac{1}{6}$

12. $2\frac{2}{3} \div 3\frac{5}{9}$

13. $2\frac{1}{2} \div 3\frac{1}{7}$

14. $1\frac{5}{7} \div \frac{6}{7}$

15. $2\frac{5}{8} \div \frac{21}{24}$

16. $3\frac{5}{7} \div \frac{13}{14}$

17. $5\frac{2}{5} \div \frac{3}{4}$

18. $4\frac{1}{3} \div \frac{26}{27}$

19. $5\frac{3}{7} \div \frac{1}{3}$

20. $3\frac{2}{9} \div \frac{1}{8}$

21. $5\frac{2}{5} \div \frac{9}{10}$

22. $8\frac{2}{3} \div \frac{1}{7}$

23. $6\frac{1}{7} \div \frac{7}{18}$

24. $5\frac{1}{5} \div 1\frac{1}{2}$

25. $2\frac{3}{4} \div 1\frac{1}{6}$

26. $1\frac{1}{7} \div 1\frac{1}{6}$

27. $1\frac{1}{8} \div 1\frac{1}{9}$

28. $13\frac{2}{3} \div \frac{1}{9}$

29. $3\frac{2}{3} \div \frac{22}{27}$

30. $3\frac{6}{7} \div 1\frac{1}{4}$

31. $5\frac{2}{7} \div 7\frac{2}{5}$

32. $2\frac{1}{6} \div 1\frac{1}{2}$

33. $1\frac{1}{12} \div 2\frac{1}{6}$

Fractions

Adding Mixed Numbers With Like Denominators

Example $3\frac{2}{7} + 1\frac{3}{7} = \blacksquare$

Solution

$$\begin{array}{r} 3\frac{2}{7} \\ + 1\frac{3}{7} \\ \hline 4\frac{5}{7} \end{array}$$

Step 1   Write in vertical form.

Step 2   Add the numerators.
$2 + 3 = 5$

Step 3   Keep the denominator.

Step 4   Add the whole numbers.

Answer $4\frac{5}{7}$

Exercise   Add. Write your answers in simplest terms.

1. $\frac{2}{5} + \frac{2}{5}$

2. $\frac{5}{7} + \frac{1}{7}$

3. $\frac{8}{12} + \frac{3}{12}$

4. $\frac{5}{8} + \frac{1}{8}$

5. $\frac{2}{7} + \frac{5}{7}$

6. $\frac{8}{11} + \frac{4}{11}$

7. $1\frac{1}{6} + 2\frac{3}{6}$

8. $2\frac{5}{8} + \frac{1}{8}$

9. $5\frac{3}{10} + \frac{2}{10}$

10. $5\frac{1}{6} + \frac{1}{6}$

11. $8\frac{1}{12} + \frac{3}{12}$

12. $5\frac{1}{6} + \frac{3}{6}$

13. $8\frac{5}{11} + 1\frac{2}{11}$

14. $9\frac{1}{10} + 3\frac{3}{10}$

15. $8\frac{2}{5} + 3\frac{4}{5}$

16. $6\frac{2}{9} + \frac{5}{9}$

17. $8\frac{2}{12} + 6$

18. $11\frac{12}{21} + 2\frac{3}{21}$

19. $5 + 2\frac{1}{7}$

20. $7\frac{1}{7} + 13\frac{1}{7}$

21. $13\frac{12}{21} + 1\frac{3}{21}$

22. $8\frac{6}{13} + \frac{6}{13}$

Fractions

Adding Fractions With Unlike Denominators

Example $\dfrac{7}{15} + \dfrac{2}{5} = \blacksquare$

Solution

$\dfrac{7}{15} = \dfrac{7 \times 1}{15 \times 1} = \dfrac{7}{15}$

$+\dfrac{2}{5} = \dfrac{2 \times 3}{5 \times 3} = +\dfrac{6}{15}$ Add the numerators.

$\dfrac{13}{15}$

Rename the fractions with like denominators.

Answer $\dfrac{13}{15}$

Adding Mixed Numbers With Unlike Denominators

Example $5\dfrac{5}{8} + 2\dfrac{7}{12} = \blacksquare$

Solution

$5\dfrac{5}{8}$ $\dfrac{5}{8} = \dfrac{5 \times 3}{8 \times 3} = \dfrac{15}{24}$ $5\dfrac{5}{8} = 5\dfrac{15}{24}$

$+2\dfrac{7}{12}$ $\dfrac{7}{12} = \dfrac{7 \times 2}{12 \times 2} = \dfrac{14}{24}$ $+2\dfrac{7}{12} = 2\dfrac{14}{24}$

Rename the fractional part with like denominators.

$7\dfrac{29}{24} = 8\dfrac{5}{24}$

Rename $7\dfrac{29}{24}$.

$7 + \dfrac{29}{24} = 7 + 1\dfrac{5}{24} = 8\dfrac{5}{24}$

Answer $8\dfrac{5}{24}$

Fractions

Exercise Find common denominators and add. Write your answers in simplest terms.

1. $\dfrac{3}{7} + \dfrac{1}{3}$

2. $\dfrac{5}{6} + \dfrac{1}{3}$

3. $\dfrac{8}{12} + \dfrac{1}{8}$

4. $\dfrac{4}{17} + \dfrac{3}{34}$

5. $\dfrac{6}{11} + \dfrac{3}{4}$

6. $\dfrac{8}{15} + \dfrac{1}{6}$

7. $\dfrac{2}{15} + \dfrac{3}{45}$

8. $\dfrac{5}{8} + \dfrac{5}{6}$

9. $\dfrac{7}{9} + \dfrac{5}{27}$

10. $2\dfrac{1}{6} + \dfrac{2}{9}$

11. $12\dfrac{3}{10} + \dfrac{1}{15}$

12. $5\dfrac{6}{72} + \dfrac{1}{8}$

13. $8\dfrac{5}{16} + 2\dfrac{1}{8}$

14. $15\dfrac{2}{17} + 1\dfrac{1}{3}$

15. $26\dfrac{5}{7} + 2\dfrac{4}{21}$

16. $10\dfrac{6}{11} + 2\dfrac{5}{121}$

17. $8\dfrac{3}{36} + 2\dfrac{1}{12}$

18. $9\dfrac{5}{18} + 2\dfrac{5}{54}$

19. $5\dfrac{1}{2} + 2\dfrac{1}{17}$

20. $7\dfrac{3}{36} + 2\dfrac{1}{12}$

21. $3\dfrac{5}{18} + 1\dfrac{5}{54}$

22. $10\dfrac{1}{2} + 12\dfrac{1}{17}$

Fractions

Subtracting Mixed Numbers With Like Denominators

Example $14\frac{5}{11}$

$-\ 6\frac{2}{11}$

$\overline{\qquad 8\frac{3}{11}}$

Step 1   Subtract 2 from 5.

$5 - 2 = 3$

Step 2   Keep the denominator.

Step 3   Subtract the whole numbers.

$14 - 6 = 8$

Answer $8\frac{3}{11}$

Exercise Subtract. Write your answers in simplest terms.

1. $\frac{5}{8} - \frac{2}{8}$

2. $\frac{6}{13} - \frac{2}{13}$

3. $\frac{4}{15} - \frac{1}{15}$

4. $\frac{12}{17} - \frac{2}{17}$

5. $\frac{8}{9} - \frac{5}{9}$

6. $\frac{6}{7} - \frac{3}{7}$

7. $\frac{8}{19} - \frac{2}{19}$

8. $2\frac{3}{5} - \frac{2}{5}$

9. $8\frac{7}{8} - \frac{3}{8}$

10. $5\frac{6}{10} - 4\frac{1}{10}$

11. $15\frac{12}{13} - 4\frac{1}{13}$

12. $7\frac{7}{10} - 5\frac{2}{10}$

13. $18\frac{15}{16} - 5\frac{7}{16}$

14. $12\frac{5}{8} - 2\frac{2}{8}$

15. $17\frac{3}{4} - 5\frac{2}{4}$

16. $31\frac{5}{18} - 2$

17. $39\frac{16}{21} - 5\frac{6}{21}$

18. $14\frac{5}{6} - 2\frac{2}{6}$

19. $22\frac{3}{10} - 5\frac{3}{10}$

20. $9\frac{35}{40} - 6\frac{10}{40}$

21. $3\frac{1}{7} - \frac{1}{7}$

22. $16\frac{3}{8} - 12\frac{1}{8}$

Fractions

Subtracting Mixed Numbers With Unlike Denominators

Example

$$18\frac{2}{3} \qquad \frac{2}{3} = \frac{2 \times 7}{3 \times 7} = \frac{14}{21} \qquad 18\frac{2}{3} = 18\frac{14}{21}$$

$$-5\frac{1}{7} \qquad \frac{1}{7} = \frac{1 \times 3}{7 \times 3} = \frac{3}{21} \qquad -5\frac{1}{7} = 5\frac{3}{21}$$

$$\overline{\qquad\qquad}$$

$$13\frac{11}{21}$$

Rename the fractional parts with like denominators.

Subtract the numerators and the whole numbers.

Answer $13\frac{11}{21}$

Exercise Find common denominators and subtract. Write your answers in simplest terms.

1. $13\frac{4}{5} - 5\frac{2}{3}$

2. $9\frac{7}{8} - 3\frac{1}{3}$

3. $5\frac{5}{6} - 2\frac{1}{3}$

4. $18\frac{4}{8} - 5\frac{2}{24}$

5. $15\frac{10}{24} - 5\frac{1}{6}$

6. $3\frac{5}{8} - 1\frac{2}{6}$

7. $10\frac{13}{14} - 3\frac{1}{2}$

8. $36\frac{2}{5} - 5\frac{1}{6}$

9. $11\frac{8}{9} - 5\frac{2}{8}$

10. $16\frac{9}{13} - 2\frac{2}{3}$

11. $8\frac{15}{17} - 2\frac{2}{3}$

12. $28\frac{10}{32} - 5\frac{1}{8}$

13. $18\frac{2}{7} - 16\frac{1}{28}$

14. $31\frac{5}{12} - 4\frac{3}{48}$

15. $16\frac{7}{13} - 5\frac{2}{39}$

16. $32\frac{5}{12} - 8\frac{2}{24}$

17. $28\frac{1}{6} - 3\frac{1}{9}$

18. $3\frac{1}{3} - 1\frac{1}{7}$

19. $56\frac{3}{11} - 5\frac{1}{9}$

20. $15\frac{32}{33} - 8$

21. $8\frac{15}{16} - 2\frac{3}{24}$

22. $23\frac{8}{15} - 6\frac{9}{20}$

Subtracting Mixed Numbers With Renaming

Example 12

$\quad\quad - 3\frac{1}{7}$

Solution

Step 1   Rename.

$12 = 11 + 1$

$12 = 11 + \frac{7}{7}$

$12 = 11\frac{7}{7}$

Answer $8\frac{6}{7}$

Step 2   Subtract.

$12 \quad = \quad 11\frac{7}{7}$

$-3\frac{1}{7} = \quad 3\frac{1}{7}$

$\overline{\quad\quad\quad\quad 8\frac{6}{7}}$

Example $21\frac{1}{5}$

$\quad\quad - 4\frac{3}{5}$

Solution

Step 1   Rename.

$21\frac{1}{5} = 21 + \frac{1}{5}$

$\quad\quad\quad = 20 + 1 + \frac{1}{5}$

$\quad\quad\quad = 20 + \frac{5}{5} + \frac{1}{5}$

$\quad\quad\quad = 20\frac{6}{5}$

Answer $16\frac{3}{5}$

Step 2   Subtract.

$21\frac{1}{5} \quad = \quad 20\frac{6}{5}$

$-4\frac{3}{5} = \quad 4\frac{3}{5}$

$\overline{\quad\quad\quad\quad 16\frac{3}{5}}$

Fractions

Exercise Find common denominators and subtract. Write your answers in simplest terms.

1. $13\frac{2}{5} - 5\frac{6}{7}$

2. $18\frac{1}{5} - 2\frac{3}{5}$

3. $14\frac{3}{10} - 2\frac{1}{2}$

4. $26\frac{5}{7} - 5\frac{13}{14}$

5. $10\frac{5}{12} - 6\frac{3}{4}$

6. $24\frac{1}{11} - 5\frac{6}{22}$

7. $8\frac{2}{9} - 3\frac{4}{5}$

8. $6\frac{1}{12} - 3\frac{1}{2}$

9. $13\frac{1}{7} - 6\frac{3}{8}$

10. $14 - 2\frac{5}{11}$

11. $28\frac{2}{13} - 6\frac{7}{8}$

12. $12 - 8\frac{3}{7}$

13. $25\frac{5}{6} - 1\frac{9}{10}$

14. $9\frac{2}{15} - 4\frac{4}{5}$

15. $42\frac{1}{5} - 3\frac{3}{8}$

16. $53\frac{6}{9} - 4\frac{17}{18}$

17. $13\frac{5}{11} - 1\frac{21}{22}$

18. $30 - 6\frac{15}{19}$

19. $18\frac{1}{9} - 3\frac{2}{3}$

20. $33\frac{12}{40} - 8\frac{9}{10}$

21. $5\frac{5}{13} - 2\frac{30}{39}$

22. $16\frac{7}{10} - 4\frac{49}{50}$

23. $7\frac{1}{18} - 2\frac{2}{3}$

24. $13\frac{1}{11} - 3\frac{4}{22}$

25. $36 - 8\frac{3}{7}$

26. $13\frac{1}{4} - 5\frac{3}{5}$

27. $27\frac{5}{13} - 6\frac{25}{26}$

28. $14\frac{1}{6} - 3\frac{5}{8}$

29. $18\frac{2}{9} - 6\frac{3}{4}$

30. $6\frac{27}{30} - 5\frac{13}{15}$

31. $7\frac{8}{11} - 1\frac{21}{34}$

32. $6\frac{1}{5} - 4\frac{7}{8}$

33. $4\frac{1}{2} - 2\frac{7}{12}$

34. $16\frac{5}{9} - 3\frac{17}{18}$

35. $14\frac{3}{17} - 2\frac{5}{34}$

36. $2 - 1\frac{5}{11}$

37. $45\frac{4}{9} - 5\frac{4}{5}$

38. $32\frac{5}{16} - 5\frac{15}{32}$

39. $8\frac{3}{14} - 2\frac{6}{7}$

40. $29\frac{1}{10} - 3\frac{10}{15}$

41. $13\frac{5}{16} - 8\frac{23}{24}$

42. $4\frac{2}{7} - 2\frac{4}{5}$

43. $13\frac{15}{35} - 1\frac{6}{7}$

44. $10\frac{2}{3} - 8\frac{8}{9}$

45. $15\frac{11}{20} - 4\frac{4}{5}$

Decimals

Identifying Place Value With Decimals

Example Write the name of the place for each underlined digit.
1. 23.0<u>6</u>71   hundredths
2. 105.106<u>2</u>   ten-thousandths

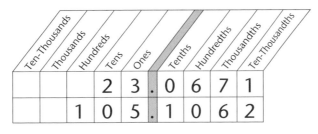

Comparing Decimals

Example Compare 2.38 and 2.4. Use the symbols < or >.

Solution Insert zeros to give each decimal the same number of places.
1. 2.38 and 2.4
2. 2.38 and 2.40 (after inserting a zero)
Since 38 is less than 40, then 2.38 < 2.40.

Example Compare 19.2 and 8.8943.

Solution Since the whole number 19 is greater than 8, then 19.2 > 8.8943.

Exercise Write the name of the place for each underlined digit.

1. 35.0<u>6</u>
2. 0.52<u>6</u>03
3. 5.681<u>1</u>
4. 1.0<u>6</u>11
5. 0.5811<u>1</u>
6. 0.40101<u>5</u>
7. 0.00<u>2</u>731
8. <u>2</u>76.03
9. 2.0<u>8</u>35
10. 0.2850<u>1</u>
11. 12.3005<u>2</u>
12. 52.083<u>1</u>
13. 0.306<u>1</u>11
14. 0.56<u>0</u>891
15. 1.0065<u>1</u>
16. 60.00<u>7</u>9
17. 14.000<u>8</u>1
18. 156.0<u>1</u>23
19. 133.0<u>1</u>
20. 15.0<u>1</u>911
21. 1.99<u>1</u>15
22. 8.567<u>2</u>3
23. 12.03587<u>6</u>
24. <u>8</u>,315.67

Decimals

Rounding Decimals

Example   Round 2.7017 to the nearest thousandth.

Solution   2.7017 ◄────── The number to the right of the thousandth place (7)
is greater than or equal to 5, so add 1 to the thousandth
place and drop all digits to the right.

Answer   2.7017 ≈ 2.702 (≈ means "about equal to.")

Example   Round 8.1649 to the nearest hundredth.

Solution   8.1649 ◄────── The number to the right of the hundredth place (4)
is less than 5, so drop the 4 and 9.

Answer   8.1649 ≈ 8.16

Exercise   Round each decimal to the places named.

		Tenth	Hundredth	Thousandth
1.	2.063	_____	_____	_____
2.	0.0891	_____	_____	_____
3.	1.0354	_____	_____	_____
4.	0.15454	_____	_____	_____
5.	32.70391	_____	_____	_____
6.	7.63	_____	_____	_____
7.	19.808964	_____	_____	_____
8.	34.00354	_____	_____	_____
9.	2.061155	_____	_____	_____
10.	139.4181891	_____	_____	_____

Decimals

Adding Decimals

Example $23 + 0.62 + 1.9 = \blacksquare$

Solution

23.	
0.62 ◄———Line up all the	
+ 1.9 decimal points.	
25.52	

23.00 ◄———Inserting zeros
0.62   may help.
+ 1.90
25.52

Answer   25.52

Exercise   Write these problems in vertical form. Then add.

1. 2.3 + 6 + 8.41

2. 0.413 + 9.6 + 0.2

3. 17 + 0.205 + 1.6

4. 2 + 0.63 + 0.5 + 1.1

5. 3.5 + 8.21 + 0.006

6. 8 + 0.15 + 1.61 + 2

7. 81.7 + 10.73 + 1.673

8. 0.02 + 0.603 + 8 + 0.11

9. 13.06 + 1.5 + 9 + 0.41

10. 2.71 + 0.031 + 8 + 9.9

11. 39.4 + 3 + 8.27 + 0.1

12. 5 + 8.4 + 0.07 + 6

13. 42 + 0.126 + 0.1 + 0.23

14. 6.28 + 0.28 + 5.4

15. 7.6 + 1 + 0.212

16. 0.561 + 4.7 + 215

17. 81.4 + 6.7 + 8.41

18. 50.51 + 2.6 + 9.15

19. 42.6 + 0.57 + 23.5

20. 39.6 + 0.003 + 1.81

21. 95.1 + 1.63 + 101.1

22. 8 + 1.53 + 0.007

23. 0.203 + 0.72 + 0.025

24. 1.56 + 1.231 + 0.07

25. 13 + 0.92 + 6.7

26. 83 + 9.6 + 1.305

27. 5.03 + 0.607 + 0.19

28. 18.95 + 1.4 + 0.071

29. 39.9 + 14.62 + 2.3

30. 2.3 + 1.78 + 0.663

31. 8.702 + 3.7 + 0.63

32. 3.0101 + 0.62 + 4

33. 2.7 + 0.063 + 1.77

34. 12.8 + 0.14 + 0.03 + 3

35. 1.9 + 5.621 + 0.03

36. 4.7 + 0.726 + 89.1

37. 1.7 + 2.31 + 0.631

38. 6.7 + 0.815 + 2

39. 0.37 + 2.9 + 8

40. 6.09 + 0.261 + 9.2

41. 23 + 1.003 + 5.4

42. 5.21 + 0.53 + 15.6

43. 63 + 1.92 + 88.8

44. 0.38 + 7.02 + 0.115

45. 5 + 0.27 + 1.919

46. 1 + 0.006 + 0.0071 + 1.8

47. 11.001 + 1.1 + 6.27

48. 3.9 + 1.06 + 0.081

Decimals

Subtracting Decimals

Example $12 - 1.68 = \blacksquare$

Solution 12.00 ◄————Line up the decimal points and insert zeros.
$$\begin{array}{r} 12.00 \\ -\ 1.68 \\ \hline 10.32 \end{array}$$

Answer   10.32

Exercise Write these problems in vertical form. Then subtract.

1. $6.59 - 0.48$

2. $36 - 2.3$

3. $19.83 - 2.3$

4. $33.89 - 0.32$

5. $5.2 - 0.156$

6. $31.4 - 8$

7. $38.5 - 1.67$

8. $7.6 - 0.67$

9. $0.091 - 0.0197$

10. $1.1 - 0.99$

11. $7.7 - 2.63$

12. $36.5 - 1.83$

13. $6.7 - 2.34$

14. $1.6 - 1.08$

15. $0.89 - 0.098$

16. $2.31 - 0.9$

17. $0.011 - 0.00201$

18. $0.3 - 0.234$

19. $1.03 - 0.89$

20. $75 - 0.108$

21. $8.7 - 2.31$

22. $1 - 0.9$

23. $8.3 - 0.99$

24. $45.1 - 0.06$

25. $0.101 - 0.0982$

26. $53.72 - 1.8$

27. $9.01 - 0.6$

28. $2.171 - 0.18$

29. $5.6 - 0.42$

30. $2.1 - 0.8$

31. $9 - 0.62$

32. $12 - 4.35$

33. $1 - 0.08$

34. $0.1 - 0.0356$

35. $0.35 - 0.19$

36. $5.51 - 0.6$

37. $19.5 - 0.34$

38. $2.81 - 0.931$

39. $11.23 - 9.9$

40. $31.3 - 0.61$

41. $4.35 - 0.6$

42. $0.68 - 0.086$

43. $0.1 - 0.06$

44. $1.63 - 0.89$

45. $7.5 - 6$

46. $3 - 0.4$

47. $5.52 - 0.66$

48. $6 - 0.9$

49. $0.32 - 0.0832$

50. $1 - 0.662$

Decimals

Multiplying Decimals

Example $0.26 \times 1.3 = $ ■

Solution $.26$ ◄——2 places plus
          $\underline{\times\ 1.3}$ ◄——1 place equals
              78
          $\underline{+\ 26}$
          $.338$ ◄——— 3 places

Example $0.321 \times 0.002 = $ ■

Solution $.321$ ◄——3 places plus
          $\underline{\times\quad .002}$ ◄——3 places equals
          $.000642$ ◄——6 places

Exercise Write these problems in vertical form. Then multiply.

1. 0.2×0.3

2. 0.7×1.2

3. 1.9×0.3

4. 2.6×8

5. 0.26×0.2

6. 0.62×0.3

7. 0.81×1.2

8. 0.42×6.3

9. 0.92×0.21

10. 0.65×0.07

11. 1.23×1.2

12. 0.128×0.52

13. 5.8×0.006

14. 0.081×0.02

15. 0.96×0.73

16. 8.03×0.67

17. 0.126×0.73

18. 25.3×0.62

19. 0.5×6

20. 1.3×0.8

21. 2.3×0.5

22. 4.3×0.8

23. 3.5×0.7

24. 0.85×3

25. 0.26×1.5

26. 1.8×0.18

27. 4.8×0.06

28. 0.31×0.09

29. 3.62×0.05

30. 0.402×0.11

31. 0.71×0.62

32. 1.62×0.71

33. 52.6×0.36

34. 4.2×0.008

35. 703×0.02

36. 0.91×0.083

Decimals

Scientific Notation

Example   Express 2,800 in scientific notation.

Solution $2,800 = 2.800 \times 10^3$ ⟵——3 places
or
2.8×10^3

Example   Express 0.00039 in scientific notation.

Solution $0.00039 = 3.9 \times 10^{-4}$ ⟵——4 places
Use the negative sign $(^-4)$ when the decimal point is moved to the right.

Exercise   Write these numbers in scientific notation.

1. 3,600
2. 35,100
3. 46,000
4. 75,100
5. 6,530
6. 391,000
7. 1,725,000
8. 5,301,000
9. 87,100,000
10. 267,000,000
11. 100,000
12. 1,700,000,000
13. 34,000,000
14. 306.2
15. 12.721
16. 0.0000623
17. 0.00002
18. 0.1602
19. 623.05
20. 0.000000005
21. 0.00000101
22. 0.00663

23. 510
24. 8,702
25. 92,300
26. 18,000
27. 980,000
28. 5,600,000
29. 7,810,000
30. 1,000,000
31. 45,000,000
32. 9,720,000
33. 5,300,000,000
34. 961,000,000
35. 171,800,000
36. 48.39
37. 150.82
38. 0.0000031
39. 0.000175
40. 0.003
41. 0.00231
42. 0.000000453
43. 0.000119
44. 0.0024

Decimals

Dividing Decimals by Whole Numbers

Example $0.168 \div 14 = \blacksquare$

Solution

$$
\begin{array}{r}
0.012 \\
14\overline{)0.168} \\
-14 \\
\hline
28 \\
-28 \\
\hline
0
\end{array}
$$

Place the decimal point in the quotient directly above the one in the dividend.

Example $68.6 \div 28 = \blacksquare$

Solution

$$
\begin{array}{r}
2.45 \\
28\overline{)68.60} \\
-56 \\
\hline
12\ 6 \\
-11\ 2 \\
\hline
1\ 40 \\
-1\ 40 \\
\hline
0
\end{array}
$$

Adding a zero may help you complete the division problem.

Dividing Decimals by Decimals

Example $8.04 \div 0.6 = \blacksquare$

Solution

$$
\begin{array}{r}
13.4 \\
0.6\overline{)8.04} \\
-6 \\
\hline
2\ 0 \\
-1\ 8 \\
\hline
2\ 4 \\
-2\ 4 \\
\hline
0
\end{array}
$$

Step 1 Move the decimal point in the divisor to the right.

Step 2 Move the decimal point in the dividend the same number of places to the right.

Step 3 Divide and bring the decimal point straight up into the quotient.

Renaming Decimals as Fractions

Example   Rename 0.13 as a fraction.

Solution $0.13 = \dfrac{13}{100}$

Example $0.026 = \blacksquare$

Solution $0.026 = \dfrac{26}{1,000}$ or $\dfrac{13}{500}$

Decimals

Renaming Fractions as Decimals

Example   Rename $\frac{13}{25}$ as a decimal.   Choose a multiplier that will give you a denominator that is a power of 10. (10, 100, 1,000, 10,000, . . .)

Solution $\frac{13}{25} = \frac{13 \times 4}{25 \times 4} = \frac{52}{100}$

$$= 0.52 \text{ or}$$

$$
\begin{array}{r}
0.52 \\
25 \overline{)13.00} \\
-\ 12\ 5 \\
\hline
50 \\
-\ 50 \\
\hline
0
\end{array}
$$

Dividing the numerator by the denominator will also give the decimal equivalent.

Exercise   Divide. Rename decimals as fractions.

1. $4.7 \div 2$

2. $0.78 \div 3$

3. $1.448 \div 0.8$

4. $2.88 \div 0.9$

5. $10.2 \div 1.2$

6. $11.55 \div 2.1$

7. $4.545 \div 0.9$

8. $2.807 \div 0.7$

9. $0.351 \div .09$

10. $4.004 \div 0.22$

11. $0.777 \div 0.15$

12. $13.7046 \div 0.91$

13. $0.0615 \div 1.5$

14. $0.00902 \div 0.41$

15. $0.01952 \div 3.2$

16. $0.00206 \div 0.002$

17. $32.92 \div 0.4$

18. $0.12741 \div 0.31$

19. $0.08833 \div 0.11$

20. $0.0084 \div 0.007$

21. $6.2432 \div 1.6$

22. $36.8 \div 8$

23. $3.51 \div 9$

24. $7.23 \div 3$

25. $2.412 \div 0.6$

26. $8.32 \div 3.2$

27. $10.44 \div 2.9$

28. $0.159 \div 0.15$

29. $0.266 \div 0.07$

30. $2.173 \div 4.1$

Percents

Solving Proportions

Example $\dfrac{25}{\blacksquare} = \dfrac{5}{6}$

Solution $\dfrac{25}{\blacksquare} = \dfrac{5}{6}$

$$5 \times \blacksquare = 25 \times 6$$
$$5 \times \blacksquare = 150$$
$$\blacksquare = 150 \div 5$$
$$\blacksquare = 30$$

Changing Percents to Decimals

Example Write 32% as a decimal.

Solution $32\% = 0.32$ Move the decimal point 2 places to the left and remove the % sign.

Example Write 6.3% as a decimal.

Solution $6.3\% = 0.063$

Changing Percents to Fractions

Example Write 45% as a fraction.

Solution $45\% = 0.45$

$$45\% = \dfrac{45}{100}$$
$$45\% = \dfrac{9}{20}$$

Renaming Decimals as Percents

Example Write 0.231 as a percent.
Move the decimal point 2 places to the right.

Solution $0.231 = 23.1\%$

Percents

Renaming Fractions as Percents

Example   Write $\frac{7}{8}$ as a percent.

Solution   First express $\frac{7}{8}$ as a decimal.

$$
\begin{array}{r}
0.875 \\
8\,)\overline{7.000} \\
\underline{-6\,4} \\
60 \\
\underline{-56} \\
40 \\
\underline{-40} \\
0
\end{array}
$$

$\frac{7}{8} = 0.875$

$\phantom{\frac{7}{8}} = 87.5\%$ or $87\frac{1}{2}\%$

Answer   87.5%

Finding the Percentage

Example   23% of 35 is what number?

Solution $0.23 \times 35 = \blacksquare$

$8.05 = \blacksquare$

Exercise Find the percentage.

1. 20% of 52 is ____
2. 35% of 60 is ____
3. 70% of 50 is ____
4. 10% of 82 is ____
5. 2% of 39 is ____
6. 5% of 7 is ____
7. 14% of 2.8 is ____
8. 39% of 6 is ____
9. 3% of 4.9 is ____
10. 6% of 0.42 is ____
11. 18% of 5.6 is ____
12. 56% of 23.5 is ____
13. 7% of 0.82 is ____
14. 32% of 0.38 is ____

15. 25% of 75 is ____
16. 62% of 35 is ____
17. 9% of 150 is ____
18. 15% of 20 is ____
19. 26% of 40 is ____
20. 3% of 35 is ____
21. 23% of 5 is ____
22. 19% of 8 is ____
23. 8% of 7.02 is ____
24. 11% of 3.6 is ____
25. 13% of 2.5 is ____
26. 70% of 0.38 is ____
27. 53% of 0.72 is ____
28. 6.2% of 32 is ____

Percents

Exercise Find the rate.

1. ___% of 72 is 1.44
2. ___% of 350 is 14
3. ___% of 380 is 34.2
4. ___% of 2.8 is 0.42
5. ___% of 4.5 is 0.18
6. ___% of 5.1 is 1.632
7. ___% of 0.26 is 0.1248
8. ___% of 1.5 is 0.48
9. ___% of 0.03 is 0.0021
10. ___% of 1.8 is 0.09
11. ___% of 30 is 0.87
12. ___% of 80 is 4.96
13. ___% of 35 is 2.065
14. ___% of 80 is 7.36

15. ___% of 90 is 5.4
16. ___% of 10 is 0.8
17. ___% of 320 is 16
18. ___% of 6.3 is 1.26
19. ___% of 6.1 is 0.61
20. ___% of 5.3 is 2.067
21. ___% of 0.41 is 0.2214
22. ___% of 4.5 is 1.71
23. ___% of 0.9 is 0.594
24. ___% of 0.3 is 0.0243
25. ___% of 50 is 2.1
26. ___% of 53 is 4.823
27. ___% of 60 is 1.68
28. ___% of 90 is 6.48

Exercise Find the base.

1. 6% of ___ is 0.03
2. 7% of ___ is 0.021
3. 8% of ___ is 0.152
4. 15% of ___ is 145.5
5. 23% of ___ is 8.05
6. 4% of ___ is 2.48
7. 3.5% of ___ is 53.2
8. 7% of ___ is 0.042
9. 15% of ___ is 0.345
10. 2.3% of ___ is 2.185
11. 0.14% of ___ is 0.0462
12. 0.91% of ___ is 0.5733
13. 0.26% of ___ is 0.0208
14. 0.9% of ___ is 0.0216
15. 28% of ___ is 82.88
16. 235% of ___ is 18.8
17. 110% of ___ is 42.9
18. 0.07% of ___ is 0.0035

19. 9% of ___ is 0.81
20. 4% of ___ is 0.52
21. 6% of ___ is 1.68
22. 22% of ___ is 75.02
23. 4% of ___ is 11.2
24. 9% of ___ is 90
25. 5% of ___ is 0.045
26. 9% of ___ is 0.153
27. 18% of ___ is 0.0234
28. 4.2% of ___ is 2.646
29. 5.9% of ___ is 11.8
30. 0.11% of ___ is 0.033
31. 20.3% of ___ is 1.827
32. 0.5% of ___ is 0.0025
33. 41% of ___ is 37.843
34. 140% of ___ is 74.2
35. 99% of ___ is 97.02
36. 0.06% of ___ is 0.0078

Percents

Exercise Find the missing numbers.

1. 2% of ___ is 0.16

2. 18% of 25 is ___

3. ___% of 150 is 43.5

4. 7% of ___ is 1.96

5. 53% of 69 is ___

6. ___% of 36 is 3.6

7. 8% of ___ is 4.48

8. 17% of 39 is ___

9. ___% of 32 is 8

10. 26% of ___ is 0.676

11. 52% of 35 is ___

12. ___% of 8.5 is 1.36

13. 75% of ___ is 19.65

14. 30% of 35.4 is ___

15. ___% of 15.2 is 13.832

16. 2.8% of 60 is ___

17. 2.9% of 60 is ___

18. ___% of 7.7 is 0.77

19. 95% of ___ is 9.5

20. 11% of 19 is ___

21. ___% of 77.1 is 21.588

22. 15% of ___ is 5.4

23. 0.07% of 276 is ___

24. ___% of 378 is 0.756

25. 0.08% of ___ is 0.0312

26. 6% of 2.8 is ___

27. 32% of ___ is 16.96

28. ___% of 16 is 0.8

29. 43% of ___ is 13.76

30. 9% of 156 is ___

31. 92% of ___ is 184

32. ___% of 100 is 3.9

33. 19% of 56 is ___

34. 75% of ___ is 28.5

35. ___% of 81 is 7.29

36. 80% of 30 is ___

37. 35% of ___ is 3.185

38. ___% of 30 is 5.4

Percents

39. 28% of 6.5 is ____

40. 20% of ____ is 6.44

41. ____% of 60 is 3.18

42. 4.3% of 50 is ____

43. 13% of ____ is 0.507

44. ____% of 31 is 1.736

45. 62% of 24 is ____

46. 3.4% of ____ is 2.754

47. ____% of 37 is 13.69

48. 29% of 300 is ____

49. 0.25% of ____ is 0.0375

50. ____% of 4.2 is 0.21

Calculator Handbook

There are many kinds of electronic calculators. Each calculator is a little different from others. Some have more keys than others. The keys may be placed differently. You may have to press the keys in a certain order. Most calculators, however, are very similar.

Here is a calculator that has the basic functions you find on most calculators.

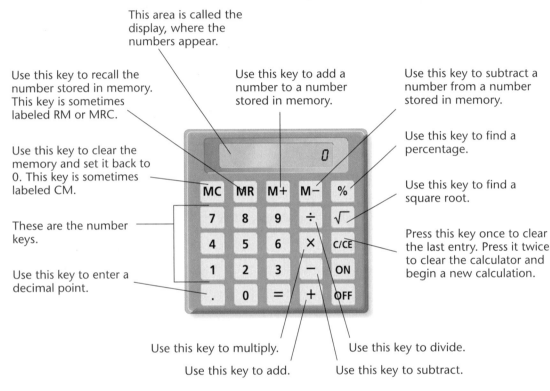

This area is called the display, where the numbers appear.

Use this key to recall the number stored in memory. This key is sometimes labeled RM or MRC.

Use this key to add a number to a number stored in memory.

Use this key to subtract a number from a number stored in memory.

Use this key to clear the memory and set it back to 0. This key is sometimes labeled CM.

Use this key to find a percentage.

Use this key to find a square root.

These are the number keys.

Use this key to enter a decimal point.

Press this key once to clear the last entry. Press it twice to clear the calculator and begin a new calculation.

Use this key to multiply.

Use this key to divide.

Use this key to add.

Use this key to subtract.

You can use a calculator to help you do arithmetic quickly and accurately. In many cases, you key the calculation the same way you would write it on paper.

Press *23* + *61* =
The display will read *84*.
23 + 61 = 84
Press *12* × *12* =
The display will read *144*.
12 × 12 = 144

Press *98* − *18* =
The display will read *80*.
98 − 18 = 80
Press *63* ÷ *9* =
The display will read *7*.
63 ÷ 9 = 7

It's a good idea to look at the display after you key in each number. It helps to check that you haven't pressed a wrong key by mistake.

The $\sqrt{\ }$ key will give you the square root of a number.

Example   What is the square root of 81?
Press 81 $\sqrt{\ }$
The display will read 9.

The $\%$ key will help you find a percentage. The $\%$ key works differently on different kinds of calculators. You may need to press $=$ after $\%$ on some calculators. The examples show how the key works on most calculators.

Examples   What is 25 percent of 44?
Press 44 $\times$ 25 $\%$
The display will read 11.
What is 10 percent more than 50?
Press 50 $+$ 10 $\%$
The display will read 55.

If you are going to use the same number, or constant, in a series of calculations, you can store it in memory. Remember to clear the memory by pressing MC before you begin.

Examples   What is 18 times 4? 18 times 12? 18 times 31?
Press 18 $M+$ C/CE
The display reads 0. The number 18 is stored in memory.
Press MR $\times$ 4 $=$ The display reads 72.
Press MR $\times$ 12 $=$ The display reads 216.
Press MR $\times$ 31 $=$ The display reads 558.

You can add to or subtract from the number in memory by using the $M+$ and $M-$ keys. Remember to clear the memory by pressing MC before you begin.

Press	Display	Number in Memory
22	22	0
M+	22	22
6	6	22
M+	6	28
20	20	28
M−	20	8

Decimal, Percent, and Fraction Conversion

Renaming Decimals as Percents

Example   Rename 0.75 as a percent.

Solution   0.75

Step 1   Move the decimal point two places to the right.

$$0.75 = 75\%$$

Step 2   Then insert a percent symbol.

Example   Rename 0.5 as a percent.

Solution $0.5 = .50$

$$0.5 = 50\%$$

Renaming Percents as Decimals

Example   Rename 80% as a decimal.

Step 1   Move the decimal point two places to the left.

Solution $80\% = 80.\%$

Step 2   Then drop the percent symbol.

$$80\% = 0.80$$

$$= 0.8 \longleftarrow \text{You can always drop zeros at the end of a decimal.}$$

Renaming Fractions as Decimals

Example   Rename $\frac{7}{20}$ as a decimal.

Solution   **Method 1**

$$\frac{7}{20} = \frac{7 \times 5}{20 \times 5} = \frac{35}{100}$$

$$= 0.35$$

Choose a multiplier that makes the denominator a power of 10 (10, 100, 1,000, . . .)

Method 2

$$\frac{7}{20} = 20 \overline{)\begin{array}{r} 0.35 \\ 7.00 \\ -\ 6\ 0 \\ \hline 1\ 00 \\ -\ 1\ 00 \end{array}}$$

Divide the numerator by the denominator.

Decimal, Percent, and Fraction Conversion

Renaming Decimals as Fractions

Example Rename 0.025 as a fraction.

Solution First, read the decimal: "25 thousandths."

Then write the fraction and simplify.

$$0.025 = \frac{25}{1,000} = \frac{25 \div 25}{1,000 \div 25} = \frac{1}{40}$$

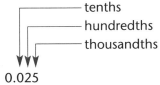

Renaming Fractions as Percents

Example Rename $\frac{9}{25}$ as a percent.

Solution **Method 1**

Write as an equivalent fraction with denominator 100.

$$\frac{9}{25} = \frac{9 \times 4}{25 \times 4} = \frac{36}{100} = 36\%$$

Percent means "per 100."
So, 36 hundredths is 36%.

Method 2

$$\frac{9}{25} = 0.36 = 36\%$$

Step 1 Divide the numerator by the denominator.

Step 2 Rewrite the decimal as a percent.

Renaming Percents as Fractions

Example Rename 2% as a fraction.

Solution $2\% = \frac{2}{100}$ ⟵ *Percent* means "per 100."

$= \frac{1}{50}$ ⟵ Simplify.

Measurement Conversion Factors

Metric Measures

Length
1,000 meters (m) = 1 kilometer (km)
100 centimeters (cm) = 1 m
10 decimeters (dm) = 1 m
1,000 millimeters (mm) = 1 m
10 cm = 1 decimeter (dm)
10 mm = 1 cm

Area
100 square millimeters (mm^2) = 1 square centimeter (cm^2)
10,000 cm^2 = 1 square meter (m^2)
10,000 m^2 = 1 hectare (ha)

Volume
1,000 cubic meters (m^3) = 1 cubic centimeter (cm^3)
100 cm^3 = 1 cubic decimeter (dm^3)
1,000,000 cm^3 = 1 cubic meter (m^3)

Capacity
1,000 milliliters (mL) = 1 liter (L)
1,000 L = 1 kiloliter (kL)

Mass
1,000 kilograms (kg) = 1 metric ton (t)
1,000 grams (g) = 1 kg
1,000 milligrams (mg) = 1 g

Temperature Degrees Celsius (°C)
0°C = freezing point of water
37°C = normal body temperature
100°C = boiling point of water

Time
60 seconds (sec) = 1 minute (min)
60 min = 1 hour (hr)
24 hr = 1 day

Customary Measures

Length
12 inches (in.) = 1 foot (ft)
3 ft = 1 yard (yd)
36 in. = 1 yd
5,280 ft = 1 mile (mi)
1,760 yd = 1 mi
6,076 feet = 1 nautical mile

Area
144 square inches (sq in.) = 1 square foot (sq ft)
9 sq ft = 1 square yard (sq yd)
43,560 sq ft = 1 acre (A)

Volume
1,728 cubic inches (cu in.) = 1 cubic foot (cu ft)
27 cu ft = 1 cubic yard (cu yard)

Capacity
8 fluid ounces (fl oz) = 1 cup (c)
2 c = 1 pint (pt)
2 pt = 1 quart (qt)
4 qt = 1 gallon (gal)

Weight
16 ounces (oz) = 1 pound (lb)
2,000 lb = 1 ton (T)

Temperature Degrees Fahrenheit (°F)
32°F = freezing point of water
98.6°F = normal body temperature
212°F = boiling point of water

Measurement Conversion Factors

To change	To	Multiply by	To change	To	Multiply by
centimeters	inches	0.3937	meters	feet	3.2808
centimeters	feet	0.03281	meters	miles	0.0006214
cubic feet	cubic meters	0.0283	meters	yards	1.0936
cubic meters	cubic feet	35.3145	metric tons	tons (long)	0.9842
cubic meters	cubic yards	1.3079	metric tons	tons (short)	1.1023
cubic yards	cubic meters	0.7646	miles	kilometers	1.6093
feet	meters	0.3048	miles	feet	5,280
feet	miles (nautical)	0.0001645	miles (statute)	miles (nautical)	0.8684
feet	miles (statute)	0.0001894	miles/hour	feet/minute	88
feet/second	miles/hour	0.6818	millimeters	inches	0.0394
gallons (U.S.)	liters	3.7853	ounces avdp	grams	28.3495
grams	ounces avdp	0.0353	ounces	pounds	0.0625
grams	pounds	0.002205	pecks	liters	8.8096
hours	days	0.04167	pints (dry)	liters	0.5506
inches	millimeters	25.4000	pints (liquid)	liters	0.4732
inches	centimeters	2.5400	pounds avdp	kilograms	0.4536
kilograms	pounds avdp	2.2046	pounds	ounces	16
kilometers	miles	0.6214	quarts (dry)	liters	1.1012
liters	gallons (U.S.)	0.2642	quarts (liquid)	liters	0.9463
liters	pecks	0.1135	square feet	square meters	0.0929
liters	pints (dry)	1.8162	square meters	square feet	10.7639
liters	pints (liquid)	2.1134	square meters	square yards	1.1960
liters	quarts (dry)	0.9081	square yards	square meters	0.8361
liters	quarts (liquid)	1.0567	yards	meters	0.9144

Addition Table

+	0	1	2	3	4	5	6	7	8	9	10
0	0	1	2	3	4	5	6	7	8	9	10
1	1	2	3	4	5	6	7	8	9	10	11
2	2	3	4	5	6	7	8	9	10	11	12
3	3	4	5	6	7	8	9	10	11	12	13
4	4	5	6	7	8	9	10	11	12	13	14
5	5	6	7	8	9	10	11	12	13	14	15
6	6	7	8	9	10	11	12	13	14	15	16
7	7	8	9	10	11	12	13	14	15	16	17
8	8	9	10	11	12	13	14	15	16	17	18
9	9	10	11	12	13	14	15	16	17	18	19
10	10	11	12	13	14	15	16	17	18	19	20

Subtraction Table

−	0	1	2	3	4	5	6	7	8	9	10
0	0	−1	−2	−3	−4	−5	−6	−7	−8	−9	−10
1	1	0	−1	−2	−3	−4	−5	−6	−7	−8	−9
2	2	1	0	−1	−2	−3	−4	−5	−6	−7	−8
3	3	2	1	0	−1	−2	−3	−4	−5	−6	−7
4	4	3	2	1	0	−1	−2	−3	−4	−5	−6
5	5	4	3	2	1	0	−1	−2	−3	−4	−5
6	6	5	4	3	2	1	0	−1	−2	−3	−4
7	7	6	5	4	3	2	1	0	−1	−2	−3
8	8	7	6	5	4	3	2	1	0	−1	−2
9	9	8	7	6	5	4	3	2	1	0	−1
10	10	9	8	7	6	5	4	3	2	1	0

Note: To use this table, look at the numbers in the far left vertical column. Select a number from the vertical column. Then subtract from that number by selecting a number in the top horizontal row. The difference is listed where the column and row meet. For example, subtract number 4 in the top horizontal row from number 1 in the vertical column. The answer is −3, which is the number located where the column and row meet. You must subtract the numbers in the horizontal row from the numbers in the vertical column for this chart to work.

Multiplication Table

×	2	3	4	5	6	7	8	9	10	11	12
2	4	6	8	10	12	14	16	18	20	22	24
3	6	9	12	15	18	21	24	27	30	33	36
4	8	12	16	20	24	28	32	36	40	44	48
5	10	15	20	25	30	35	40	45	50	55	60
6	12	18	24	30	36	42	48	54	60	66	72
7	14	21	28	35	42	49	56	63	70	77	84
8	16	24	32	40	48	56	64	72	80	88	96
9	18	27	36	45	54	63	72	81	90	99	108
10	20	30	40	50	60	70	80	90	100	110	120
11	22	33	44	55	66	77	88	99	110	121	132
12	24	36	48	60	72	84	96	108	120	132	144

Division Table

÷1	÷2	÷3	÷4	÷5
$0 \div 1 = 0$	$0 \div 2 = 0$	$0 \div 3 = 0$	$0 \div 4 = 0$	$0 \div 5 = 0$
$1 \div 1 = 1$	$2 \div 2 = 1$	$3 \div 3 = 1$	$4 \div 4 = 1$	$5 \div 5 = 1$
$2 \div 1 = 2$	$4 \div 2 = 2$	$6 \div 3 = 2$	$8 \div 4 = 2$	$10 \div 5 = 2$
$3 \div 1 = 3$	$6 \div 2 = 3$	$9 \div 3 = 3$	$12 \div 4 = 3$	$15 \div 5 = 3$
$4 \div 1 = 4$	$8 \div 2 = 4$	$12 \div 3 = 4$	$16 \div 4 = 4$	$20 \div 5 = 4$
$5 \div 1 = 5$	$10 \div 2 = 5$	$15 \div 3 = 5$	$20 \div 4 = 5$	$25 \div 5 = 5$
$6 \div 1 = 6$	$12 \div 2 = 6$	$18 \div 3 = 6$	$24 \div 4 = 6$	$30 \div 5 = 6$
$7 \div 1 = 7$	$14 \div 2 = 7$	$21 \div 3 = 7$	$28 \div 4 = 7$	$35 \div 5 = 7$
$8 \div 1 = 8$	$16 \div 2 = 8$	$24 \div 3 = 8$	$32 \div 4 = 8$	$40 \div 5 = 8$
$9 \div 1 = 9$	$18 \div 2 = 9$	$27 \div 3 = 9$	$36 \div 4 = 9$	$45 \div 5 = 9$

÷6	÷7	÷8	÷9	÷10
$0 \div 6 = 0$	$0 \div 7 = 0$	$0 \div 8 = 0$	$0 \div 9 = 0$	$0 \div 10 = 0$
$6 \div 6 = 1$	$7 \div 7 = 1$	$8 \div 8 = 1$	$9 \div 9 = 1$	$10 \div 10 = 1$
$12 \div 6 = 2$	$14 \div 7 = 2$	$16 \div 8 = 2$	$18 \div 9 = 2$	$20 \div 10 = 2$
$18 \div 6 = 3$	$21 \div 7 = 3$	$24 \div 8 = 3$	$27 \div 9 = 3$	$30 \div 10 = 3$
$24 \div 6 = 4$	$28 \div 7 = 4$	$32 \div 8 = 4$	$36 \div 9 = 4$	$40 \div 10 = 4$
$30 \div 6 = 5$	$35 \div 7 = 5$	$40 \div 8 = 5$	$45 \div 9 = 5$	$50 \div 10 = 5$
$36 \div 6 = 6$	$42 \div 7 = 6$	$48 \div 8 = 6$	$54 \div 9 = 6$	$60 \div 10 = 6$
$42 \div 6 = 7$	$49 \div 7 = 7$	$56 \div 8 = 7$	$63 \div 9 = 7$	$70 \div 10 = 7$
$48 \div 6 = 8$	$56 \div 7 = 8$	$64 \div 8 = 8$	$72 \div 9 = 8$	$80 \div 10 = 8$
$54 \div 6 = 9$	$63 \div 7 = 9$	$72 \div 8 = 9$	$81 \div 9 = 9$	$90 \div 10 = 9$

Glossary

A

Advance (ad vans´) to move forward (p. 56)

Area (âr´ ē ə) amount of space inside a shape (p. 20)

Assist (ə sist´) a defensive play by a fielder that helps to make a putout (p. 199)

Average (av´ ər ij) the number obtained by dividing the sum of two or more quantities by the number of quantities (p. 42)

B

Balance (bal´ əns) the amount due (p. 231)

Base (bās) an amount that a percent is taken of (p. 217)

Baserunning average (bās run ing av´ ər ij) ratio of stolen bases to attempted steals (p. 197)

Batting average (bat´ ing av´ ər ij) a ratio of hits to at bats; a measure of how well a batter hits (p. 192)

Beading (bē´ ding) a cord of beads used for jewelry or woven into designs (p. 90)

Beneficiary (bən ə fish´ ē er ē) a person who receives the face value of an insurance policy (p. 262)

Budget (bud´ jit) a plan for managing money (p. 215)

C

Calculate (kal´ kyə lāt) to find an answer by using mathematics (p. 40)

Calorie (kal´ ər ē) unit of measure of the energy in food; the amount of heat needed to raise the temperature of one gram of water one degree Celsius (p. 2)

Celsius (sel´ sē əs) a thermometer on which 0 degrees is the freezing point and 100 degrees is the boiling point of water (p. 303)

Circle graph (sėr´ kəl graf) way to show comparisons by using segments of a circle (p. 219)

Clockwise (klok´ wīz) in the direction in which the hands of a clock rotate (p. 57)

Compare (kəm pâr´) to examine two numbers to determine which is larger (p. 81)

Compound interest (kom´ pound in´ tər əst) interest computed on principal plus interest (p. 231)

Compute (kəm pyüt´) to calculate or figure out (p. 40)

Construction class (kən struk´ shən clas) type of house (p. 252)

Consume (kən süm´) to use; to eat or drink up (p. 2)

Conversion factor (kən vėr´ zhən fak´ tər) a number you multiply a measurement by to obtain an equivalent measurement (p. 166)

Convert (kən vėrt´) to change to something of equal value (p. 72)

Coverage (kuv´ ər ij) insurance for a loss (p. 246)

Credit (kred´ it) the right to buy now and to pay later (p. 236)

Cubic (kyüb´ ic) the volume of a cube whose length, width, and depth each measure the same (p. 282)

Currency (kėr´ ən sē) money (p. 166)

D

Decimal (des´ ə məl) a whole number followed by a point and places to the right. The numbers to the point's right equal less than one. (p. 120)

Decimal place (des´ ə məl plās) position to the right of the decimal point (p. 120)

Degree (di grē´) 1/360th of a circle (p. 219)

Denominator (di nom´ ə nā tər) the part of a fraction that is below the line and that tells the number of parts in the whole (p. 74)

Dice sum (dīs sum) the total points shown on two or more dice (p. 54)

a	hat	e	let	ī	ice	ô	order	ů	put	sh	she		a	in about
ā	age	ē	equal	o	hot	oi	oil	ü	rule	th	thin	ə	e	in taken
ä	far	ėr	term	ō	open	ou	out	ch	child	ŦH	then		i	in pencil
â	care	i	it	ȯ	saw	u	cup	ng	long	zh	measure		o	in lemon
													u	in circus

Die (dī) (plural: **dice**) (dīs) a small cube of bone, plastic, etc., marked on each side with from one to six spots and used usually in pairs (p. 53)

Discount (dis´ kount) the amount taken off the usual price (p. 213)

Double roll (dub´ əl rōl) wallpaper that covers twice the wall area of a single roll (p. 26)

Double time (dub´ əl tīm) payment of 2 times the hourly rate (p. 138)

Draw (drȯ) to pick at random (p. 61)

E

Earned run average (ERA) (ėrnd run av´ ər ij) (ē är ā) a statistic the describes how many runs a pitcher allows; ERA = 9 × Earned Runs ÷ Innings Pitched (p. 200)

Elapse (i laps´) to slip by; to pass (p. 176)

Elapsed time (i lapst´ tīm) the difference between the starting time and the ending time (p. 176)

Endowment insurance (en dou´ mənt in shür´ əns) insurance where premium is paid and face value is paid to the insured (p. 262)

Equivalent (i kwiv´ ə lənt) equal to another in a particular way (p. 72)

Error (er´ ər) misplay in fielding a ball that allows a player to advance (p. 199)

Estimate (es´ tə māt) to give a reasonable or approximate number; to make a general but careful guess of the number, size, or value of something (p. 11)

Expect (ek speckt´) to look forward to (p. 59)

Experiment (ek sper´ ə mənt) a procedure used to test a theory; trial or test (p. 59)

F

Fabric guide (fab´ rik gīd) chart showing the amount of material needed to make garments (p. 88)

Face value (fās val´ yü) the worth printed or written on a policy (p. 256)

Factors (fak´ tərz) numbers that when multiplied together form a product; numbers being multiplied (p. 74)

Fahrenheit (far´ ən hīt) a thermometer on which 32 degrees is the freezing point and 212 degrees is the boiling point of water (p. 303)

Fat calories (fat kal´ ər ēz) calories that come from the fat in food (p. 5)

Fielding percentage (fēld´ ing pər sen´ tij) ratio of assists and putouts to total chances (p. 199)

Finance charge (fī´ nans chärj) money paid for the use of money (p. 236)

Fixture (fiks´ cher) toilet, sink, bathtub, or shower (p. 250)

Formula (fôr´ myə lə) a rule or method of doing something (p. 53)

Frame (frām) in bowling, any of the divisions of a game in which all ten pins are set up anew (p. 34)

G

Games back (gāmz bak) difference in wins and losses between a team and the first-place team (p. 205)

Geometric (jē ə met´ rik) formed of straight lines, triangles, circles, etc., as a pattern (p. 90)

Graph (graf) a pictorial way to display information (p. 10)

Gross pay (grōs pā) pay before deductions (p. 132)

H

Height (hīt) the distance from top to bottom (p. 20)

I

Improper fraction (im prop´ ər frak´ shən) a fraction whose numerator is equal to or greater than its denominator (p. 74)

Income (in´ kum) money earned (p. 215)

Increase (in krēs´) to make greater (p. 10)

Insurance (in shür´ əns) coverage by a contract in which one party guarantees another against loss (p. 246)

Interest (in´ tər ist) amount paid for the use of money (p. 228)

Interest rate (in´ tər ist rāt) percent paid or charged for the use of money (p. 228)

Invert (in vėrt´) to reverse in position (p. 111)

a	hat	e	let	ī	ice	ȯ	order	ù	put	sh	she		a	in about
ā	age	ē	equal	o	hot	oi	oil	ü	rule	th	thin	ə	e	in taken
ä	far	ėr	term	ō	open	ou	out	ch	child	ᴛʜ	then		i	in pencil
â	care	i	it	ȯ	saw	u	cup	ng	long	zh	measure		o	in lemon
													u	in circus

K

Kilowatt (kil′ ə wot) unit of electrical power equal to 1,000 watts (p. 292)

L

Lend (lend) to loan (p. 233)

Length (lengkth) the distance from end to end (p. 20)

Liability (lī ə bil′ ə tē) insurance that protects the owner against claims resulting from an accident that is his or her fault (p. 258)

Limited-payment life insurance (lim′ ə tid pā′ mənt līf in shùr′ əns) insurance that covers the policyholder until death (p. 262)

Line segment (līn seg′ mənt) a part of a line (p. 274)

Loan (lōn) money given to a borrower that is to be returned with interest (p. 228)

Location multiplier (lō kā′ shən mul′ tə plī ər) a chart that helps determine a house's replacement cost based on its ZIP code location (p. 254)

M

Macramé (mak′ rə mā) a coarse fringe or lace of cord knotted into designs (p. 90)

Major medical insurance (mā′ jər med′ ə kəl in shùr′ əns) insurance to cover larger medical expenses (p. 248)

Meter (mē′ tər) an instrument for measuring and recording how much gas, electricity, water, etc., passes through it (p. 294)

Metered parking space (mē′ tərd pärk′ ing spās) a space where you must put money in a parking meter (p. 181)

N

Numerator (nü′ mə rā tər) the part of a fraction that is above the line and that tells how many parts are used (p. 74)

O

Odometer (ō dom′ ə tər) an instrument for measuring the distance traveled by a vehicle (p. 154)

Ordinary life insurance (ôrd′ n er ē līf in shùr′ əns) insurance where payments are made as long as the insured is alive (p. 262)

Overtime (ō′ vər tīm) time beyond the estimated limit (p. 138)

P

Peak hours (pēk ourz) the time when usage is greatest (p. 298)

Per (pėr) for each; for every (p. 132)

Percent (pər sent′) number per hundred (p. 195)

Percentage (pər sent′ ij) a given part or amount in every hundred; the part in a percent (p. 212)

Perimeter (pə rim′ ə tər) the distance around all the sides of a polygon (p. 272)

Possibility (pos ə bil′ ə tē) outcome that can occur (p. 54)

Possible outcome (pos′ ə bəl out′ kum) a result that can happen (p. 52)

Predict (pri dikt′) to state what will happen (p. 60)

Premium (prē′ mē əm) amount paid for insurance (p. 246)

Premium chart (prē′ mē əm chärt) list of amounts to be paid for insurance (p. 246)

Principal (prin′ sə pəl) amount of a loan or a deposit (p. 228)

Probability (prob ə bil′ ə tē) the chances that an outcome will happen; the number of successful outcomes divided by the total number of possible outcomes (p. 53)

Probability tree (prob ə bil′ ə tē trē) a diagram showing all possible outcomes (p. 52)

Proper fraction (prop′ ər frak′ shən) a fraction in which the numerator is less than the denominator (p. 75)

Protractor (prō trak′ tər) an instrument in the form of a half-circle marked with degrees, for drawing and measuring angles (p. 219)

Putout (pùt′ out) a play in which the batter or runner is retired (p. 197)

a	hat	e	let	ī	ice	ô	order	ù	put	sh	she	ə	a	in about
ā	age	ē	equal	o	hot	oi	oil	ü	rule	th	thin		e	in taken
ä	far	ėr	term	ō	open	ou	out	ch	child	ᴛʜ	then		i	in pencil
â	care	i	it	ȯ	saw	u	cup	ng	long	zh	measure		o	in lemon
													u	in circus

Q

Quarterly (kwôr′ tər lē) happening at regular intervals four times a year (p. 231)

R

Radius (rā′ dē əs) a line from the center to the edge of a circle (p. 219)

Rate (rāt) percent (p. 212)

Rate factor (rāt fak′ tər) an amount by which the basic premium is multiplied (p. 260)

Recipe (res′ ə pē) directions for making something (p. 72)

Rectangular prism (rek tang′ gyə lər priz′ əm) a solid figure with bases or ends that are parallel and sides that are rectangles (p. 282)

Regroup (rē grüp′) to reorganize (p. 92)

Rename (rē nām′) to express in another form equal to the original (for example, 1 hour = 60 minutes) (p. 75)

Repeat (rē′ pēt) something that appears again (p. 96)

Replacement cost (ri plās′ mənt kȯst) the cost to replace insured property (p. 254)

Round up (round up) to round to the next highest number (p. 26)

Rummy (rum′ ē) card games in which the object is to match cards into sets of the same denomination or run of the same suit (p. 62)

S

Sacrifice out (sak′ rə fīs out) out made to advance base runners (p. 192)

Salary (sal′ ər ē) a fixed amount of money paid to a worker regularly (p. 144)

Sale price (sāl prīs) reduced price of an item (p. 213)

Sales tax (sālz taks) a tax on sales or services, added to the price (p. 212)

Scale (skāl) ratio of the map size to the true size of an object or area (p. 276)

Scale drawing (skāl drȯ′ ing) a picture that shows relative sizes of real objects (p. 276)

Semimonthly (sem i munth′ lē) twice per month (p. 248)

Simple interest (sim′ pəl in′ tər əst) interest computed on principal only (p. 228)

Slugging percentage (slug′ ing pər sent′ ij) ratio of total bases to official at bats (p. 193)

Spare (spâr) in bowling, knocking down all the pins with two rolls of the ball (p. 36)

Speedometer (spē dom′ ə tər) an instrument that measures how fast a car is traveling (p. 154)

Standard (stan′ dərd) a rule or model for measuring (p. 24)

Statistic (stə tis′ tik) fact collected and arranged so as to show certain information (p. 192)

Strike (strīk) in bowling, knocking down all ten pins on the first roll of the ball in a frame (p. 37)

Suit (süt) any of the four sets of thirteen playing cards (p. 61)

Symbol (sim′ bəl) a character that stands for something else (p. 81)

T

Term insurance (tèrm in shùr′ əns) insurance where payments and insurance last for a fixed amount of time (p. 262)

Time (tīm) duration of a loan or deposit (p. 228)

Time and a half (tīm and ə haf) payment of 1.5 times the hourly rate for work (p. 138)

U

Unit (yü′ nit) any fixed amount, quantity, etc., used as a standard (p. 20)

Unit count (yü′ nit kount) a way to determine a house's size for insurance purposes (p. 250)

V

Vary (vâr′ ē) to differ in characteristics (p. 10)

Volume (vol′ yəm) the amount of space occupied in three dimensions (p. 282)

W

Watt (wät) a unit of electrical power (p. 292)

Width (width) the distance from side to side (p. 25)

Won-lost percentage (wun lost pər sent′ ij) ratio of wins to games played (p. 202)

a	hat	e	let	ī	ice	ô	order	ù	put	sh	she	ə	a in about
ā	age	ē	equal	o	hot	oi	oil	ü	rule	th	thin		e in taken
ä	far	èr	term	ō	open	ou	out	ch	child	ᴛʜ	then		i in pencil
â	care	i	it	ȯ	saw	u	cup	ng	long	zh	measure		o in lemon
													u in circus

Index

order of operations in, 303
  pictures or diagrams in, 31, 101
Proper fraction, 75
Proportion, 285
Protractor, 219, 225
Putout, 197

Photo Credits

Cover images: © comstock.com; p. xvi, © David Young-Wolff/PhotoEdit; p. 4, © David Young-Wolff/PhotoEdit; p. 11, © Tony Freeman/Photo Edit; p. 14, © Jonathan Nourok/PhotoEdit; p. 18, © Michael Newman/PhotoEdit; p. 28, © Mary Kate Denny/PhotoEdit; p. 32, © Courtesy of Brunswick; p. 44, © Michael Newman/PhotoEdit; p. 45, © Michael Newman/PhotoEdit; p. 50, © Michael Newman/PhotoEdit; p. 70, © T. Tracy/Getty Images; p. 73, © Tom Pantages; p. 75, © David Young-Wolff/PhotoEdit; p. 82, © Mark Richards/PhotoEdit; p. 86, © Michael Newman/PhotoEdit; p. 91, © Michael Newman/PhotoEdit; p. 98, © David Young-Wolff/PhotoEdit; p. 102, © Gary Conner/PhotoEdit; p. 106, © Jonathan Nourok/PhotoEdit; p. 110, © Michael Newman/PhotoEdit; p. 111, © Spencer Grant/PhotoEdit; p. 114, © Bill Aron/PhotoEdit; p. 118, © Bill Aron/PhotoEdit; p. 125, © Chip Henderson/Tony Stone Images; p. 130, © David Young-Wolff/PhotoEdit; p. 136, © Bill Bachmann/PhotoEdit; p. 137, © Lawrence Migdale/Tony Stone Images; p. 138, © David Young-Wolff/PhotoEdit; p. 144, © Charles Thatcher/Tony Stone Images; p. 148, © Robert Brenner/PhotoEdit; p. 152, © David Young-Wolff/PhotoEdit; p. 155, © Ron Rovtar/Getty Images; p. 157, © Michelle Bridwell/PhotoEdit; p. 157, © David Young-Wolff/Tony Stone Images; p. 165, © Ron Chapple/Getty Images; p. 168, © Joachim Messerschmidt/Getty Images; p. 174, © A. Ramey/PhotoEdit; p. 186, © VCL/Getty Images; p. 190, © Tony Freeman/PhotoEdit; p. 194, © Inga Spence/Index; p. 198, © Jim Cummins/FPG International; p. 201, © Mark Richards/PhotoEdit; p. 210, © SW Productions/Getty Images; p. 215, © David Young-Wolff/PhotoEdit; p. 222, © Michael Newman/PhotoEdit; p. 226, © Tony Freeman/PhotoEdit; p. 232, © Superstock; p. 237, © Amy Etra/PhotoEdit; p. 240, © Bill Aron/PhotoEdit; p. 244, © Michael Newman/PhotoEdit; p. 249, © Tony Freeman/PhotoEdit; p. 256, © James L. Shaffer; p. 260, © Tony Freeman/PhotoEdit; p. 263, © John Fortunato/Tony Stone Images; p. 266, © Myrleen Ferguson/PhotoEdit; p. 270, © Lawrence M. Sawyer/Getty Images; p. 281, © Mary Kate Denny/PhotoEdit; p. 286, © Courtesy of The Container Store; p. 290, © Courtesy of Commonwealth Edison; p. 292, © Superstock; p. 304 (left), © Robert J. Bennett/Getty Images; p. 304 (right), © Amy Biller